Zapata's Revenge

Free Trade and

the Farm Crisis in Mexico

by Tom Barry

South End Press

Boston, Massachusetts

Cover design by Mark Vallen
Text design and production by South End Press collective
Printed in the U.S.A.

Library of Congress Cataloging-in-Publication Data

Barry, Tom, 1950-
Zapata's Revenge: Free Trade and the Farm Crisis in Mexico/ Tom Barry.
p. cm.
Includes bibliographical references and index.
ISBN 0-89608-500-7 (cloth) : $35.00.—ISBN 0-89608-499-x (paper) : $16.00
1. Peasantry—Mexico 2. Land reform—Mexico 3. Agriculture—Economic aspects—Mexico—Farming and Agricultural issues. 4. Free trade—Mexico I.Title.
HQ1531.M6B375 1995
338.1'0972—dc2095-3031
CIP
South End Press, 116 Saint Botolph Street, Boston, MA 02115

99 98 97 96 95   2 3 4 5 6 7 8 9

CONTENTS

TABLES

Acknowledgments

I would like to acknowledge my appreciation of the hospitality and the help offered to me by the many campesinos, rural promoters, researchers, and analysts with whom I consulted during my trips to Mexico. Special thanks go to Luis Hernández and the staff of CECCAM in Mexico City.

The book is a product of the dedicated cooperation of the staff of the Interhemispheric Resource Center. Harry Browne, Erik Leaver, and Steve Whitman contributed excellent research support throughout this long project. I also counted on research assistance by interns Hugh Bartling, Debbie Swander, and Cristina Wagner. Beth Sims edited the first draft of the manuscript. As always, the administrative direction and emotional support of Debra Preusch, the center's executive director, was greatly appreciated and critical to the book's completion.

I am grateful to Kirsten Appendini, David Barkin, Jonathan Fox, Neil Harvey, and Michael Kearney for reading and commenting on parts of the manuscript. I am especially indebted to Michael Foley and David Myhre for reading the entire manuscript, to Jonathan Fox for his support and guidance in this project, and to all three for giving me the benefit of their extensive knowledge about the Mexican *campo* and agricultural affairs.

Financial support for the center's ongoing U.S.-Mexico food and farm project came from the Presbyterian Hunger Fund, Sisters of St. Francis, and the Evangelical Lutheran Church of America. The J.D. and Catherine T. MacArthur Foundation provided essential support for analysis of U.S.-Mexico relations, and the Ford Foundation provided financial support for the center's focus on U.S.-Mexico rural development issues.

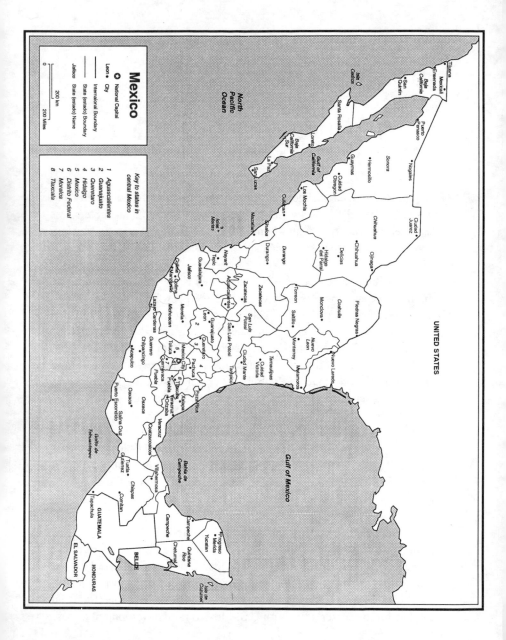

ZAPATA LIVES

"We're all *zapatistas*, not just the *compañeros* with the rifles. Our demands are the same, and they have been the same for the last one hundred years: land and liberty."

—Interview with Francisco Lozano, campesino
of the Altos de Chiapas, February 1994

Emiliano Zapata, hero of the Mexican Revolution that overthrew the Porfirio Diaz dictatorship in 1910, died a victim of that revolution. With his call for *tierra y libertad* (land and liberty), Zapata helped make and shape the revolution. The governments that followed the toppling of the Porfirio Díaz dictatorship (1877-1910), while professing a commitment to the country's *campesinos,** fell short of meeting the demands of the *zapatistas* for land and political freedom. In the end, the campesino general became an outlaw in the postrevolutionary state.

Ten years after he took up arms to defend the campesinos of his home state of Morelos, Zapata was assassinated by government emissaries

---

* Campensino means one who works the *campo* (land) and is used interchangably with peasants to refer inclusively to small-scale private farmers, *ejiditarios* (ejido members) and *journaleros* (farmworkers). When referring to campesinos collectively, the English term peasantry and the Spanish term *campesinado* are used.

in 1919. But his murder did not silence Zapata's Liberation Army of the South. Instead, cries of *Viva Zapata* emboldened the *zapatistas* in their struggle to win back control of ancestral community lands. Even after the original *zapatistas* put away their guns, Zapata's name continued to inspire campesino militancy. Whenever campesinos have gathered to seek land or confront the state, the image and name of Emiliano Zapata have been present. Campesino militants inevitably invoke his legacy to build support for their own causes. In the history of campesino struggles, the memory of Zapata has never died.

Zapata is not only a hero for Mexico's *hombres de maíz*, the millions of small farmers and farmworkers who are the heart of rural Mexico. He is also a national hero, a member of the country's pantheon of men who led the country to independence, who fought foreign invaders, and who made revolution. Their names—Hidalgo, Juárez, Madero, Zapata, Carranza, Obregón—grace boulevards, towns, monuments, and subway stops. Unlike the other mythic figures of Mexican history, Emiliano Zapata is a truly popular hero, never having compromised himself in government or wavered from his commitment to the rural masses. Zapata's name has also found a place in presidential rhetoric. Whenever a president addresses campesino or rural development issues, homage is inevitably paid to Zapata. When announcing the end of agrarian reform in 1992, President Carlos Salinas de Gortari boldly declared that he was doing only what Emiliano would have wanted.

Although initially counting on the support of the *zapatistas* of the South and the followers of Pancho Villa in the North, the postrevolutionary governments never fully incorporated the interests of the peasantry. The persistence of Zapata and other advocates of the peasantry did ensure that land reform found a place in the Constitution of 1917. But with the one major exception of Lázaro Cárdenas (1934-40), Mexican presidents regarded land distribution more as a way to pacify the peasantry and ensure their political support than as a central component in an integrated rural development program.

Zapata continues to live because the peasantry has refused to die. Agricultural modernization and industrialization strategies pursued by Mexican governments have failed to move Mexico beyond the rural problems of the third world. Today, more than one-fifth of Mexico's workforce is employed in agriculture, and there are more campesinos than existed at the time of the Mexican Revolution.

The failure of industry and export agriculture to provide sufficient employment has meant that some six million campesino families continue to see the land and farming as fundamental to their families' fights for daily survival. With a piece of land, they at least have a home and a chance to provide food for themselves. Without land, they might end up selling scissors in the Mexico City subway, roaming the countryside for temporary work, or taking their chances crossing into the United States.

The problems and the demands of today's campesinos mirror those who banded together with Zapata in 1911 to make revolution and also strike at the core of the nation's economic and political crises. Like the early *zapatistas*, campesinos in Mexico increasingly see their agrarian and political demands as being closely linked. While they insist on control over local government and resources, they recognize that local problems cannot be changed until there is a revamping of national policies.

On January 1, 1994, the day that the North American Free Trade Agreement (NAFTA) took effect, the Mexican government and economic elite came face to face with its old nemesis, an armed rebellion of campesinos whose rallying cry was land, justice, and democracy. Out of the Lacandón Jungle in the southeastern state of Chiapas arose the first challenge to the trade agreement that linked Mexico, the United States, and Canada. The Zapatista National Liberation Army (EZLN) let it be known that the plight of the peasantry could not be ignored. No longer could Mexico pursue modernizing strategies on the backs of campesino laborers. No longer could exploitation and repression of its native people be ignored. Years of petitions and protests had failed to alert the Mexican government to the deepening poverty of the rural population. It would now have to listen to firearms carried by indians who also called themselves *zapatistas*.

The EZLN's dramatic entry into Mexican politics sent a message to Mexican society: Don't forget us, the rebels were saying, you depend on us for your political and economic stability. We, the campesinos of Mexico, grow your corn, cut your cane, and pick your coffee. We have not gone away during the past 75 years of postrevolutionary governments, and we will not go away with neoliberalism and free trade. Like the early *zapatistas*, the EZLN saw a close connection between their poor economic circumstances and their lack of political control. It was this combination of political and economic demands and their linking of local and national issues that won the latter-day *zapatistas* such broad national support.

The call of the indian peasants for economic justice and democracy reverberated around the world, not just as headline news but as a broad challenge to a financial and political order that excludes the poor. Their inclusive rhetoric, lack of dogmatism, and expressions of outrage in the face of economic globalism gave their rural revolt an international relevance.

The special circumstances of Chiapas—the militarization of this frontier state, the persistence of colonial elites, the lack of agrarian reform, the ethnic tension, and the social stratification—help explain why an armed campesino army formed in the Lacandón Jungle and not in other regions of the country also characterized by pervasive rural poverty and landlessness. But just as it is important to recognize the local context for the Chiapas uprising, its national and international framework should not be overlooked.

Throughout Mexico, campesinos—and even the more privileged sector of commercially active farmers—have felt betrayed by the government and left out of its development plans. Campesinos with their machetes at their side, more well-heeled small farmers with their felt *sombreros* and leather boots, and medium- and large-scale farmers with their pickups and tractors are all frustrated and angry with the rapid economic policy changes that have withdrawn government support and left them competing with the more productive U.S. farm sector.

Mexico's farm sector, except for a small group of large-scale agroexporters with secure markets, see more risk than opportunity in the trade opening that NAFTA brings. But the risks are different according to the type of grower. Most farmers are among the poorest of the poor in Mexico. They have no pickups or tractors to lose. They wear *huaraches* of old tire rubber, not engraved leather *norteño* boots. For them, the farm crisis is a threat to the survival of their families. The same lament echoes from one village to another, from Chihuahua to Chiapas. "We are campesinos," observed a young indian man from a lowlands village in Chiapas. "The land is all we have, all we know. Without the land, what will happen to us and our children? We will be begging on the streets of Mexico City or working as *peones* like our grandfathers did."

For the *zapatistas* of the Chiapas jungles, this bleak prognosis gave rise to the age-old conclusion of agrarian revolution: *Tierra o Muerte*

(Land or Death). Other campesino militants, especially in the more indigenous regions of Guerrero, Oaxaca, Hidalgo, Puebla, and Veracruz, have also concluded that violent confrontation is the only recourse to neoliberal restructuring and free trade. Many other angry campesinos have responded with dramatic marches to Mexico City, occupations of state buildings, and seizures of uncultivated land. They are saying that they have a rightful place in Mexico's economic and political future.

A Death Foretold

The demise of the peasantry as an economic class has been a death foretold. Throughout Mexican history, many government planners, economists, and social scientists on both the left and the right have predicted the disintegration of the peasantry as capitalist market relations penetrated the countryside. But Mexican campesinos have endured. Their tenacity and pugnacity has seen them through the liberal reforms of the last century and the modernization of Mexican state capitalism.

The persistent presence of the *campesinado* in Mexico can be attributed in part to the government's agrarian reform program and other attempts to keep the campesino sector pacified. The campesino role in supplying the country with cheap food and labor also helps to explain their survival as a social sector and economic class. But neither politics nor economics fully explain how the *campesinado* has been able to evade their apparent historical fate.

More than a way of earning a living, the *campo* (land) is a way of life for many Mexican campesinos. It is an ideology with roots in the pre-Columbian past that has been sustained by the agrarian reforms and rhetoric of the revolution.[1] Being a campesino is different from having a job. It is a way of relating to land and community. It is a sense of place and identity not easily shaken. The *campo* is the heart and soul of Mexico—all readily discovered in the deep melancholy and joy for life tapped by its *ranchera* music, the instinctive hospitality of its people, the resonance of its rituals, and the easy acceptance of life's natural rhythms.

Having withstood and in large part adapted to the winds of economic modernization, the peasantry may finally be facing its meeting with fate. The grim reaper comes in the form of neoliberal economics and free trade. Although many in the countryside are heroically resisting, bitter resignation is probably more common than protest in rural Mexico. This pessimism mirrors the deepening stagnation of the agricultural sector. In the 1960s the agricultural GDP (gross domestic product) averaged 3.8 percent annual growth, falling to 3.4 percent in the 1970s, 1.1 percent in the 1980s, and 0.9 percent in the 1990-93 period. In other words, the growth of the agricultural sector has increasingly fallen behind population growth and overall GDP growth.

Many rural villages are turning into ghost towns as entire families choose economic exile in the United States or look for a new life along city streets. The options for those who remain in their villages are few. Only those with large extensions of good land and access to low-cost capital will be able to take advantage of the new market "freedoms" and capture a share of the more liberalized, integrated markets. As a result, the less competitive efficiency of small-scale production with its labor-absorption capacity and usually less environmentally destructive agricultural practices is devalued. As the prices of agricultural inputs rise and those of commodities fall, many small farmers are being pushed out of the market and some are adopting a survival strategy of self-provisioning. For rising numbers of young campesinos, the life of rural banditry and narcotrafficking has become an increasingly alluring alternative to the dead-end future of farming. Deteriorating conditions have, in the case of the Tarahumara indians of Chihuahua, led to famine and starvation in late 1994.

Yet the farm crisis in Mexico extends beyond the fate of campesino society. As described in the chapters that follow, the fate of land and farmers in Mexico is seen as an indicator of a wider development crisis that brings together issues of food security, productivity, democracy, economic progress, and sustainability.

Chapters One and Two seek the historical origins for today's rural problems and conflicts, reviewing the evolution of Mexico's agrarian and agricultural policies and the tensions between populism and economic modernization. Chapters Three and Four set the international framework for Mexico's farm crisis, looking first at the internationalization of farm and food systems and then more specifically at the implications of NAFTA. Having set the historical and global context, these chapters then look more closely at the dimensions of Mexico's agricultural system and its campesino sector.

Chapters Five and Six explain two leading components of the agricultural economy: agroexports and basic grains. Each sector is evaluated in terms of its ability to compete in the international market, spark economic growth, provide jobs, and promote broad development. Chapter Seven, titled, "People of the Land," focuses on the campesinos themselves—the men, women, and children who till the land and pick the crops. It examines their problems and their attempts to shape their own future. Chapter Eight analyzes the changes to Mexico's hallowed agrarian reform laws.

Chapter Nine examines the farm crisis in light of its impact on indians, women, and migrant patterns. Chapter Ten evaluates the options for sustainable agricultural development in Mexico, looking at the contradictions between environmental conservation and the agricultural economy as currently structured. The concluding chapters summarize the major issues raised in the preceding chapters and review some of the options for rural development in Mexico.

Financial Crisis and Farm Crisis

In early 1995, as this book was going to press, the financial crisis overshadowed the farm crisis. In many ways, however, farm and financial crises in Mexico are integrally related. Both emanate from a model of development crafted by a technocratic elite with little concern for the welfare of the vast majority of the population. Both crises had the same symptoms: a widening trade imbalance, the lack of productive investment, and an almost exclusive focus on foreign capital and foreign market conditions (with little concern about the fate of domestic producers and consumers).

The profound lack of democracy and government accountability in Mexico created the breeding grounds for the unstable conditions that prevail in the country's farm and financial markets. The Mexican people and their leaders bear the main responsibility for allowing this undemocratic state to endure. But the U.S. government and the other foreign nations and institutions that lavished praise on the Mexican technocrats and shored up the neoliberal model with generous loans and credit guarantees, also share responsibility for the deteriorating socioeconomic conditions and shaky political conditions in Mexico.

The financial crisis that set off the uncontrolled devaluation of the peso was also a crisis in faith. Bolstered by financial support from the U.S.

Treasury and the World Bank and riding on a wave of speculative investment in the country's stock market, President Salinas declared that Mexico was leaving its third world status behind. With borrowed money, Mexico was able to cover its widening trade deficit, control inflation, spur modest economic growth, and uphold the value of the peso through the Salinas administration.

Mexico's apparent economic stability earned the country the reputation of being one of the world's most promising emerging markets and recognition as a leader in implementing needed economic reforms. This illusion of economic dynamism also helped explain why so many Mexicans maintained their passive allegiance to the ruling party and accepted the official wisdom that free trade and neoliberalism were in the country's best interests. But Mexico's purported economic stability was built on a house of cards—a stacked deck in the hands of a corrupt, self-serving elite. When it became obvious to insiders that the country no longer had the reserves to pay its import bill and honor its short-term debt obligations, the house of cards came tumbling down, bringing with it the value of the peso and the belief that Mexico was joining the ranks of the more developed nations.

For those who had been lulled to sleep by neoliberal promises, the financial crisis was a rude awakening. But for those who kept their eyes open and had seen the signs of disaster in the rising trade deficit, growing unemployment, lack of direct investment, and deepening desperation in the countryside, the financial crisis was tragic confirmation of their common sense conclusion that the magic of the international marketplace was so much hocus-pocus.

The omens of the 1995 crisis were hard to miss, just as they were before the crisis of 1982. But Mexico's political leaders were too busy to notice or care. They were creating attractive conditions for foreign capital, winning new World Bank loans, selling off state enterprises to insiders, and pushing through NAFTA. Instead of devoting the necessary attention to expanding Mexico's domestic market, building its productive capacity, and developing a base for export production, the technocrats were in the business of selling illusions.

Fearing that the crisis in Mexico would spread and that it would undermine the free trade agenda, the International Monetary Fund, the United States, and other industrialized countries like Japan plied Mexico with new loans, loan guarantees, and credit guarantees. Stabilizing the weak peso and allowing Mexico to avoid defaulting on its ballooning debts were the stated objectives of this emergency response. Mexico's creditors—including lenders, portfolio investors, and anyone exporting to Mexico—stood to benefit immediately from the various financial packages. The emergency assistance to Mexico was predicated on the belief that Mexico's neoliberal economic model was fundamentally sound, although in need of better financial management.

Largely unacknowledged by foreign lenders, however, were the inherent weaknesses and failings of Mexico's economic policies. In fact, the increase in Mexico's external debt burden, which resulted from the various financial bailout efforts sowed the seeds of further economic destruction and political instability in Mexico. To regain stability, the government faced the dual challenge of increasing it monthly debt-service payments and shaking its deepening dependence on foreign food products and other imports. In the near future, Mexico may also face the hard choice between declaring a debt moratorium and tending to the basic needs of its own population and producers.

For the Mexican people, the financial crisis and devaluation mean facing a future of decreased consumption, inflation, reduced employment opportunities, and higher-cost, harder-to-get loans. In the farm sector, the 1995 crisis offered some relief for producers of domestic food crops since imports had suddenly become more expensive, and exports were more profitable because of the further reduction in wage costs in Mexico. For the most part, however, the financial crisis deepened the already severe farm crisis. The liberalization of international trade, deregulation of domestic prices, and the dismantling of the government's agricultural institutions that had occurred as a result of neoliberal reforms made it difficult for the government to protect food producers and to assist food consumers in these times of declining buying power and rising poverty.

A Common Destiny

Lamenting the difficulties facing the peasantry in these times of free trade and the withdrawal of state support, an indian *ejidatario* concluded an interview saying, "We feel so alone, all alone facing our destiny as campesinos." Throughout Mexico campesinos are deciding whether to fight, flee, or simply continue the daily battle for survival. A campesino's lack of security in a globalizing economy in which production, marketing, and finance have become increasingly integrated, is an intensely personal affair. But this feeling is also a central element in a development dilemma that extends far beyond the dirt roads of rural villages.

At the very least, the political stability of Mexico depends on finding a productive place for the millions of rural families who are now being told that they are relics of a bygone era. Sustained economic growth will depend on a healthy agricultural economy and the country's ability to provide income for all its citizens, not just the ones who can compete on the international market. Moreover, Mexico, with its large peasantry and underemployed labor force, cannot replicate the development model followed by more technologically advanced nations.

In the industrial world, countries like the United States are counting on spurring their own economies by boosting exports to less industrialized countries like Mexico. But without broad-based development there will be few customers for U.S. goods. More directly, the United States sees the impact of stagnating rural economies in Mexico and other Latin American nations in rising immigration pressures on its southern border. The individual survival problems of the Chiapas indian who feels abandoned by the national economy reflect the global challenge of charting development strategies that work for the large majority.

The following pages explore the development questions raised by the deepening desperation of Mexico's *campesinado*. In the process, there are lessons to be learned but no easy solutions. Neither the state nor the market is adequate to address the complexity of the interconnections among farmers, markets, and the land. However, it is from a better understanding and broader acknowledgment of the integral connections that join society, economy, and environment that any lasting resolution to the farm and free trade crisis will emerge. *Zapata's Revenge* was written with that conviction and hope.

REFORM, REVOLUTION, AND COUNTERREFORM

"It never crossed your mind that revolution should be for the benefit of the masses. Instead, to keep the people—already semifree and strong—from taking justice into their own hands, you developed the creation of a novel revolutionary dictatorship."

—Open letter from Emiliano Zapata to President Carranza,
March 17, 1919

The problems of rural Mexico keep coming back to haunt Mexico's policymakers. Each time the government and business believe they are on the right road to economic modernization, yet another crisis in the countryside emerges. Sometimes it is a matter of declining production and increasing imports, while at other times the crisis has more to do with rising social tensions in rural areas. The armed rebellion in Chiapas of the neo-*zapatistas* in early 1994, which challenged the neoliberal restructuring plans of the PRI (Institutional Revolutionary Party) government, added the most recent dimension to Mexico's ever-expanding rural crisis.

Beginning with the Mexican Revolution of 1910 the government has shaped two different sets of farm policies to deal with the dual character of its rural problems. One has addressed production and economic issues; the other has addressed people and politics. Agricultural policies have aimed to boost production, while agrarian policies have responded to demands by campesinos for land and to the state's own need to retain political support in rural areas.

For the most part, these two policies—agrarian and agricultural—have been complementary. Agrarian reform, for example, established the foundation for capitalist agriculture by reducing the number of inefficient *haciendas* or *latifundios* (large rural estates not intensively cultivated) and establishing a stable source of low-cost rural labor. But agrarian and agricultural policies can operate at cross-purposes, as when attempts to build political support among campesinos clash with policies that facilitate capital accumulation by the commercial farm sector.[1]

As a rule, the government's agricultural policies have disproportionately benefited capitalist growers and ranchers. An estimated 90 percent of public sector investment in infrastructure for agricultural development has historically been channeled to large-scale producers in the North and Northwest. In contrast, less attention has been given to the irrigation, marketing, and productive needs of campesino farmers who produce only limited surpluses.

The government has managed, at least until recently, to maintain its political hold on the peasantry through its agrarian program. Since 1917 more than 95 million hectares have been distributed to some 3.1 million beneficiaries.[2] By holding out the possibility that more land would be distributed, the government has practiced a "politics of promises" that has given it a "renewable lease on political legitimacy (Table 1)."[3]

Driven by their own ideological principles and the promised rewards of free trade with the United States, Mexican policymakers since the mid-1980s have gradually abandoned the country's traditional agrarian policies. In 1992 President Salinas pushed through a constitutional amendment that went a long way toward making the country's farm policies fully consistent with the government's new commitment to private property and the free market. The amendment to Article 27 of the Mexican Constitution ended the land distribution program and opened the way for ejido privatization.* At the same time that it was dismantling the

---

* The ejido is a community-based system of land tenure in which the government protected privately held parcels and communal lands within the community from the market. Before changes to the constitution in 1992, ejido lands could

agrarian programs of its populist past, the government subjected the entire farm sector to its neoliberal restructuring and macroeconomic policies. The overall objective was to make Mexican agriculture more efficient and competitive and less dependent on state support. It has done this by cutting subsidies for such agricultural inputs as fertilizer and seeds, reducing farm credit, and liberalizing prices so they will drop to international levels.

The government soon found that the special needs of the peasantry and the more general needs of its farmers could not be so easily disregarded. Growers, small and large, began organizing against the government and the liberalization of agricultural trade. Farmers seized government offices, blocked highways, and marched to Mexico City to protest price, credit, and farm subsidy policies. The deepening farm crisis is one that affects not only the small farmer (with ten hectares or less) population. In its pursuit of neoliberalism, the state has also dramatically affected the fortunes of medium-scale farmers (generally those with ten to forty hectares) who are becoming an endangered species in Mexico. Too big to escape into self-provisioning and too small to compete with Mexican and U.S. agribusinesses, they have become increasingly militant, complaining that while the industrialized nations continue to subsidize their farm sectors, Mexico is dropping all support for its family farmers.

It was, however, the uprising of mainly indigenous peasants in Chiapas that brought the rural crisis of Mexico to national and international attention. It highlighted the political risks facing the government as it abandoned the campesino-oriented component of it rural program. This chapter and the one that follows review the history of the Mexican state's attempts to modernize agricultural production in Mexico while maintaining rural political stability. Over the years, different solutions have been proposed and implemented, but many of the same problems keep boomeranging back to Mexico's policymakers.

not be bought, sold, or rented—although a widespread clandestine rental market existed. The ejidos existed under state sponsorship, which encouraged political patronage, corruption, and centralization of power within the ejidal communities. Also part of the social sector are the agrarian communities, which are indigenous lands based on historical claims and which have operated more autonomously than the ejidos.

Table 1

Land Use and Tenure by General Type (1988)

Type	Percentage*	Area (millions hectares**)
Livestock Grazing	57.6	112.8
Private Property	(32.6)	63.8
Ejidos	(25.0)	49.0
Agriculture	12.6	24.7
Private	(3.2)	(6.3)
Ejidos	(9.4)	(18.4)
Forestry	12.3	24.1
Private	(4.7)	(9.2)
Ejidos	(7.6)	(18.4)
Federal Government Land	6.2	12.1
Urban Real Estate	2.2	4.3
Other uses	9.4	18.4
TOTAL AREA*	**100.3**	**196.4**

* Percentage does not add to 100 because of rounding.
** 1 hectare equals 2.47 acres.
Sources: Data from INEGI and the Ministry of Planning and Budget (SPP) reported in Banco Nacional de México (Banamex), *Review of the Economic Situation in Mexico* , LXVII/No.798 (May 1992).

Liberals and Científicos

The continuing struggle to win control of land and the state's central role in promoting economic development are among the leading factors shaping today's Mexico. Although the Mexican Revolution did usher in an entirely new political order and set the stage for the economic modern-ization strategies of this century, it did not represent a complete break from the political and economic forces active in the 1800s.

Postindependence politics in nineteenth-century Mexico revolved around the often violent struggle between Liberals and Conservatives.

The Conservatives represented the continuation of the colonial power structure in Mexico, while the Liberals wanted to rid the country of precapitalist economic and political structures. Guided by the liberal ideology popular in the United States and Europe, Mexico's Liberals sought to redefine property relations, loosen restrictions on private capital, and establish a strong role for the state in supporting market development.

The 1857 constitution represented the triumph of liberalism. Central to the liberal agenda was an agrarian program that called for the redistribution of clerical and communal property. By privatizing the property of the church and the indians, the Liberals sought to undermine precapitalist economic relations and promote new economic growth. For the Liberals, the Catholic Church and its extensive landholdings obstructed the development of a modern state, as did the communal lands of the indians. Liberals in Mexico, like their counterparts in Europe, equated citizenship in a modern republic with property ownership. Ironically, the leader of the Liberals was a full-blooded Zapotec indian, Benito Juárez, who regarded the Catholic Church as an oppressor of the poor and an obstacle to the creation of a modern republic.

Rather than leading to the creation of a large number of property owners and a broadened internal market, the liberal reforms of the 1860s facilitated the concentration of lands in the hands of a privileged few. While brandishing their ideals of individualism and private property, the Liberals set about furthering their own economic interests by occupying lands formerly held by the church and indians. They further justified this expropriation by claiming that the indians were an inferior race whose society and culture stood in the way of modernization. Behind the dispossession of indian land also lay the need of the new agrarian bourgeoisie for an unencumbered rural workforce.

The liberal ideology of private property and free markets proved a powerful weapon in the toppling of the entrenched power structure of the military, church, and associated elites. As a guide to modernization, however, liberalism proved less adequate. Unlike the countries from which the ideology had been imported, Mexico lacked the domestic market, economic infrastructure, and civil society necessary for a political economy that functioned according to the principles of liberalism.[4] Nonetheless, the Liberals' assault on clerical and communal property did set the stage for the long period of economic growth and modernization that characterized the rule of General Porfirio Díaz (1876-1910), known as the *Porfiriato.*

The prominence of populist, agrarian, and nationalist policies in postrevolutionary Mexico can largely be explained by the social and economic conditions of the *Porfiriato.* A look back at those three decades of economic growth and political stability presided over by the *científicos* (professionals who espoused a positivist philosophy) of the regime also helps place current trends in Mexico in their historical context.

The Liberal/Conservative conflict that shaped Mexico's postindependence history had faded before General Porfirio Díaz took power. Positivism, a derivation of liberalism, was the ideology of the new regime and the *científicos* that administered its policies. Instead of abstract promises and speculation about improved social structures, the positivists proclaimed the importance of order and work. "Peace and prosperity" was the slogan of the *Porfiriato* and the few that benefited from the dictatorship. For most Mexicans, however, this period preceding the 1910 revolution was one of violence and destitution.

According to liberal ideals, privatizing land ownership implied the creation of a large independent class of yeoman farmers who would form the backbone of a modern republic. In Mexico, however, liberalism opened the way not to a broad distribution of property but to its concentration in the hands of a powerful few. This process accelerated during the Díaz regime, which granted immense land concessions as favors to supporters of the regime and to firms hired to survey national land. The communal lands of indian and peasant communities were deemed "vacant" and expropriated. By 1910 President Díaz had presided over what would be the most extensive land distribution in Mexico's history, leaving the indian population deprived of 90 percent of its land.[5]

By 1910 Mexico had become a country of landless peons forced to work for a pittance in the mines and plantations owned by foreign investors and the *hacendados* (owners of large rural estates) favored by the regime. Only 4 percent of rural family heads owned any land. An estimated 92 percent of Mexico's population was landless.[6] Federal troops pushed indians off their lands, which were then turned over to cattle, agribusiness, mining, and surveying companies that were granted vast land concessions.

Exports fueled the steady economic growth of the Díaz years. Having been driven off their ancestral lands, the rural masses no longer produced chile, corn, beans, and squash but were forced to work in the mines and agroexport plantations owned mostly by U.S. investors. Declining food production resulted in widespread hunger and desperation. During the *Porfiriato*, corn and bean production declined by 20 percent and 25 percent respectively.[7]

Paradoxically, at the same time that the *Porfiriato* was maintaining and reinforcing the use of feudal and even slave forms of production in agriculture and resource extraction, México was also modernizing economically.[8] Railroad construction throughout Mexico created the infrastructure for mining, forestry, agroexport production, and a nascent industrial sector. More than three-quarters of the new investment in infrastructure and production came from foreign capital.[9]

Economic modernization resulted in constant economic growth in Mexico, but its people were starving. At the start of the *Porfiriato*, 4 percent of the agricultural production was exported, rising to 20 percent by 1907. In contrast, land devoted to corn production dropped from 52 percent to 33 percent.[10] With no land to grow their own food and unable to afford to buy food, Mexico's campesinos scavenged the countryside for roots and wild plants to stave off starvation.

Localized rebellion among the country's *jornaleros* (day workers) and peons became increasingly common, as did strikes and protests against foreign investors in northern Mexico. A downturn in the world economy in 1907 caused the Mexican economy to stagnate, leading to new sources of discontent with the Díaz dictatorship. But it was not until Francisco Madero, a progressive politician from a wealthy landowning family, challenged the reelection of Díaz in 1910 that the widespread discontent with the *Porfiriato* coalesced into a national campaign to overturn the dictator. Counting on the support of such rural militants as Emiliano Zapata and Francisco "Pancho" Villa, who were pursuing their own revolutionary objectives, Madero succeeded in ending the dictatorship and was elected president.

Porfirio Díaz had shaped an economic and social order characterized by exploitation and repression that endured more than three decades. The infusion of foreign capital, the state's support for export production, a repressive social order that guaranteed stability, and the state's role in facilitating capitalist expansion (mainly through natural resource extraction, plantation agriculture, and commerce) all helped maintain economic growth.

But these strengths were also the principal weaknesses of the *Porfiriato*. The economy proved extremely vulnerable to contractions in U.S. demand and capital flows, and the population was so impoverished that there was no effective demand to spur domestic production. Those ranchers and traders not favored by the regime were early supporters of Madero, and they were joined by peasants who demanded the return of expropriated lands.

Origins of Zapatismo

In 1909 the villagers of Anenecuilco, in the state of Morelos, elected Emiliano Zapata to be their council president. His uncle, the previous president, handed the 30-year-old Zapata the titles to the community's land, much of which had already been lost to the sugar mills and *hacienda* owners. Committed to defending his village from further land-grabbing, Zapata became a supporter of Madero, who had made vague promises to return stolen lands if he became president. Zapata and other campesino leaders were also sympathetic to Madero's appeal to the liberal principles of rule by law instead of vested economic interests.

The campesinos of Anenecuilco had armed themselves before in the defense of their community's land and water, and under Zapata's leadership they joined the revolutionary movement to support Madero. As president, Madero rejected demands from the *zapatistas* for extensive agrarian reform that would revolutionize land-ownership patterns. Madero tried to mollify his campesino supporters by proposing legislative initiatives that would prevent further land loss but would do little to meet the immediate demands of the land-hungry campesinos.

Frustrated with the weak-willed Madero government, Zapata and Villa kept their armies mobilized. The two rural *caudillos* (strongmen) each had different programs. Villa, although of peon origin himself and backed by campesinos victimized by the Díaz dictatorship, had no systematic agrarian or political program. In contrast to the militarism of Villa, Zapata had a well-defined set of goals, including the demand for the recognition of communal rights to land and the right of small farmers to control their own villages. Shortly after Madero became president, Zapata issued his famous Plan of Ayala, which translated the local demands of the Morelos villages into a national platform. Unlike Madero's Plan of

San Luis Potosí, which was largely a restatement of liberal principles, the Plan of Ayala was a radical platform that stressed the importance of local self-government and land reform. It called for restoration of community lands that had been lost to *hacendados* and politicians as a result of the liberal reforms of the 1850s and the land grabs of the *Porfiriato*.

Intra-elite conflict and continued attacks on federal troops by campesino armies created a brief opening for the campesino movement in 1914, but neither Villa nor Zapata was prepared to direct a national government. Their own failure to unify forces and create a common popular political agenda allowed northern elites led by Generals Venustiano Carranza, Alvaro Obregón, Adolfo de la Huerta, and Plutarco Elías Calles to regroup and gain control of the state.

Instead of the populist, agrarian, vaguely socialist revolution envisioned by the *zapatistas*, the postrevolutionary state was dominated by *caudillo* generals who represented the interests of the northern agrarian bourgeoisie and other ascendant economic interests. For the capitalists, the postrevolutionary government renewed the hope of instituting the bourgeois economic order promised by the liberal reforms of the 1850s but distorted by the favoritism and foreign orientation of the Díaz dictatorship. The strong national state that coalesced in the postrevolutionary period continued the tradition of state interventionism advocated by the Liberals and exercised during the three decades of the *Porfiriato*.[11]

Hardly a strong advocate of agrarian reform, President Carranza (1914-20) recognized that land distribution would contribute to the stability of his own regime. In an ambiguously worded decree, the Carranza government in 1915 announced a land distribution program that promised to return land to communities whose land had been expropriated during the *Porfiriato*. A year and a half later he canceled the program, believing that it was threatening the rights of private property by allowing the reconstitution of indigenous lands and fanning populist agrarian demands. Like Madero, Carranza approached land reform from the liberal tradition, which stressed the importance of private property.[12] This elite concept of agrarian reform contrasted with the more radical positions advocated by Pancho Villa, Emiliano Zapata, and other populists who were responding to a mass movement of dispossessed campesinos and unemployed workers.

Despite Carranza's opposition, the constitution of 1917 incorporated principles more in concert with the reformist than the liberal concept of agrarian reform. In Article 27 of the constitution the state's right of eminent domain was broadly defined to include its right to distribute the land and waters of the nation in the interests of "public wealth." Instead of regarding land as "naturally private," the constitution defined land socially. Still, for the many delegates to the constitutional convention who were pushing for stronger measures such as the socialization of property, Article 27 was a compromise, not a victory for populism.[13]

Article 27 represented a major step away from the liberal tradition's narrow focus on private property, but it was certainly not the fulfillment of the *zapatista* demand, "Down with the *haciendas*, and long live the *pueblos*." By setting limits on land ownership and by giving the state strong powers of eminent domain, the reform language of the constitution did facilitate the modernization of Mexican agriculture and the expropriation of inefficient *haciendas*. For the most part, however, it was used more to pacify the peasantry than to build a strong agrarian reform sector in Mexico. By keeping alive the promise of land distribution, the state could maintain pressure on estate owners to use or lose their land while at the same time retaining the political support of the peasantry.

Under the pressure of the land reform program, the vast *haciendas* of the *Porfiriato* gradually disappeared. But they were not replaced by the thriving sector of democratically controlled agrarian communities envisioned by Zapata and other agrarian revolutionaries. Instead, the large landowners kept the core of their estates intact, allowing the state to distribute more marginal lands. Assisted by a greatly strengthened state, a capitalist farming sector developed in Mexico with the reform sector relegated to lands of little agricultural potential and denied the technical and financial assistance it needed.

During the 1915-34 period the indigenous agrarian community and the ejidos were regarded by the government not as fundamental parts of an overall agricultural development strategy but as transitory forms of property ownership. The land distribution that did occur in this period was not aimed so much to increase economic progress or better the lot of poor campesinos but as an instrument to pacify rebellious peasants and to create communities of cheap workers near commercial farm operations.

In terms of economic development, the real division in land ownership patterns was not between private and communal property but between what was considered commercially viable and the rest, which was only for the subsistence of the large peasant population. In the latter category were the agrarian communities, small private holdings of rainfed land, and most ejidos. By providing a source of farm labor, these marginal holdings would complement a more dynamic farm sector, consisting largely of irrigated small- and medium-scale landholdings and large agribusiness operations.[14]

Although the return of communal lands was central to the *zapatista* struggle, it was not the only demand of the revolutionaries. Like Madero, they demanded democracy. They wanted local control and did not join Madero's revolution only to have the Díaz dictatorship replaced by an even stronger and more centralized state. As the sugar mills and *haciendas* had extended their hold on land and economic power in Morelos, the villages had lost their autonomy. Agents of the Díaz government and the large landowners had gained increasing influence in their communities. Their cry, "Long Live the Pueblos" was a political demand to return power to the village assemblies, where decisions about the use of land and water would be decided by direct vote.[15]

Dismissed as *bandidos* and *indios* by the elite, the *zapatistas* were fighting for a political platform that resonated with democratic conviction. According to the General Law on Municipal Liberties advocated by the campesino revolutionaries of Morelos, "Municipal liberty is the first and most important and democratic institution since nothing is more natural or worthy of respect than the right that the citizens of any settlement have of arranging by themselves the affairs of their common lives and of resolving them as best suits the interests and needs of their locality."

Like Madero before him, Carranza was murdered as part of the intra-elite struggle for power. General Alvaro Obregón, a rancher from Sonora, took over the presidency in 1920. To restore a measure of political stability, Obregón successfully pacified the *zapatistas* with an extensive land distribution in Morelos. It was not until the presidency of Lázaro Cárdenas (1934-40), however, that the Mexican government undertook a serious agrarian reform. In the meantime, land distribution, although part of state policy, did not have a great impact on the skewed patterns of land ownership in Mexico. Not having much of an agricultural policy other than encouraging private capitalist agriculture, the governments that preceded Cárdenas had only a halfhearted commitment to distributing land to the landless and to reconstituting communal holdings.

Except in certain regions, like the state of Morelos where the organized campesino movement was strong, the Mexican countryside was still dominated by the old *haciendas* and *latifundios*. Rather than confronting the landed elite, Obregón's successor, President Plutarco Elías Calles, favored colonization schemes that settled petitioners on a portion of the federal lands that came into government control as a result of the revolution.

By the early 1930s Mexico was still a turbulent country in which the power of the newly constituted states was continually threatened by agrarian violence, rebellions by disaffected generals, and rule by regional *caudillos*. Compounding this instability was a deepening recession that sparked increased labor and peasant militancy.

Statism and Populism

General Lázaro Cárdenas, governor of Michoacan, became president in 1934.[16] In contrast to his predecessors, Cárdenas did not believe that the revolution was fully consolidated. In his view, Mexico needed to overhaul its economic and political structures if it were to modernize and develop economically. With the economic elite debilitated by the recession in the agroexport and mining sectors in a state of collapse, Cárdenas set out to reshape state institutions and reorder the economic structures of Mexico. To ensure political stability, he created a network of corporatist institutions that brought the military, peasantry, and workers under the direct control of the state political party.[17] The cornerstone of his economic policy was an extensive agrarian reform that gave the newly formed ejidos a central place in agricultural production.

Until Cárdenas, the Mexican state regarded the ejido sector not as a pillar of economic development but as a politically expedient and transitory part of the country's social fabric. In the agricultural economy it was seen as complementing the capitalist sector by providing a ready source of cheap labor and acting as a repository for landless campesinos.

Cárdenas, however, had different plans for the ejido. He envisioned a productive ejido sector that would be given fertile lands and would receive state assistance to ensure productivity. The collectivized *ejidatarios* would supply the country with the food it needed. Equally important, they would form the economic base necessary for industrialization by generating foreign exchange through increased agroexport production and by expanding the market for manufactured consumer goods.

The Cárdenas *sexenio* (standard six-year presidential term) was the apex of the agrarian reform in Mexico. More than 20 million hectares (1 hectare equals 2.47 acres) of land were distributed, more than twice as many as had been distributed under his predecessors. More important was the quality of the land and the new government attention to the needs of the ejidos. Instead of just doling out lands of questionable agricultural value, Cárdenas turned over agroexport estates to collectivized ejidos. By the end of the Cárdenas presidency in 1940, ejidos accounted for one-half of Mexico's cultivated area, and the number of landless laborers had declined from 68 percent to 36 percent of the rural workforce.[18]

To carry out such an extensive redistribution of land, Cárdenas shaped a state/campesino alliance that overpowered the opposition of regional agrarian power structures. He put teeth into the government's expropriation decrees by arming more than 60,000 campesinos to defend their lands from attacks by the security forces employed by or allied with the affected landowners. Cárdenas encouraged local and regional campesino mobilization while channeling it within a national federation created by the state. In 1938 Cárdenas formed the National Campesino Federation (CNC), a pyramidal mass organization shaped along corporatist lines to include all the beneficiaries of agrarian reform.[19]

Zapata had called for the return of communal lands to rural communities. Instead of actually turning over lands to campesinos, the Mexican government gave the beneficiaries of agrarian reform rights to land or *derechos agrarios* but not direct ownership. All those with *derechos agrarios* automatically became members of the CNC and the state's national political party (which under Cárdenas changed its name to the Party of the Mexican Revolution in 1938).[20] Called the social sector, *ejidatarios* depended on the state for usufruct rights to the land and on state institutions such as the Ejido Bank for credit and technical assistance.

During its first few years, the CNC represented the convergence of campesino mobilization and the government's effort to control the peasantry. But when the reformist Cárdenas government was succeeded by more conservative ones, the grassroots component of CNC faded and the organization became more a top-down instrument of state control.

The Cárdenas presidency had a lasting impact on Mexico.[21] Before Cárdenas, political power was more personal than institutional and counted on the support of a conservative coalition of interests. With his populist policies and the creation of corporatist structures linked to the national party, Cárdenas succeeded in forging a progressive coalition and in legitimizing the state among the popular sectors. A commitment to agrarian reforms or *agrarismo* assumed a central place in Cardenista populism. But unlike the agrarian focus of Zapata, which stressed the importance of local control, the agrarian policies of Cárdenas expanded the role of the state.

The populism of Cárdenas was two-edged. It proved an effective weapon when used to dismantle the *haciendas* and to reduce the influence of the agrarian elite. But because it was so closely linked to the expansion of state power, Cardenista populism successfully undermined independent popular organizing. Cardenista populism—and *agrarismo* as its main manifestation—had a sharp revolutionary impact when used against the regional landholding *caudillos* and on behalf of landless campesinos. But Cardenismo also had a pacifying, counterrevolutionary character that contributed to the formation of a powerful, centralized state and allowed little room for autonomous organizing by either workers or campesinos. With the masses of workers and campesinos unable to represent their own interests, government-sponsored sectoral organizations like the CNC served to strengthen the authoritarian state.

Cárdenas made the ejido a fundamental part of the agricultural economy. Previous governments had seen the ejidos as playing only a marginal role in economic development and capital accumulation. During the Cárdenas *sexenio*, however, there was hope that the ejidos could assume a more dynamic role in furthering economic progress. Because of the extensive reform program, the ejido sector soon accounted for half of the country's agricultural production. But government commitment to ejido agricultural production, which was already on the wane by the final year of the Cárdenas *sexenio*, declined dramatically in the 1940s. The ejidal sector never became a nationally important source of capital accumulation, although it was an important player in the steady economic progress experienced by Mexico in the 1940-70 period. Cárdenas left Mexico with a strong corporatist state capable of effectively mediating class conflicts. In the interests of both economic and political stability, Cárdenas pursued populist policies that reduced the power of the agrarian bourgeoisie while eliminating most of the *latifundios* left over from the *Porfiriato*. In place of a personalistic political order, he forged a political system based on a multi-sector ruling party.

To restore the social peace necessary for economic development, he further strengthened the centralized state and rid the provinces of militant campesino organizations that challenged the new federal order. More than simply a vehicle to maintain social peace, the state under Cárdenas assumed an ever more interventionist role in economic development. Recognizing that the nation's narrow capitalist class did not have the capacity to move Mexico toward industrialization, Cárdenas used the expanded economic and political capacity of the state to modernize agriculture and lay the base for industrialization.[22]

Counterreform and Modernization

In the three decades after Cárdenas, the state turned away from populism and toward business.[23] Reform turned to counterreform, and the corporatist structures given form during the Cárdenas *sexenio* became little more than bureaucratic channels of political control. The official rhetoric of the 1940-70 period included obligatory references to the populist and nationalist commitments of the state. But the government's policies and programs did not honor the social promises made by Cardenismo and instead shifted to accommodate dependent capitalism.[24]

With the corporatist mechanism of political control in place, the old agrarian order debilitated, and a strong interventionist state posed to support economic modernization, post-Cárdenas governments concentrated on promoting capitalist development. It was not until three decades later that the state once again recognized that a new round of populism and reformism was necessary for its legitimation.

Like other nations, Mexico equated industrialization with economic development.[25] Part of the eagerness to industrialize arose from the belief that only by emulating industrialized nations would Mexico rise above its undeveloped status. The commitment to industrialization was also based on the objective appraisal of international terms of trade, which showed a consistent decline in prices for agricultural commodities contrasting with the steady rise in value of industrial goods.

Prioritizing industrialization did not mean that agriculture was ignored, only that it played a subservient role to the industrial sector. Rather than being the motor of economic progress, agriculture partly financed and otherwise supported the industrialization process. Capital accumulated by agriculture provided significant foreign exchange to import manufacturing plants and equipment and the local currency needed to build the required urban and industrial infrastructure.[26]

The capital-generating capacity of commercial agriculture was to a large degree a product of the small farm sector's provisioning of cheap food and low-cost labor. Having their own small plots to provide them with most of their own basic foods and in some cases a net surplus, campesino farmers required only small quantities of cash to maintain their families. They therefore served as a source of low-cost labor to the commercial agricultural sector, which has customarily paid seasonal workers below-subsistence wages. The large campesino population of corn and bean farmers then not only supplied much of the nation's food, but it also directly helped keep down farm wages and food prices, as well as indirectly helping to keep industrial wages down through its contribution of cheap food and labor. Agriculture's expanding need for farm machinery, agrochemicals, and infrastructure also helped push industrialization forward.

Like the presidents who preceded Cárdenas, those that followed the populist leader saw only a marginal role for the ejido in the agricultural economy. Beginning with the Manuel Avila Camacho government (1940-46) and especially during the Miguel Alemán *sexenio* (1946-52), the state's commitment to developing ejido agriculture was discontinued as government support was directed almost exclusively to private agribusiness.[27]

Agrarian reform and its bureaucracy remained part of the post-Cárdenas government, but the pace of land distribution dramatically decreased, and the quality of the land that was parceled out greatly deteriorated. Changes to the agrarian code in 1942 set the tone for the land reform program for the next three decades. The new code repudiated the focus of the Cárdenas years and reaffirmed the state's commitment to private property. Regarding collectivized ejido administration and production as socialist and a threat to private property, the government denied them credit and prevented the formation of new collectivized ejido structures.

To further limit the reach of agrarian reform, the government in the late 1940s began issuing *certificados de inafectibilidad* (certificates of immunity) that granted landholders exemptions from the property limits spelled out in the agrarian code. Protected by these government guarantees, landowners with close ties to government officials could accumulate vast amounts of land without facing the threat of government expropriation. Among the main beneficiaries of these exemptions were cattle ranchers who accumulated large estates, while other ranchers and growers skirted the agrarian reform by placing properties in the names of relatives and friends (called *prestanombres* or names on loan).

Two-Tiered Agriculture

Revolutionary Mexico had initiated the first agrarian reform program in Latin America. Although the massive distribution of land did substantially reduce land concentration, it did not create an equitable structure of land ownership and use. Instead, what agricultural economists call a bimodal or dual structure of agricultural production gradually took shape in Mexico, especially after Cárdenas left office in 1940. As a general rule, small private farmers and *ejidatarios* were once again relegated to rainfed parcels and less fertile lands, where they cultivated mainly basic grains (largely corn and beans). With the exception of a few collectivized ejidos located in the irrigation valleys of the Northwest, commercial agriculture became the province of the medium- and large-scale privately owned farms that had access to irrigation or had high-quality rainfed lands.

Campesino and commercial agriculture, however, were not two worlds apart. In fact, the success of the bimodal structure depended on the functional integration of the commercial and noncommercial sectors. Campesino agriculture provided cheap basic foodstuffs to the rapidly urbanizing nation and the cheap seasonal labor required by the agroexport estates and other commercial operations. This cheap food and cheap labor, together with the flow of state-subsidized inputs and infrastructure projects, ensured the success of agribusiness and provided an economic base for industrial expansion.

The classification of the structure of Mexican agriculture as bimodal does capture the large gap that exists between the large-scale commercial producers and the vast majority of farmers in Mexico that rely on family labor. In Mexico, capitalist producers control about one-fifth of the arable land although they constitute less than 2 percent of total farmers. Beyond the capitalist sector is a continuum of medium- and small-scale farmers who have less than forty hectares. They range from those who produce large surpluses and regularly employ nonfamily labor to those who produce limited or no surpluses and only rarely or never employ nonfamily farm labor. Included among the latter grouping are infrasubsistence landholders, generally with five hectares or less, who depend on wage labor themselves to maintain their families.

As land becomes more scarce, population increases, and government supports diminish, this latter category is becoming ever larger. It is this desperate rural underclass that joined the ranks of the *zapatistas* in Chiapas. Although the bimodal classification accurately conveys the polarized character of Mexican agriculture, the term *trimodal* better describes the three major categories of farmers and their relations with the market: 1) capitalist producers, 2) medium- and small-scale farmers who are surplus-producing but rely primarily on family labor, 3) infrasubsistence or subsistence farmers together with the landless, many of whom regularly work as *jornaleros*, or wage farmworkers.

Campesino farming in Mexico is mostly an infrasubsistence operation. Few campesino families can survive solely from the production of their land. While able to provide a good part of their family food needs, campesinos must leave their villages to seek cash income from seasonal farm work. Because campesinos do not depend on wage labor for the totality of their survival needs, commercial farmers can pay the migrant workers wages that do not cover the costs of their basic needs. Moreover, the surplus grains that campesino farmers are able to produce on their own parcels are commonly sold for prices that do not cover the real costs of production.[28]

Having demobilized the campesino population and substantially reduced the number of landless campesinos with the massive land distribution of the 1930s, the Mexican government in 1940 concentrated on modernizing commercial agriculture. For three decades it largely neglected campesino agriculture. But rather than attempting to develop its own version of agricultural modernization, the government looked to the United States and other industrialized countries for its model of agricultural development.

Modernization thus implied a reliance on mechanization and chemical inputs to increase productivity on commercial lands. Considering the relatively undeveloped state of capitalist agriculture in Mexico, it also meant a pivotal role for the state in providing infrastructure, subsidized inputs, financing, and technical assistance. Encouraging this move toward capital-intensive agriculture was the arrival in the 1940s of the so-called "Green Revolution" in Mexico.[29] To increase productivity of basic grains (especially wheat), researchers sponsored by the Rockefeller Foundation and Ford Foundation advocated the widespread use of hybrid seeds and chemical fertilizers.

The focus of the Green Revolution was on commercial, irrigated agriculture. Remarkably, campesino agriculture, which accounted for most of the country's corn and bean production and more than 50 percent of the agricultural workforce, was virtually ignored.[30] The Green Revolution technicians exhibited little concern for the problems and concerns of the vast majority of Mexico's farmers, preferring instead to assist proven commercial farms. They believed that techniques that worked on the larger farms would also work for campesino subsistence farmers.

Underlying the Green Revolution was a conviction that agricultural techniques were transferable: What was good in the United States was good for Mexico and appropriate for commercial and noncommercial agriculture alike. Problems of agricultural development were reduced to technical considerations, ignoring the structural obstacles that faced a peasantry isolated from national markets, handicapped by poor soil, dependent on rain water, and subject to the manipulation of local *caciques* (bosses) and moneylenders.[31] The narrow focus of the Green Revolution accentuated the bimodal division in Mexican agriculture. Two decades after the first agreement for technical assistance was signed by the Mexican government, wheat yields by the targeted farmers of north and central Mexico were the highest in Latin America, but the average yields of corn (grown mainly by small farmers on rainfed parcels) were among the lowest.[32]

First Signs of the Crisis

The agricultural sector experienced an impressive record of growth during this three-decade period (1940-70). Both agroexports and basic grains production steadily increased as overall farm production outdistanced the rate of population growth. By the late 1960s, however, agricultural stagnation slowly began to replace the impressive growth experienced since 1940. Annual growth in the sector declined from nearly

6 percent in the first half of the 1960s to just 1 percent in the final half of the decade. Mexican agriculture, which had helped push the economy forward since 1940, was in crisis—and this same crisis continues today, albeit with new dimensions and challenges. There is no single explanation for the crisis. But the bimodal structure of agriculture and the failure of the state to develop an agriculture policy that responded to small farmers as well as to commercial ones and that addressed regional circumstances set the stage for stagnation.

Increased farm production has come at a high price, and one that could not continue indefinitely. The government channeled most of its support to the commercial sector, disproportionately providing it with irrigation, storage facilities, cheap rail transportation, long-term agricultural credit, low fuel costs, and (especially in the case of wheat) high guarantee prices. Increased production of agroexports and Green Revolution grains were bought with billions of dollars from the government treasury.[33]

At the same time that the government was pouring vast sums into agribusiness, it was also opening up public lands to cattle ranching and subsistence agriculture. Colonization programs that brought landless campesinos into the humid tropical forests of the southeast served to keep grain reserves high and provide beef to the expanding urban middle class. But just as the federal treasury is limited, so is the country's natural resource base. As the agricultural frontier began to shrink, *milpas* (traditional farms with shifting cultivation) were converted to pastures, land conflicts intensified, percapita grain production began to fall, and grain imports started to rise. Total production continued to increase, but overall population growth, particularly in urban areas, outstripped the less rapid increases in productivity.

Despite impressive advances in wheat production, Mexico by the 1970s also began importing wheat. Farmers that had earlier switched to wheat production because of high guarantee prices shifted to other crops as prices fell as part of the government's attempt to maintain cheap food for its urban population. Because domestic corn prices were also kept low as a way to keep food prices and inflation down, commercial production of corn declined as these farmers also changed to agroexport or to sorghum production. Higher fixed prices for sorghum, a feed grain, resulted in a dramatic transfer from the production of food grains (for human consumption) to feed grains (for animals, especially poultry and pigs) in central, north-central, and northeastern Mexico.[34]

As a modernization strategy, the increased mechanization of agriculture during this period never matched the expectations of the developmentalists. To encourage mechanization, the government exempted farm machinery from import duties and provided ample financing to facilitate purchases of tractors and harvesters. Mexico became the Latin American nation with the highest degree of agricultural mechanization. But the resulting increase in productivity was minimal, especially when compared with the gains from irrigation and the use of Green Revolution inputs.[35] One factor was that high-power, heavy-duty, and very expensive farm machinery imported from the United States did not meet the needs of many farmers, especially small- and medium-scale producers. Another reason that yields fell short of projections was the persistence of extensive agricultural practices common to precapitalist farming and ranching. Many growers were not accustomed to making intensive use of land, labor, and machinery.[36]

Mechanization as a centerpiece of agricultural modernization seemed inappropriate for a country with such a large idle workforce. Industrialization was unable to meet the demand for jobs, and mechanization was actually eliminating jobs in the commercial agricultural sector. Each tractor put to work on the farm meant that three to four workers lost their jobs. Moreover, rather than relying on sharecroppers or *colonos* (as in a traditional *latifundio* system) or hiring permanent wage workers, Mexico's *neolatifundios* relied on temporary farmworkers.

Among the main beneficiaries of agricultural modernization were foreign traders and investors. Capital-intensive production relied on inputs supplied mainly by foreign companies, such as John Deere, Massey Fergusen, and Monsanto, many of which set up plants in Mexico to meet the high demand. Although not directly involved in agricultural production, foreign capital became central to the fruit and vegetable export business as well as to the expanding livestock industry in northern Mexico through contracting and financing arrangements. With the government having backed away from the nationalist convictions of the Cárdenas era, transnational corporations also came to dominate such agroprocessing industries as animal feed, snack food, and meatpacking. Foreign investment did help modernize the sector, but this modernization also brought increased dependence on foreign capital, rising food imports, and the widespread adoption of U.S.-style consumption patterns, including the purchase of more processed foods.

During the 1950s the agricultural sector, at least on the surface, seemed in good shape. Agroexports were increasing, and they accounted for more than half of total export production as late as 1970 (decreasing sharply to 25 percent by the end of the decade because of rising petroleum exports). Although there was no dramatic improvement in the yields of corn and beans, total production had increased steadily mainly because of the extension of the country's agricultural frontier into the humid tropics. Coffee and sugarcane production also increased with the expansion into formerly uncultivated tropical regions.

Sluggish agricultural production together with rising food imports were the first economic indicators of the agricultural crisis. Perhaps more alarming were the social indicators of crisis in rural Mexico. The benefits of three decades of economic growth were not proportionately distributed throughout the farm sector, but most campesino families did experience some improvement in their percapita income levels. This flow of cash into rural Mexico did not, however, offset the deepening sense of insecurity felt in the countryside.

As population pressures increased and environmental degradation worsened, complete self-provisioning in basic foodstuffs became increasingly rare. As a result of the government's cheap-food policies, the terms of trade between rural and urban Mexico steadily deteriorated. The conversion of farmland to pastures and the unwillingness of the government to distribute arable lands to campesinos increased rural landlessness and migration. By the late 1960s the rising intensity of rural conflicts, including the guerrilla struggle in Guerrero, accentuated the seriousness of Mexico's agricultural crisis.

The Legacy of Zapata

Emiliano Zapata was a central figure in the Mexican Revolution. He is not just another stone monument to the glories of Mexico's heroic past— Zapata is a living legend. Although he died at the hands of the postrevolutionary regime, subsequent governments have attempted to bolster their own populist and agrarian credentials by paying homage to the campesino general. Through the decades, however, campesino militants have rejected the state's attempts to associate its limited version of land reform with Zapata. Instead they have appropriated the slogans and familiar image of the "Caudillo from the South" to build popular support for their own attacks against the authoritarian and elitist state.

Zapatismo is synonymous with *agrarismo* in Mexico. Both as an instrument of state control and as a force for social justice, agrarianism has, like Zapata himself, been fundamental to the shaping of the Mexican political economy. But does *agrarismo* in any form remain functional as either a political, economic, or social remedy? This is an issue that has long divided policymakers, academics, and activists in Mexico. Population pressures, international market competition, and the closing of Mexico's agricultural frontier have created a new context in which land use and distribution issues are debated. Yet the problems of landlessness, the lack of alternative employment opportunities, and the stagnation of agricultural production persist in Mexico and show signs of worsening as the state's commitment to agrarian policy diminishes.

While steadfast in their claims of staying true to the spirit of Zapata, recent neoliberal governments have attempted to shed *agrarismo* in their efforts to modernize the farm economy and move away from the paternalistic political structures of the past. But *zapatismo* sentiment still runs deep in the Mexican countryside. In the absence of other remedies to economic insecurity, the old agrarian slogans, "Land and Liberty," "Land to the Tiller," and "Down with the Haciendas, Long Live the Pueblos," have not been forgotten.

As Mexico seeks to respond to the multiple challenges of maintaining political stability, boosting agroexports, guaranteeing an adequate food supply, fostering rural development, and protecting its badly degraded environment, the legacy of Zapata is at issue. In determining the future direction of agricultural policy, Mexicans will have to decide whether there is still room for *zapatismo*.

It has been said that the *zapatistas* were a "country people who did not want to move and therefore got into a revolution."[37] The campesinos of Morelos became revolutionaries to resist the rapacious advance of capitalist agriculture in Mexico. Not wanting to become wage laborers on land that was once theirs, they became guerrillas who helped ensure that a land distribution program to campesinos became part of the new Mexico. Was this not wanting to budge from the communal lands a premodern response that is at least part of the reason why Mexico remains a country with such an uncompetitive agricultural sector and large destitute rural population? Or did it prefigure a postmodern solution to such problems as excessive urbanization, unsustainable development, and undemocratic and overly centralized government? In evaluating Zapata's legacy, such questions must be answered.

The showdown between free trade and the indian rebels in Chiapas in the 1990s highlights the widening differences of opinion about the legacy of Emiliano Zapata and the nature of the current farm and development crisis in Mexico. The revolt in the Selva Lacandona called attention to a new Mexico, one in which the historic connections between the state and the peasantry had been severed and substituted by international market solutions to the country's persistent economic and social problems. Chapter Two will look at the recent background to Mexico's current rural crisis by cataloging the resurrection of the populist and nationalist tendencies within the ruling party in the 1970s, their economic and political failures, and the triumph of the neoliberal technocrats.

POPULISTS AND TECHNOCRATS

"Zapata still has his boots on and his horse saddled."

-President Echeverría, 1976

One way to regard Mexican history is as a pendulum that swings back and forth between progressive and conservative, activist and consolidating currents within the PRI.[1] Generally, the oscillation represents more of a readjustment of policies than a contest between two fixed ideological positions, although the political shift between *sexenios* has occasionally been quite dramatic. After three rightward-shifting decades punctuated by minor adjustments to the left, the pendulum swung dramatically back to progressive reformism in 1970 when Luis Echeverría became president. Cardenista-style populism returned to Mexico under Echeverría, and with it a revival of *agrarismo*.

The country needed a new injection of populism to ease rural and student unrest. The social peace that Cárdenas had established in the countryside was threatened by rising campesino militancy, and the impressive economic growth that had once characterized the agricultural economy was no longer even keeping pace with population growth. Not only were food imports up, but agroexport production had lost its former dynamism. To make matters worse, the import-substituting industrialization that since World War II had constituted the motor of the country's economic development policy badly needed an overhaul. The legitimation and capital accumulation functions of the state were both being put to test.

Recognizing the threats to the country's stability, Echeverría quickly let it be known that under his watch there would be a major shake-up in the balance of power. The capitalist class (including the foreign investors) that had profited under the state's protective wing was judged to have grown so powerful that it was threatening the populist pact that the government had with the peasantry. Grassroots activism and leftist agitation propped up Echeverría's populism from below, and *tercermundismo* (third worldism), then gaining prominence in academic and international circles, provided the ideological foundation. Echeverría's return to agrarianism as an economic development strategy also counted on foreign funding from multilateral sources, most prominently the World Bank, in the form of program support for newly conceived "integrated rural development" projects.

For both political and economic reasons, the state elite realized that the peasantry could no longer be ignored if the agricultural crisis were to be solved and campesino militancy pacified. For the first time in thirty years, the government looked to the ejido and *minifundio* sectors as valid economic actors that needed state support. Adopting a program of "shared development," Echeverría criticized past development efforts that assumed that the benefits of agricultural growth would trickle down to all rural sectors.

Understanding that campesinos themselves needed to participate actively in the development of rural Mexico, Echeverría became the first president since Cárdenas to promote local and regional campesino organization. He promoted the agrarian reform agency to cabinet status and revised the agrarian reform code in 1971 to restore the importance that Cárdenas had given the ejido sector. Although Echeverría did not withdraw support for private agribusiness, he greatly angered the agricultural bourgeoisie who felt threatened by the rising tide of campesino militancy, which they felt was fueled by the government's populist rhetoric.

The Echeverría *sexenio* is remembered by many, especially in the Northwest, as a period in which the government handed over huge tracts of lands to militant campesinos, but land distribution was not the primary focus of President Echeverría's reform program. Instead, the government turned its attention to providing services, organizational support, and infrastructure to small producers ignored by previous administrations.

This emphasis was a reflection of the development philosophy coming into vogue within the World Bank and other foreign lending institutions.

Mexico was not the only third world nation facing a crisis in the countryside. Other Latin American nations had enjoyed the postwar boom fueled by import-substituting industrialization and nontraditional agroexport production. But the resulting economic growth was uneven, with the countryside and the peasantry seeing few of the benefits. Recognizing the severity of the rural crisis, the World Bank in 1973 spearheaded a worldwide rural development program that concentrated on improving conditions for those left behind by earlier development strategies. By targeting credit, infrastructure, technical assistance, health care, marketing support, and educational projects to the rural poor and small producers, rural development projects would not only improve socioeconomic conditions in the *campo* but also boost national economic growth.

Before the Echeverría presidency, virtually the only government outreach to small producers had been the credit programs of the Ejido Bank. By the end of his term, however, there existed an array of government agencies providing services to the peasantry. PIDER, Mexico's lead rural development agency funded by the World Bank, was complemented by new state marketing institutions for coffee, sugar, and tobacco, all of which benefited small producers.[2] Conasupo established warehouse facilities for basic grains producers, and Banrural and ANAGSA became important sources for credit and crop insurance.

President Echeverría encouraged the collectivization of ejidos and the creation of ejido associations. In practice, collectivization did not usually mean unified production but rather the collective administration of credit, use of agricultural machinery, purchase of inputs, and marketing. The government also promoted the formation of ejido associations that joined ejidos together to increase their efficiency. Beginning in the mid-1970s there appeared an array of so-called second level organizations known as Ejido Unions (UE) and third-level organizations that joined UEs into what are known as Rural Collective Interest Associations (ARICs). By authorizing the formation of local and regional organizations, the government laid the foundation for expanded campesino mobilization. But the government's populist commitments were at odds with its insistence on corporatist stability. Localized campesino mobilization was repressed in Guerrero, Chiapas, Oaxaca, and Chihuahua. The government also ably applied divide-and-conquer tactics to debilitate regional and national-level campesino organizations that challenged the top-down control of the CNC and the government's rural agencies.

The lack of respect for democratic, grassroots organizing explained why many of the UEs and ARICs soon became just paper organizations. In a few cases, however, these associations did become important channels for *ejidatarios* to challenge local power structures and to create more efficient and profitable units of production.[3] Although the impact was limited at first, the Echeverría reforms that created the new legal framework for campesino organizing set the stage for the emergence in the 1980s of a new national campesino movement focusing on production issues.[4]

The progressive reformists within the ruling party came to the fore again in Mexico during the Echeverría *sexenio* to renew the severely debilitated populist pact and reorder Mexico's development model. Despite the similarities to the Cárdenas period—its nationalism, agrarianism, and attention to ejido production—the Echeverría government, unlike that of Cárdenas, was unable to establish new foundations for economic and political stability in Mexico. Part of this failure can be attributed to the opposition of a private sector that was much more powerful relative to the state than it was in the 1930s. Because of the limited reach of Echeverría's reforms and the government's ambivalent response to campesino organizing, the state failed to build a strong campesino/state alliance that could effectively counter private-sector reaction.

Agrarismo under Echeverría was an adulterated version of Cardenista agrarianism. One Mexican analyst described the Echeverría government's policies as "technocratic populism."[5] Its focus was on providing government services to campesinos producing for the market, while the 30 percent to 50 percent who existed on the margins of the market were largely ignored by Echeverría's populism. Moreover, the rural reforms did not directly challenge the concentration of land, water, and capital in agribusiness. The polarized structure of agricultural production that had taken shape from 1940-70 was left untouched.

Rural development programs were not "integral" as their promoters proclaimed because they failed to recognize the functional links that existed between subsistence and commercial agriculture. The emphasis of the programs was on improved organization and increased state participation, not on equity and redistribution. The government believed that the circumstances of the subsistence sector could be improved without affecting the privileges enjoyed by agribusiness.

At the same time that the Echeverría administration was spending unprecedented sums on rural development, it did not cut back government subsidies for agroexport agriculture. To fund its rural development programs, the government relied on multilateral loans and deficit financing rather than adopting a progressive tax structure. With few exceptions, especially the expropriation of agroexport estates in Sonora and Sinaloa, Echeverría opted for distributive measures that minimally improved rural conditions rather than backing campesino demands for land and water rights that would have reduced the concentration of land and wealth.

While declaring its commitment to improve the lot of the campesino, the government discouraged farmworker organizing despite deplorable conditions and the fact that most *ejidatarios* were also farmworkers. Moreover, Echeverría contributed to the hardening of bimodal agriculture by channeling public-sector investment to agroexport agriculture, granting new exemptions for the importation of farm machinery, and promoting cattle ranching—all of which increased rural unemployment.[6]

By 1976 the populist agenda was in ruins. Having failed to establish a fiscal foundation for the expansion of government services and subsidies, Echeverría ushered in an era of inflation and debt crisis. Another legacy of his reformism was the dependency of small producers on state rural development and marketing agencies over which they had little control. In many instances, the middlemen or *coyotes* who had exploited isolated campesino producers were replaced by inefficient and insensitive state institutions. Because of the lack of attention to inequitable patterns of land and resource control, tensions remained high in the *campo,* and the agricultural crisis persisted.

A Mixed Bag

The business community was relieved to have the populist demagogue Echeverría replaced in 1976 by the moderate José López Portillo (1976-82). It expected the political pendulum to swing back to conservatism, but these expectations were not fully realized. Instead, progressive and conservative currents within the administration struggled for policy control. Attempting to maintain stability, the president shifted back and forth from left to right. As a result, government policy sometimes marked a return to the nationalist populism of Cárdenas and Echeverría. But in other instances government policy foreshadowed the neoliberalism of the De la Madrid, Salinas, and Zedillo governments.

By the end of his term in 1982, however, political and economic instability had pushed López Portillo to adopt policies that responded more to the advocates of populist and nationalist policies. These included the nationalization of the private banking system, the government's withdrawal from General Agreement on Trade and Tariffs (GATT) negotiations, the decision to limit oil exports to the United States, and the creation of the Mexican Food System (SAM).

López Portillo's ambivalent agrarian policy contributed to his uncertain identity. The government's decision not to overturn Echeverría's expropriations of agroexport estates in Sonora angered the landed elite, but generous compensation and his promise that the agrarian reform program would end with his term helped placate the large landholding class. But López Portillo did not want to be remembered as the first postagrarian president, and especially during the first half of his term he occasionally distributed land and recognized land takeovers as a way of defusing rural tensions.[7] He stressed, however, that there was little left to distribute and warned campesinos that they should focus on increasing production not on seeking more land. López Portillo set out to create the ideological, political, and administrative conditions to terminate agrarian reform as a fundamental component of rural political economy in Mexico.[8]

In March 1980, on the forty-second anniversary of the nationalization of Mexico's petroleum industry, the López Portillo government announced the SAM program, an ambitious effort to raise basic grains production and to improve food distribution to the Mexican poor.[9] The creation of SAM was an implicit recognition that agricultural modernization had not touched campesino farmers. It was also an acknowledgment that the agricultural crisis identified in the late 1960s had not gone away. SAM was designed to tackle the dual problem of falling percapita grain production and widespread rural hunger.

Mexico was awash with petrodollars and foreign loans when the program began. The discovery of vast oil reserves in the 1970s had given Mexico a new-found sense of confidence and had opened up seemingly unlimited loan funds from international banks. But all was not well. In 1979 food imports rose sharply, leading some economic planners to conclude that Mexico's oil income was flowing out of the country in the form of food purchases. With the decision of the United States to embargo Soviet grain that same year for political reasons, advocates for a stronger food security policy argued that Mexico's growing dependence on imported grains left the country vulnerable to U.S. political manipulation. This discomfort with the country's deepening food dependence combined with a sense of embarrassment and concern that oil-rich Mexico had a broad stratum of citizens who were malnourished, especially in the *campo*.

Along with good weather conditions, the higher grain prices and reduced costs of production inputs (mainly fertilizers but also pesticides) offered by the SAM program reversed the downward slide in grain production and resulted in national food self-sufficiency in 1981-82. But like Echeverría's rural development program, SAM stood on shaky fiscal grounds. The precipitous drop in oil prices in 1981 and the ensuing debt crisis meant that the government could no longer afford the generous subsidies to grain farmers. In 1982 President Miguel de la Madrid (1982-88) closed the doors of the SAM program.

SAM constituted a last hurrah for the nationalists and populist reformers before the onslaught of neoliberalism. Although only for a short period, it demonstrated that Mexico could be self-sufficient in basic grains with adequate government support. Another less commonly recognized accomplishment of SAM was its creation of a network of autonomous peasant organizations that coordinated the distribution and warehousing of basic foodstuffs for the rural poor.[10] Many of the activists associated with these community food organizations later in the 1980s became key figures in the social enterprises (*empresas sociales*) that were created to help small producers adapt to new market conditions.

Reformism during the López Portillo presidency experienced many of the same limitations and weaknesses seen during the Echeverría term. Like the rural development programs of the previous government, SAM did not set out to restructure agriculture's inequitable bimodal system. Such issues as the concentrated control of land and water and the exploitation of farmworkers were not addressed for fear of upsetting the state's alliance with agribusiness and of sparking increased campesino mobilization.

Accepting the framework of the dual agricultural system, the government never seriously attempted to boost the efficiency and productivity of campesino agriculture. Such a commitment would require not only further agrarian reform but also a comprehensive agricultural extension service that would reach out to the most isolated areas. Instead, the conditions of small farmers were viewed by the government as more of a welfare and political problem than one of stagnating agricultural production.

Even the SAM program, which focused on basic grains production, disproportionately benefited the small sector of ejidos and private farms that had a history of producing commercially and taking advantage of guarantee prices. In other words, only the players in the market benefited, while the poorest campesinos just became poorer. Moreover, the fundamental orientation toward agribusiness of the López Portillo administration was seen in its failure to pursue violations of land limits established by agrarian reform law, the government's close cooperation with agribusiness associations, and its support for the Agricultural Development Law of 1980, which authorized joint ventures between private investors and the ejido sector.[11]

SAM, with its commitment to achieving national food security, represented the end of an era in Mexican politics. During the López Portillo presidency, a debate raged within government and academia over whether to return to a more inward, nationalist approach to development or to link national development more closely to the international market. For a brief period in the last years of the López Portillo presidency, the nationalists had the upper hand in this "dispute for the nation."[12] But the debt crisis and the failure of nationalists and populists to articulate a credible alternative to the neoliberal reformism of the 1980s left the dispute behind.

In this new era shaped by trade liberalization, the price and availability of basic grains has been increasingly left to the market. With free trade, the earlier concerns about food dependency and its impact on national security have been pushed aside by the conviction that a national food policy has no place in a globalized economy. Many of the social and economic problems that SAM attempted to rectify have not gone away. Malnutrition has become more widespread in Mexico, and worsening terms of trade and ecological crises have forced many campesinos to abandon their lands. The agricultural trade deficit and low consumption in the countryside impede economic development. Closely tied to these economic considerations is the threat of rural violence and political instability.

World Bank Backs Neoliberal Policies

With U.S. backing and the leverage provided by the escalating debt crisis, the IMF and the World Bank gained considerable influence in Mexico's economic policy process beginning in 1982. Washington and the multilateral financial institutions operated on parallel tracks in guiding the neoliberal restructuring. The dramatic turnabout in Mexico's economic development policies, long the symbol of inward-looking development, represented a major victory. Mexico took the lead in renegotiating its debt, entering GATT, and joining a regional trade agreement, putting pressure on its Latin American competitors to follow suit. With multilateral guidance, Mexico became a model for deregulation and trade liberalization. As a GATT director remarked, "Mexico has helped maintain the pace for bringing about an ambitious reform of the world trading system."[13]

From 1980 to 1991 Mexico received thirteen structural and sectoral adjustment loans from the World Bank, more than any other country. It also signed six agreements with the IMF, all of which brought increased pressure to liberalize trade and investment. After Mexico acceded to multilateral pressure to join the GATT in 1986, the World Bank granted the country a huge loan. During the Salinas administration, the World Bank further opened the spigots of loans with low-interest rates and easy payback terms.[14]

Although overhauling Mexico's macroeconomic policies has been the recent priority of the World Bank, since the 1950s, it has also taken a leading role in restructuring the country's food system and its agricultural and rural development policies. Along with the Inter-American Development Bank (IDB), the World Bank was a major supporter of the colonization schemes in the humid tropics that were responsible for much of the deforestation in the 1950-80 period. Likewise, in the interests of "development," the multilateral banks provided credit, technical assistance, and investment funds for the expansion of the country's cattle industry. In the

1970s the World Bank backed Mexico's state involvement in the agricultural sector, supporting the expansion of a state-owned fertilizer company.

In the 1980s, however, neoliberal philosophy reshaped World Bank lending. Instead of promoting the state as an important element in agricultural modernization as it had previously done, the World Bank in 1989 directed the Mexican government to "promote greater private-sector participation in the modernization of the food-distribution system," support "further reductions in interest-rate subsidies to farmers," and boost agricultural exports. A commitment to opening markets and deregulating the agricultural economy had replaced the World Bank's previous commitment to equitable rural development.[15]

Although Mexico's political leaders were firm believers in market-based solutions, World Bank loans provided financial rewards for privatizing or dismantling such state institutions as Fertimex and Conasupo, following the Bank's directives of "rationalization [meaning reduction] of public investments in agriculture."[16]

The World Bank conditioned a 1991 sectoral adjustment loan for Mexican agriculture on the implementation of a laundry list of specific measures, including eliminating import permits for more than a dozen food products, removing or slashing agricultural tariffs, canceling price controls on a range of basic food items, privatizing state-owned monopolies, and, most dramatically, eliminating price guarantees for corn.

Having succeeded in a radical restructuring of the agricultural sector and the country's macroeconomic policy, the World Bank after 1991 focused on loans designed to ease the socioeconomic and political repercussions of those measures in rural areas. Its support for the Mexican government's National Solidarity Program (Pronasol) and its targeted spending for the rural population in southern and southeastern Mexico replicate similar social investment funding in other Latin American countries affected by neoliberal restructuring.[17] This contrasts with previous World Bank programs that supported integrated rural development projects in the Mexican countryside. The objective of recent rural spending is more to stave off a rapid deterioration in social welfare and resulting political instability than to promote broad-based development. For the most part, the social investment projects funded by the World Bank do not replace cutbacks in government social services. Instead, they support infrastructure projects that create jobs but have no impact on income distribution and little long-term impact on social welfare. Like its restructuring support, social investment funding attempts to avoid interventions that would distort relative prices, which means that there is little or no support for projects that support campesino production and marketing.

Without the financial support and policy assistance provided by the World Bank, the neoliberal restructuring of Mexico's economy probably would not have proceeded so steadily. However, the tight monetary and market liberalization policies instituted after 1982 were entirely consistent with the neoliberal convictions of the clique that took over from López Portillo. The PRI technocrat elite is at least as committed to the liturgy of privatization, deregulation, liberalization, and international market solutions as are the World Bank planners.

Conservative Restructuring by Technocrats

A continuum of gradually escalating neoliberal restructuring marked the 1982-94 period. Political control of the ruling party fell out of the hands of the old guard and into the hands of a new breed of technocrats. Agrarian and agricultural issues became components of a larger macroeconomic policy that responded to the principles of neoliberalism. The market, free of distortions resulting from state intervention, would be left to shape the direction of economic development and the dimensions of Mexican society. The regulations guiding international trade, domestic farm prices, land markets, and private investments would all be liberalized.

The populism of former state policies received most of the blame for the country's galloping inflation, gaping budget deficit, and debt crisis. The first order of business was a stabilization program that cut government expenditures, kept wages down, and devalued the currency. Piggybacked on the stabilization program was an economic restructuring recommended by foreign creditors that began to privatize state companies and to liberalize trade and investment.

The De la Madrid/Salinas (1982-94) era was a period of counterreform and conservative reformism much like the Avila Camacho and Alemán governments (1940-52) that followed Cardenista populism (1934-40). By early 1995 Ernesto Zedillo, who succeeded Salinas as president on December 1, 1994, had made clear his commitment to the neoliberal policies of his predecessor. Although the party leaders of each era were careful to frame policies in populist rhetoric, they rejected the populist policies of the past and introduced new reforms designed to modernize the economy and increase capital accumulation. In charge of government economic and social policies were foreign-educated economists and planners sometimes called technocrats. Winning control of the PRI from the old-style *políticos*, technocrats set out to modernize Mexico. Discarding former populist pretensions of charting national development strategies, they believed that closer integration with the global market was the only possible path to economic and social progress.

Both agrarian and agricultural policy came to reflect the broad macroeconomic policy that took shape in the 1982-94 period. In other words, how the government responded to the concerns of farmers was increasingly determined not by the special problems of the agricultural sector but by the general outlines of the economic stabilization and restructuring programs. Beginning in 1982 the government began cutting back subsidies and funding for agriculture and privatizing government services. Dramatic changes in agricultural policy came early in the Salinas administration, first with the liberalization of most domestic farm prices and later with the revisions of the agrarian reform law. By freeing growers from the protectionism and paternalism of the past, the government argued that the agricultural economy would become more efficient and productive. Furthermore, rural socioeconomic conditions would improve as trade and investment increased and state interventionism decreased.

The agricultural sector clearly needed help. Internationally, the country still faced serious agricultural deficits, which were aggravated by rising imports of processed foods and feedgrains. Domestically, economic crisis had reduced consumption levels while rural poverty and landlessness were worsening. Government sector support for the agricultural sector was declining, and there was widespread dissatisfaction with the state's rural development and marketing agencies. When the neoliberal reforms were introduced in the mid-1980s, there was little disagreement that a major restructuring of Mexico's agricultural system was in order.

Since 1986 the country's farm sector has experienced a dizzying array of reforms designed to ensure that market relations prevail in production and land use patterns. The relationship between producers and the state has been reordered by the privatization, dissolution, or contraction of state agencies that formerly supplied credit, fertilizer, insurance, technical assistance, and marketing services. The number of parastatals depending on the agricultural minority dropped from ninety-four in 1982 to fewer than ten by 1993. Guarantee prices were eliminated for most farm produce, and the borders were opened up to cheap imports. State subsidies for irrigation, electricity, and chemical inputs were mostly eliminated, and in October 1993 another direct subsidy program called Procampo that was designed to be more compatible with the principles of free trade was put in place.

Topping off all these changes was a constitutional amendment that terminated Mexico's agrarian reform program and opened the way for the privatization of the ejidal sector. After eight decades, the technocrats abandoned the hallowed revolutionary tradition of agrarian populism. According to the government's 1992 program for agricultural conversion, some two million campesino families—about three-quarters of the nation's corn farmers—"will have to search for alternatives in other crops, reorganize their landholdings, associate with private capitalists, or become wage laborers."[18] The administration's vision of rural development was one of a *campo sin campesinos* (land without landworkers).

Pushing forward the conservative reforms of the 1982-94 period were the technocrats with their philosophical commitment to the free market and the private sector. The technocrats increased their influence during the De la Madrid *sexenio* and gained the complete dominance in policymaking during the Salinas years. They believed that only through uncompromising market-oriented reform could the state encourage capital accumulation and economic progress. Furthermore, as the economy expanded and the interventionist state shrunk, social improvement and stability would necessarily follow, thereby eliminating the need for the populist policies of the past. A liberalized market would simultaneously cure the country's deep-seated economic ills and help legitimate a state whose legitimacy was increasingly questioned by all social sectors.

By the end of the Salinas administration, the neoliberal policies of PRI's technocrats, while still firmly in place, were being put to the test not only by the rebellion in Chiapas but also by signs of an unstable economy, including the rising trade deficit, expanding unemployment, an overvalued peso, and lack of private investment in agriculture. Particularly hard hit by trade liberalization, privatization of parastatals, and budget reductions were the rural population and the farm sector (Tables 2-4).

Despite these problems and others, the new PRI government of Ernesto Zedillo seemed intent on continuing and perhaps even deepening the free-market policies of his predecessor. The financial crisis that broke out during his first month as president highlighted the debility of the neoliberal model. Nonetheless, there seemed no turning away from dependence on foreign loans and free market remedies. Indeed, the emergency loans offered Mexico pushed the government to deepen its austerity, privatization, and liberalization reforms. Among the Mexican people, however, there was rising sentiment that Mexico's technocrats had sold their proud past and mortgaged their future all in the name of free trade and free markets.

At each stage in Mexico's history, from the liberalism of the mid-nineteenth century through the reforms and counterreforms of this century, the ideological convictions of Mexican leaders have molded economic and social policies. But this history of changing state policy has at each stage paralleled and responded to changing international economic and political conditions. The debt crisis, foreign pressure for economic restructuring, and the expanding globalization of production, communications, and capital flows constituted the global context for the ascent of neoliberalism in Mexico. It is to this context that we now turn in our examination of free trade and the farm crisis in Mexico.

Table 2

Mexico's Economic Indicators

Growth of Percapita Gross Domestic Product (Average Annual Growth)

1970-1980	3.7
1980-1990	-0.7
1990-1993	0.1
1994	1.3

Percapita GDP (92) — $3,470

Average Annual Growth of Real Wages

1980-1992	-0.8%
1988-1992	3.8%

Terms of Trade (Value of goods exported/imported)

1981-90 (cumulative variation)	-30.2%
1991-94 (cumulative variation)	-8.9%

Outstanding external debt as % of GDP (92) — 53%
Debt servicing as % of Exports (92) — 44%

Trade Balance (Goods) (94) — -$23,645 million

Sources: USAID, Latin America and the Caribbean, *Selected Economic and Social Data, 1994*; CEPAL, *Preliminary Overview of the Economy of Latin America and the Caribbean 1994*; 1993 figures projected; U.S. Census Data, 1990; IDB, *Economic and Social Progress in Latin America, 1994 Report.*

Table 3

State of Population

Population (1994)	92 million
Population growth rate (1980-91)	2.3%
Population growth rate (1993)	2.0%
Urban population growth rate (1990-93)	2.9%
Rural population growth rate (1990-93)	0.2%
% of population living in urban areas (1993)	74%
% of population living in urban areas (1950)	43%
Projected population by year 2020	136 million
Population under 16 years (1992)	40%
Human development index rank among 173 countries (1993)	52
% of rural population living in extreme poverty (1988)	24%
% of urban population living in extreme poverty (1988)	8%

Sources: Bread for the World Institute, *Fourth Annual Report on the State of World Hunger*; CEPAL, *Indicadores sociales básicos: América Latina y el Caribe 1950-92*, July 1993; Inter-American Development Bank, *Social and Economic Progress, 1990*.

Table 4

State of Mexican Agriculture

Agriculture as % of total GDP	7.4%
Industry as % of total GDP	32.9%
Services as % of total GDP	59.7%

Valued added by agricultural sector (average annual growth rates)
1970-80	3.4%
1980-90	1.1%
1990-93	0.9%

Leading agricultural exports: Vegetables, feeder cattle, coffee, tropical fruits
Leading agricultural imports: Sugar, dry milk, corn, meat and cattle products, sorghum, oilseeds, dry beans, and soybeans

Sectoral breakdown of agricultural economy
Farming	57.7%
Livestock	32.7%
Forestry	5.4%
Fishing	4.2%

Average agricultural wage as % of avg manufacturing wage	13%
Average agricultural wage as % of avg construction wage	20%

% of public sector investment in agricultural sector (1980)	15.0%
% of public sector investment in agricultural sector (1991)	7.6%

Average daily family income in rural areas	$5.10
Average daily family income in urban areas	$10.30

Food and agricultural trade balance worldwide in billions (1992)	-$3.1
Mexico's world rank among food importers	12

Sources: USDA statistics; *Comercio Exterior*; Banamex statistics; INEGI statistics; World Bank International Economics Department, April 1993; Economist Intelligence Unit; United Nations, *Handbook of International Trade and Development Statistics;* FAO, "Global Imports and Exports of Agricultural Products by Country," 1992.

A farmworker preparing the ground for planting corn. Alejandro Stuart/Impact Visuals

THE INTERNATIONAL CONTEXT

"It is something like Social Darwinism, the survival of the most capable."

—Prominent Mexican business owner referring favorably to
the government's free trade policies, quoted in
El Financiero International, October 24, 1994.

The reshaping of Mexico's farm sector, the dismantling of its food system, and the social and political turmoil in the countryside are more than manifestations of changing national policies. The radical restructuring of Mexican agriculture responds primarily to the forces of economic globalization. In the context of an integrated world economy, it is increasingly difficult, if not impossible, for countries like Mexico to maintain independent farm and food programs or to pursue national economic development policies.

Advances in communications and transport systems, the emergence of global financial networks, and technological changes serve as the foundation for the closer integration of international markets and production. Spearheading these changes are the transnational corporations (TNCs) that reach beyond national borders and see the entire world as their workplace and market. In its ads on public television, U.S. agribusiness corporation Archer-Daniels-Midland boasts that it is the "supermarket to the world."

In this transnational world, the Marxist maxim that power is in the hands of those who control the means of production needs modification. Ownership of the means of production is still important. But financial power also means controlling the means of distribution, access to world markets, technological research and development, and processing facilities.[1]

National economic policies that have attempted to bolster government legitimacy by protecting domestic production and meeting domestic consumer demands have been among the main obstacles to this economic globalization. In breaking down these barriers, international traders and investors have relied on the assistance of the multilateral financial institutions established at the close of the World War II. In the 1970s and increasingly in the 1980s, the International Monetary Fund (IMF) and the World Bank have taken aim at the farm and food policies of less industrialized countries.

The ascendance of neoliberalism, a set of economic beliefs that subordinates all social and development considerations to the demands of private capital and the world market, has given ideological force to this campaign to deregulate, to privatize state-held industries, and to liberalize trade and investment. Promoted by President Reagan in the United States and by Prime Minister Margaret Thatcher in Great Britain, neoliberalism soon came to dominate the policies of multilateral banks and an emerging class of technocratic politicians in Mexico and elsewhere in Latin America. Neoliberal politicians operate in concert not only with transnational traders and investors but also with national exporters and financiers who have an interest in a more globalized economy.[2]

Mexico's debt crisis and the drop in oil prices in 1981-82 made the country especially vulnerable to pressure for neoliberal restructuring. Encouraged by an influx of stabilization funding and some debt relief, the Mexican government set the country on the path of economic liberalization and integration. The pace accelerated after Mexico joined GATT in 1986, and then again at an even greater pace in 1988 when Carlos Salinas de Gortari became president.

Partly as a response to the financial crisis of the 1980s and also as a result of their own ideological convictions, the De la Madrid and Salinas governments restructured government policy to match the demands of international capital. State policy in the 1980s and early 1990s became a more coherent and focused response to economic globalization, but this adaptation process had been evident for several decades.[3]

In the agricultural sector, the internationalization of capital had been gradually reorganizing local, regional, and national systems of production and trade.[4] Global market prices, technology, and agroindustrial structures increasingly formed the context in which state policy was made. In Mexico, this was seen in the expansion of the feedgrain industry, the greater integration of agriculture and food processing, the expanding role of the TNCs in agroindustry, and increasing government attention to the most technologically advanced and profitable farm sectors. International grain prices influenced state food policies. The high returns of producing exports for affluent foreign markets relative to the low returns of production of goods for low-wage domestic consumers shaped agricultural development efforts. Increasingly, international market structures and the demands of the industrialized nations determined what was produced and local prices.

Although changing international market prices and the evolving demands of capital accumulation established the context for setting national economic policy, the government still attempted to modify the imperatives of the international market with its own political needs for legitimation. Over the past few decades, Mexico has retained modes of economic regulation—guarantee prices, subsidized consumer goods, state supports for agricultural inputs, land distribution, and other policy mechanisms—that either respond to or preempt popular unrest.

But the inroads of global economic integration have made it ever more difficult for Mexico to orient its economy to provide primarily for the needs of its own population. Policies aimed at balancing the needs of national capital accumulation and consumption are undermined by the easy flow of international trade and investment and new global regimes of profit taking. Instead of trying to regulate the national economy, Mexican government officials have acceded to the demands of economic globalization by restructuring economic policy to make the country more attractive to foreign investors and traders.

The old development strategies based on satisfying the demands of the domestic market have been gradually abandoned. The mild redistributive policies of corporatist populism have been rejected as too costly and as obstacles to integration into the global structures of trade and investment. By the late 1980s the broader vision of capitalist growth accompanied by a commitment to improving socioeconomic conditions had given way to a more focused and coherent economic policy designed to mold Mexico to the "requirements" of the global economy.

Although resisted by dissenting elements within the PRI and criticized for its crass economism by the popular political opposition, there have been no comprehensive, credible alternatives offered to the neoliberal strategy. Bolstered by their own confidence and supported by the international community, Mexico's planners have designed economic policies that are a perfect fit for global capital and trade. This has meant liberalizing international commodity exchange, meeting investors' demands for highly flexible, low-wage export production, and facilitating the international circuit of capital.

The dramatic overhaul of Mexico's agricultural economy—the end of land distribution, the opening of the ejido to privatization, liberalization of agricultural commodity prices, the termination of most food and production subsidies, and the abandonment of the state's role in agricultural marketing and distribution—has been a logical extension and indeed a key part of neoliberal restructuring. By opening up the farm sector and the food distribution system to international market forces, the Mexican government turned its back on the nationalist and populist policies of the past and embraced the agroindustrial imperative of today's globalized economy.

Revamping Old Food Systems

Under the pressure of globalization, old food systems are breaking down both in industrialized countries like the United States and less-industrialized ones like Mexico.[5] Most food systems in the post-World War II period were modeled loosely on the one in the United States, which stressed national regulation of the agricultural economy through import barriers and export subsidies. In the United States and Europe, such policies bolstered the farm sectors and quickly resulted in chronic grain surpluses that helped improve a country's trade position. Policies protecting national farm sectors also created a ready source of inputs for burgeoning agroindustries. In less-industrialized nations like Mexico, national food policies helped create a base for industrialization, with the peasantry supplying the nation with both cheap food and cheap labor.

In the capitalist industrial world, trade in manufactured goods became increasingly liberalized in the 1950s and 1960s. But the United States, which played a leading role in shaping international trade policy, insisted on the right to protect and subsidize its farm sector, thereby precluding the possibility of submitting national farm economies to international rules. Yet just as the rising flow of investment capital and changes in technology were restructuring global manufacturing, so too was the world's agricultural economy being reshaped. It was not until the 1980s, however, that the United States began pushing for free trade of agricultural as well as of manufactured goods.

Although farm subsidies have been costly to U.S. taxpayers, the U.S. food system served the nation's postwar economic and political interests. Cheap food and food aid were used to push open national markets in the third world and to reward countries that stayed aligned with U.S. foreign policy. In marked contrast to most other third world nations, Mexico managed to stay relatively self-sufficient in grains at least until the 1970s, mainly because of its agrarian policies. Unlike many food-dependent nations, Mexico was able to maintain an independent foreign policy. The costs of sustaining a national food system and the availability of subsidized grains from the United States led to the Mexican government's decision to dismantle its own food system and to abandon its own structure of agricultural price structure and subsidies.

Having obtained technological superiority in farm production and world dominance of agroindustry, the United States reversed its earlier position and became the leading advocate of liberalized agricultural trade within GATT and other trading agreements. Freeing commodity trade will allow the United States access to new markets without having to compete with the high levels of subsidies offered to European farmers. Mexico, having lost its own food self-sufficiency and grown dependent on imported cheap grains, dropped its previous commitment to maintain control over its food system in the belief that better access to the world market and international capital will guarantee that the food needs are met.

The New Agrofood System

The increased flow of U.S. grains to Mexico, the blossoming of the fast-food industry in Mexican cities, and the presence of more Mexican produce in U.S. supermarkets are all part of the internationalization of the agricultural economy.[6] The new agrofood system is still evolving, but its essential structure has already been put into place by transnational capital. Like manufacturing, agriculture and food distribution are being shaped by the increasing global integration of labor and production. The global market dictates which crops will be produced in which countries. In the hope that this global integration will benefit all trading partners, concerns about food security, the fate of the peasantry, and the future of the family farm are being pushed aside.

Among the main characteristics of this internationalization of farm and food are:

- *Central Place of Agroindustry*

No longer is the family farm the center of the agricultural economy. In both industrialized and less industrialized nations, agroindustry has become the nexus around which agricultural production and food distribution revolve. Farms are simply the suppliers of raw materials to food processing industries, which, like manufacturing industries, have become increasingly globalized. Technological change and new communications systems have facilitated the global sourcing of commodities and the fragmentation of production across borders.

- *Importance of Agroexports*

As countries become more integrated into the global market, agroexport production often takes precedence over production for the domestic market. Agroexports provide the foreign exchange needed for debt payments and to pay for rising food imports. Increased agroexport production also responds to the global sourcing requirements of the internationalized agrofood system.

The major beneficiaries of agroexport production are transnational corporations that supply inputs, extract surpluses, and provide markets. Local producers, especially small farmers, find it difficult to enter the international market when faced with the economies of scale, advertising, marketing resources, access to credit and technology, and flexibility in input-sourcing enjoyed by large commercial producers and TNCs.

- *International Division of Labor*

Under the international division of labor in the agrofood system, the less-industrialized South specializes in the export of labor-intensive crops and traditional tropical agroexports, while the North exports grains and processed foods. This is a fundamentally asymmetric relation in that the

North maintains its food security and dumps its surpluses on the food-poor South, which exports luxury foods to the North. The presence in the United States and Europe of large communities of immigrant workers who work for substandard wages adds another dimension to the international division of labor. In the United States, 70 percent of hired, nonfamily agricultural workers are Latino, 62 percent are foreign-born, and 20 percent are undocumented.[7] As unions are broken and wages fall, the food processing industry in the United States also increasingly depends on foreign-born workers.

- *Economic Factors Dictate Distribution of Global Production*

The internationalization of agriculture enforces a distribution of production more closely based on a region's or a nation's competitive position. As trade barriers fall, production shifts to areas where productivity is higher and costs lower. The cost of producing sugar in the United States rather than importing it from the Caribbean or of growing rice and alfalfa in California deserts becomes more difficult to defend. But the internationalization of agricultural production responds more to the economic rationale of the industrialized, grain-surplus North than it does to the development needs of the labor-surplus South with its lower productivity. Moreover, global sourcing might make good economic sense for a transnational agroindustry, but it makes little environmental sense given the dependence on high-energy inputs and the transportation costs.

- *Liberalized Trade*

National restrictions regulating the entry of foreign goods and capital are breaking down. But national interests still mean that some protections remain in place. Internationalization has not ushered in free trade in the sense of a complete disintegration of regulations but a new system of trade management with new forms of implicit and explicit regulation that facilitate marketing and production on a global scale.[8] GATT and NAFTA have pushed this process forward in Mexico, putting in place trade policies that better reflect the structural realities of the internationalization of agriculture.[9]

- *Asymmetry of Benefits and Impacts*

The impact of the internationalization of agricultural trade is more severe in the South, where food dependency on the North has become a major obstacle to political and economic stability and where traditional agroexports have decreased in value. Instead of flowing South, where it is most needed, capital is flowing to the industrialized nations in the form of debt payments and profits from agroexport and agroindustry investments.[10] Although the internationalization of agriculture clearly favors the TNCs and industrialized countries that are the command centers of the agrofood system, the restructuring of labor and production is also having a destabilizing impact in the North, evident in the deterioration of the family farm economy.

- *Reduced Farm Protection and Subsidies*

Farm subsidies and price supports are decreasing in industrialized and less-industrialized nations as the new agrofood system displaces old food regimes that protected farmer incomes. Most affected are highly protected farm sectors and the most subordinated growers: family farmers in the United States and in Mexico. Domestic farm prices come closer to international market levels, which are still determined by large surpluses generated by industrialized grain exports, which results in more efficient allocation of production but reduces national food security. Mexico has dramatically reduced farm subsidies and public-sector support of agriculture, making its farm sector less competitive in the face of an agribusiness system in the United States that is still based on a vast array of government programs ranging from soil conservation and disaster relief to marketing services and export promotion.

- *Limits to National Strategies for Food Production and Distribution*

With the globalization of agricultural production and distribution, governments are left with little room to develop strategies to increase food production and stimulate the rural economy. As a result, countries are losing their food self-sufficiency capabilities, small farmers are being forced off the land, and rural impoverishment is deepening.

Down on the Farm, Up with Agroindustry

At the center of the new agrofood system is the food processing industry.[11] With the increased control of corporate agribusiness over food processing, the food system is moving farther away from the traditional vision of family farms and local markets. In all farm subsectors—basic grains, dairy, livestock, and even fruit and vegetables—farmers have been subsumed by an industrial process that stretches from petrochemical products and bioengineered genetic inputs to frozen and highly processed food products. Taken together, farmers form a crucial link in this agroindustrial chain, but individually each is replaceable and enjoys no control over the conditions in which they market their products.

Efforts by agribusiness to become independent of the vagaries of weather, international politics, and natural diversity have spurred research efforts to replace agricultural products with synthetics and substitutes. To increase and redirect consumer spending, agroindustries have diversified food products. Cheap and plentiful agricultural products are broken down into basic components and then recombined with texturizers and seasonings to create "designer" foods and food supplements such as flavored nondairy coffee creamers, TV dinners, and nonfat ice cream.

The industrialization of the agrofood system is evident in 1) the concentration in food processing and distribution, 2) the vertical integration of chemical and seed input industries, 3) a high ratio of mostly temporary farmworkers and food-processing workers to actual farmers, and 4) the capture of only a relatively small portion of the value of processed foods by primary producers.

Agroindustry has assumed a distinctly international flavor resulting from cross-border homogenization of diets and global sourcing of inputs. Food processing industries are altering agricultural structures and eating habits around the world, as seen in the following trends:

*Constant search for substitute inputs to reduce costs and increase control, giving companies greater flexibility in response to political and economic developments. This search has given rise to synthetic replacements (hydrogenated soy oil for butter, for example), food substitutes (high fructose corn syrup substituting for sugar, for example), and food engineering (scientifically balanced pet foods and hybrid horticultural products, for example).

* Diversification of input sources (from different countries or regions) to bolster the price-setting capabilities of agribusinesses and obstruct the formation of producer organizations or cartels aimed at winning higher prices for unprocessed commodities.

* Increased control by agroindustry over the production process to guarantee quantity and quality.

* Quality standards set by biochemical engineers and company scientists rather than determined by farmers and natural conditions.

* Creation of consumer needs for new, packaged processed food products, giving rise to specialized niche markets with higher markups.

* Research, development, and marketing expenses for new products, resulting in further concentration of the food processing industry by
marginalizing smaller companies and obstructing competition.

Defense of intellectual property rights in the form of copyrights,
trademarks, and patents is crucial to maintaining this system, which
explains why transnational corporations demand that these "rights" be
protected in all international and regional trade agreements. The resulting
concentration of research and development in the hands of the TNCs
blocks easy access to the industrialized food system, skewing profits
toward technologically advanced countries whose companies retain the
rights over hybrid seeds, genetic materials, and processing technology. In
recent years, nine of every ten patents issued by the Mexican government
went to foreigners, generally for products and manufacturing processes
developed by TNCs.[12]

The extension of international trade agreements to cover such
nontrade issues as the respect for intellectual property rights will further
facilitate TNC control over the world's food system. With the rising
importance of biotechnology—meaning the manipulation of molecular
and cell biology in the search for new products and forms of life—the
control of TNCs over virtually all the related research and technology will
make countries like Mexico more dependent on the purchase of geneti-
cally altered plant and animal life (seeds, crops with enhanced photosyn-
thetic capability, growth hormones, etc.) that has higher productivity and
greater resistance to disease. According to one analysis, the coming
"biorevolution" will result in "the intensification of international trade
linkages, the exacerbation of international scientific disparities, and the
furtherance of national market penetration."[13]

Opponents of neoliberal policies and free trade often charge that
such policies will facilitate increased foreign control over farming and
agroindustry in Mexico. Few dispute this. But is foreign control of
agriculture any worse for farmworker conditions, quality of food, and
food security in Mexico? There is little evidence that domestic firms are
any more or less responsive to Mexico's development needs than are
foreign firms. Simply because domestic capital is involved does not mean
that broader national interests are placed above narrow profit considerations. Instead, the issue is the uncontrolled and rapacious character of the
agrofood system in which Mexican investors participate as willing junior
partners.[14]

The Green Revolution, which aimed to replicate the productivity of agriculture in the North, stimulated the internationalization of Mexico's farm sector by increasing its dependency on inputs and machinery manufactured largely by TNCs. The increasing production of feedgrains, which displaced foodgrain cultivation, also opened the doors to the increased penetration of foreign and Mexican-owned agroindustries.

Such U.S. firms as Ralston Purina and Anderson Clayton quickly assumed control over the animal-food processing industries. As a whole, agroindustry in Mexico rapidly expanded in the 1960s to serve the food needs of the country's expanding middle class. It was in agroindustry that TNCs concentrated their investment in Mexico.[15] Agroindustrialization changed the face of farming and food distribution throughout Mexico, but the new agroindustries and the jobs they created were not evenly distributed throughout the country. Many of the new food-processing industries were established in the major cities or in central states such as Guanajuato, not in the poorest and most isolated regions of rural Mexico.

The postrevolutionary Mexican government took measures to restrict foreign investment in natural resources—land, mining, oil—and public utilities, but since the 1940s it has generally welcomed foreign investment.[16] Rather than investing in direct agricultural production through land ownership, foreign companies invested in agroprocessing and to a lesser extent in contracting for export. Nestlé, for example, produces virtually all the condensed, evaporated, and powdered milk consumed in Mexico, while British American Tobacco and Phillip Morris control more than 95 percent of cigarette sales.[17] An estimated one-third of Mexico's total food-processing capacity is in the hands of U.S.-based TNCs.[18] According to the U.S. Department of Agriculture, Mexican subsidiaries of U.S. firms in 1992 sold $4.6 billion of processed foods in Mexico, in addition to the nearly $2 billion imported from the United States.

Even before Mexico joined GATT and started liberalizing trade, grocery shelves in Mexico were dominated by food products processed by top names in international agribusiness. In recent years the foreign presence in Mexico's agroindustry has broadened. Pepsico recently bought out Gamesa, Mexico's largest cookie and pasta company, and investments by U.S. poultry giants Tyson and Pilgrim's Pride have positioned the companies to take advantage of the boom in chicken consumption. U.S. firms account for most foreign investment in Mexican agroindustry, although two of the largest TNCs, Unilever and Nestlé, are European-owned (Appendix 1).[19]

Agroindustrialization subordinates food production and distribution to corporate interests that regard food only as a source of profits. The rising control of agroindustry and the declining importance of family farms parallels the globalization of the manufacturing industry that has fragmented production across national borders and shaped a flexible international labor force.

In Mexico, as in the United States, farmers have a reduced role in the new food system shaped by agroindustry and export competition. Worse off are those growers who are weakly linked or not connected at all to large-scale agroindustry and who find they have no place in the international economy.

Four

NAFTA PUSHES AGRICULTURAL INTEGRATION FORWARD

"For us campesinos, the problem is that we are just beginning to understand all the implications of free trade and having to compete against U.S. farmers. We don't know why it has to be this way, but it probably means the end to our communities."

—Margarito Sánchez of Tuxtepec, Veracruz, February 1994.

Pressure from the United States and the multilateral banks, along with Mexico's own determination to secure a prominent place in the global economy, helped launch the NAFTA negotiations in 1990. Desperate for foreign capital to finance its widening trade deficit and eager to gain better access to the world's largest market, Mexico proposed that the U.S.-Canada free trade region be extended south to include all three North American countries. The United States, however, had been suggesting hemispheric free trade since the early 1980s. After having decided to renege on its promise to join GATT in 1980 because of nationalist pressures within the López Portillo government, Mexico did sign the multilateral trade agreement in late 1985 and quickened the pace of trade liberalization.[1]

In the 1980s the U.S. government pursued its free trade strategy by entering into bilateral economic liberalization talks with most Latin American and Caribbean nations. In 1987 Washington and Mexico entered into their first "framework agreement" to facilitate trade and investment negotiations, which was followed by a more ambitious agreement in 1989. The multilateral GATT and the bilateral framework agreements, together with the Canada-U.S. Free Trade Agreement of 1988, formed the foundation for the NAFTA talks.

As a rule, international trade agreements have treated agriculture differently from other traded goods. NAFTA represented a precedent-setting step away from this tradition in that agricultural trade was treated prominently in the agreement.[2] Agricultural goods were also emphasized more in the recent Uruguay Round agreement of GATT, but NAFTA liberalization in agricultural goods went far beyond the GATT accord.[3]

In broad terms, NAFTA resulted in the gradual opening of the Mexican grain market to U.S. exports in exchange for the opening of the U.S. fruit and vegetable market to Mexican exports. Also significant was the opening of the U.S. market for sugar and cotton and the Mexican market for dry beans, oilseeds, apples, meat, and dairy products. NAFTA's full impact on the U.S.-Mexico agricultural balance of trade will not be felt until 2009 when all tariffs are phased out. However, unless there is dramatic growth in Mexico's agroexport sector, it is likely that NAFTA; together with Mexico's own economic policy reforms, will weaken Mexico's farm sector, deepen its dependence on U.S. trade and investment, and widen its agricultural trade deficit with the United States (Table 5). Projections by the U.S. Department of Agriculture indicated that the U.S. agricultural trade surplus with Mexico rose in 1994 and will rise again in 1995.

Although tariff barriers are explicitly addressed in NAFTA, even before NAFTA was signed Mexico unilaterally began dropping its tariffs to demonstrate to the U.S. government its abiding commitment to liberalized trade. During the negotiations, the many U.S. nontariff barriers in fruits and vegetables were largely ignored, raising the possibility that even as tariffs decrease, Mexican agroexports may be blocked by other trade barriers. Both nations are allowed to maintain domestic standards concerning the classification, grading, and marketing of domestic goods, which can also apply to imported produce. Since the U.S. regulatory system, which frequently responds to the protectionist demands of domes-

Table 5

Asymmetries of U.S.-Mexico Economic Integration

% of Mexican exports to the United States (93)	74%
% of U.S. exports to Mexico (93)	8%
% of Mexican imports from the United States (93)	72%
% of U.S. imports from Mexico (93)	6%
% of foreign investment in Mexico from United States (92)	63%
% of foreign investment in United States from Mexico (92)	0.15%

Sources: U.S. Embassy, *U.S. Direct Investment in Mexico;* Congressional Research Service, *North American Free Trade Agreement: U.S.-Mexico Trade and Investment Data,* May 19, 1993; FAO, "Global Imports and Exports of Agricultural Products by Country," 1980-1992.

tic growers, is more developed, such "marketing orders" will likely limit Mexican exports to the United States more than U.S. exports to Mexico.[4]

Even after NAFTA, federal marketing orders remain effective for nearly fifty fruits, vegetables, nuts, and other specialty crops, representing continuing indirect trade barriers for such products as avocados, grapefruit, limes, oranges, olives, table grapes, potatoes, onions, and tomatoes.[5] In addition, as a safety mechanism to ensure that certain farm sectors in each country are not dramatically impacted during the tariff phase-out period, NAFTA incorporated special safeguards that provide "tariff snapbacks" to higher levels.[6]

Some free trade opponents feared that NAFTA would mean a downward harmonization of phytosanitary (plant health) measures that protect consumers. But consumer rights advocates succeeded in pressuring negotiators to adopt standards that at least on the surface appear to protect U.S. producers and consumers against downward harmonization. NAFTA allows a country to maintain higher standards as long as those standards do not arbitrarily discriminate against other products.[7] In the event that an aggrieved party feels that such measures are discriminatory, that nation will have the burden of establishing proof.

Not solely a trade agreement, NAFTA also addressed such nontrade issues as intellectual property rights, services, and the movement of capital. Exceptions to liberalized trade and the incorporation of nontrade issues made NAFTA both more and less than a textbook free trade agreement. Rather it was a "managed trade" agreement that incorporated measures to ease the flow of capital but not labor.

The agreement studiously avoided all discussion of the movement of labor in the region, allowing the United States to keep its southern border closed to northbound labor flows. Mexico hoped that a free trade agreement with the United States would ease U.S. investors' concerns about its political and economic stability and thereby lead to an greater flows of U.S. private capital—on which the country's neoliberal development model was becoming increasingly dependent.

NAFTA prohibits Canada, Mexico, and the United States from requiring foreign investors to meet export targets, buy inputs from domestic suppliers, and sell equity to national citizens. Since the Mexican Revolution the government has used each of these techniques to shape the beneficial impact of foreign investment. NAFTA also protects investors from expropriation and guarantees firms the right to repatriate profits and capital in hard currency. In addition, the agreement requires Mexico to grant "national treatment" to foreign investors—that is, not to favor domestic businesses over foreign ones (with a handful of exceptions).[8]

Although NAFTA did address investment restrictions in Mexico, the impact of NAFTA on investment flows in agriculture will probably prove minor given the measures that Mexico had already unilaterally undertaken to promote foreign investment.[9] Most important were the new foreign investment regulations adopted in 1989 and the 1992 reforms to the agrarian law, both of which eased restrictions on foreign investment in land and production.[10] Changes in the country's investment and agrarian laws had already removed many of the restrictions that U.S. investors opposed. By making specific reference to the rights of foreign investors in the free trade agreement (which has treaty status in Mexico), foreign investors felt doubly assured that Mexico would not adopt new policies restricting the flow of investment capital or the activities of foreign corporations.[11]

U.S. and other foreign investment in Mexican agriculture is likely to increase in coming years, although probably not to the extent the Mexican government has been counting on or free trade advocated predicted. Other reasons for scant agricultural investment is the limited profitability of agriculture and its high-risk compared to other investments in Mexico. Some sectors are likely to see increased foreign investment include citrus, frozen vegetables, poultry, fish, and alcoholic beverages.

Not affected by NAFTA are government subsidies to bolster exports by making them more competitive with products subsidized by competing governments.[12] Along the same lines, NAFTA preserves the right of countries to impose countervailing duties on NAFTA partners when confronted by product dumping. In general, NAFTA did not affect the policies of its signatories regarding domestic farm supports. Each party agreed, however, to work toward measures for domestic support that do not distort trade or production. In recent years, Mexico has taken major steps to "rationalize" its market and cut public-sector spending, including reducing or eliminating farm input subsidies and price supports.

NAFTA Farm Provisions

NAFTA assigns all agricultural products to one of four categories: immediate tariff and import quota elimination; and five-, ten-, and fifteen-year eliminations (Appendix 2). The first category of full and immediate elimination as of January 1, 1994 affected nearly 60 percent of the value of U.S.-Mexico agricultural trade (based on 1991 figures), while approximately another 5 percent of trade will be liberalized in five years, another 30 percent in 10 years, and the remaining 5 percent in fifteen years. Tariffs on the most "import-sensitive" products—for instance, orange juice, sugar, and peanuts for the United States and corn, beans, and some dairy products for Mexico—will be phased out over the longer period of fifteen years. As trade barriers fall, it is likely that the current mix of trade between the two countries will change.

NAFTA also eliminated all existing import and export quotas and licenses. Items previously subject to quotas or licenses are now subject to tariff-rate quotas, which specify a certain quantity of goods that can annually enter free of tariffs or at lower tariff rates. Higher tariff rates, which will be phased out over five to fifteen years, will affect the balance of goods that enter a country. In the case of corn, 2.5 million metric tons of duty-free corn was allowed to enter Mexico the first year of NAFTA (with duty-free access increasing 3 percent annually for the remaining fourteen years of that transition period), while all U.S. corn exports that exceed the annual duty-free quota will be subjected to a tariff that gradually declines to zero over fifteen years.

In horticultural products, trade negotiators based the tariff-elimination timetables on the seasonality of products and the degree to which Mexico's exports compete with U.S. produce. Summer crops were phased out immediately, while trade in spring crops will be totally liberalized in five years. Winter crops will be protected by tariffs for ten years. Where grains are concerned, NAFTA specifies transition periods of fifteen years for phasing out restrictions on imports of dry edible beans and corn, and ten years for barley and malt, rice, soybeans, and wheat. Immediate duty-free status was provided for sorghum.

Uneven Impact

NAFTA pushes both the United States and Mexico away from the special protected status enjoyed by their respective agricultural sectors. However, impacts in the two countries will be entirely uneven. The United States' farm-support programs, its research and development capabilities, its more abundant natural resources, and the more technological character of U.S. agriculture make it easier for U.S. producers to compete in the international arena, especially when compared to a country like Mexico where the infrastructure for agricultural production and marketing is so minimal. In basic grains cropping, there are enormous differences in yields and labor productivity between the two countries (Table 6).[13] Generally only Mexico's low-cost labor, its counter-seasonal production cycles for vegetables, and its tropical and subtropical climates—not any greater productivity—create a niche in the U.S. market for its export offerings.

Since the mid-1980s both the United States and Mexico have been steadily reducing their support for domestic farmers. Measured by what are called Producer Subsidy Equivalents (PSEs), support levels in the U.S dropped from 32-34 percent in 1986 to 18-19 percent in 1992. In Mexico, the levels dropped from 30 percent to 13 percent during approximately the same period. Going into NAFTA, then, the Mexican agricultural sector was less protected than the powerful and competitive U.S. farm community.[14]

As a result of both NAFTA and trade liberalization under GATT, it will become more difficult for Mexico to reduce its trade deficit by regulating the flow of food imports. During NAFTA's first year, U.S. agricultural exports to Mexico jumped by 24 percent while food imports from Mexico increased by only 4 percent. Large increases in U.S. exports of grains, oilseeds, and animal products accounted for most of the U.S. trade surplus. The agricultural and food trade gap with the United States has been widening since the mid-1980s as U.S. exports to Mexico increase at a faster pace than Mexican exports to the United States. Trade liberalization, while generally favoring the more competitive U.S. agricultural and food-processing sectors, is negatively impacting elements of the U.S. farm and farmworker community. As tariffs decrease and import quotas disappear, protected sectors like the sugar and tobacco industries will be forced to compete with lower-cost producers in tropical regions. Although vegetable growers in Texas and California will be relatively unaffected by winter vegetables from Mexico, tomato growers in Florida may prove unable to compete. Already, many hundreds of farmworkers in Florida have been left without jobs as Florida growers cut back production.

Trade liberalization, however, is taking a far greater toll in Mexico. Rice farmers in Veracruz, sorghum producers in Durango, apple farmers in Chihuahua, and cotton growers in Tamaulipas have been hard hit as the government has eliminated price supports on most grains and opened the border to cheaper agricultural imports. Most dramatic will be the impact on small farmers who have traditionally sold corn on the domestic market and benefited from guarantee prices more than double the international market price. As support prices for corn are eliminated, most corn farmers will find they can no longer cover their costs and will drop out of the market. Mexico hopes that as the U.S. market opens up its nontraditional agroexports will increase to cover the costs of increased food imports. The prospects for Mexico's agroexport economy, which are discussed in the following chapter, are at best mixed, especially considering that substantially increased investment in export production has not been forthcoming.

NAFTA along with GATT opened Mexican borders to cheaper agricultural commodities and often better-quality food products. The main beneficiaries of the increased offering of imported food were not the half of Mexico's population that is poor but members of the middle class who purchased the bulk of processed food and the government, which saw cheap U.S. grains as a justification to eliminate costly support prices and subsidies for foodstuffs. Meanwhile, the poor experienced rising food costs as the government has adopted a neoliberal program of market deregulation.

In Mexico, NAFTA represented the triumph of the neoliberals over the populists and nationalists. The trade accord was both a response to the forces of globalization and a stratagem to ensure that the neoliberal program of Mexico's doctrinaire technocrats will remain firmly in place. The forces of globalization constructed the framework for regional economic integration. The impact of NAFTA cannot be separated from a series of neoliberal measures, including the end to agrarian reform, privatization of state companies that served farmers, cutbacks in government credit, and domestic-market deregulation.

Together with NAFTA and GATT, this neoliberal restructuring blindly handed over Mexico's farm and food sector to the leveling forces of the international market. Straitjacketed by their uncompromising market philosophy and using NAFTA as a cover for domestic restructuring, Mexican technocrats dodged the responsibility of designing a farm policy that would respond to Mexico's own development and food needs. This lack of responsibility on the part of Mexico's government became all the more obvious in early 1995 when a plummeting peso meant that the country would have to pay a higher price for its increasing dependence on food imports.

Table 6

U.S. and Mexican Agriculture Comparisons

Contributions to Economy

Mexican agricultural sector as % of GDP (93)	7.4%
as % of EAP* (93)	24%
U.S. agricultural sector as % of GDP (93)	1.4%
as % of EAP (93)	2.4%
Agriculture income per farmer in Mexico	$556
Agriculture income per farmer in United States	$30,766
Mexican agriculture exports as % of agriculture GDP (92)	12%
U.S. agriculture exports as % of agriculture GDP (92)	52%
% of Mexico's agriculture exports sold to U.S. (92)	82%
% of Mexico's agriculture imports supplied by U.S. (92)	64%
% of U.S. agriculture exports sold to Mexico (93)	8.8%
% of U.S. agriculture imports supplied by Mexico (93)	9.6%
Mexico's trade deficit with the United States in total agricultural products in billions (94)	-$1.5
Increase of U.S. agricultural exports to Mexico (93-94)	24%
Increase of Mexican agricultural exports to U.S. (93-94)	4%

	U.S.	*Mexico*
Arable land**	189.9 million ha.	24.7
Arable land/person	.75 ha.	.27
Use of hybrid seeds	~100%	12-16%
Irrigated land/ agricultural EAP	6.5 ha.	.55

	U.S.	Mexico
Crop Yields (92)		
Corn	8.25 MT/ha.	2.13
Dry Beans	1.66	0.66
Rice	6.41	4.15
Wheat	2.65	3.85
Sorghum	4.57	3.58
Soybeans	2.53	2.13
Tomatoes	57.7	21.9
Milk	6,774 (kg/cow)	1,237
Labor productivity		
Corn, kg/wrkr-hr.	1,000	7.3
Beans, kg/wrkr-hr.	130	2.5
Tractors/	164	1.8
100 agricultural EAP		
Combines/	231	2
1000 agricultural EAP		
Fertilizers (kg.)/farmer	5,812	192

---

* EAP refers to Economically Active Population.

** One hectare (ha.) equals 2.47 acres.

Sources: Congressional Budget Office, Agriculture in the North American Free Trade Agreement (Washington: 1993); "Sumario Estadístico," *Comercio Exterior,* 1994; Economist Intelligence Unit Limited, *Country Profile: Mexico* (London, 1993); Interview, Lee Schatz, FAS Grain and Feed Division, Oct. 3, 1994; U.S. Census Data, 1990; USDA/FAS U.S. Trade Data Collection; North American Free Trade Agreement: U.S.-Mexican Trade and Investment Data; José Luis Calva, *Probables Efectos de un Tratado de Libre Comercio en el Campo Mexicano* (Mexico City: Fontamara, 1991); FAO, *Quarterly Bulletin of Statistics* 6 (1), 1993; *FAO Production Yearbook,* 1992.

Five

THE EXPORT SOLUTION

"Nowhere in the mountain villages of the campesino economy does one see the kind of misery and exploitation that
farmworkers suffer in modern agriculture regions. The
wealthier a region is, the poorer are its peasant workers. Just
look at the miserable settlements that surround the richest
valleys and irrigated zones of the country."

—Enrique Astorga Lira, *Mercado de trabajo rural en México:*
Ya mercancía humana (Mexico's Rural Labor Market: Human
Merchandise), 1985.

Along with the increased importance of food processing, agroexport
production is the other main pillar of the new internationalized agrofood
system. Agroexports are not new in Mexico or in other less industrialized
nations. Mexico has been exporting products to Europe and the United
States ever since colonial days. What is new is that some of the world's
most industrialized nations have also become major food exporters. The
industrialized nations of Europe and North America now account for more
than 60 percent of the world's total agricultural exports. The United States
alone accounts for approximately 30 percent of world wheat exports and
60 percent of world corn exports.[1]

Less-developed nations like Mexico, under pressure to pay off
foreign debts and increase sources of foreign exchange, have prioritized
agroexport production within their farm sectors. Having rejected former
development models based on meeting expanding domestic demand with

increased production, these countries have accepted the principle that economic development is best guaranteed by attracting foreign investment to stimulate increased production for wealthier foreign markets.

Yet unlike the United States, which also tries to bolster agroexports, Mexico is not dumping domestic food surpluses on the foreign market. Instead it exports such nonessential produce as strawberries and coffee. Although there is a complementary character to U.S.-Mexico agricultural trade, Mexico needs imported inexpensive grains and milk products far more than the United States needs Mexican feeder cattle or tomatoes.[2] Problems arise when food imports outpace the growth in the volume of agroexports and when growers find themselves competing for a place in a limited market with an ever-rising number of growers from other areas of Mexico or other countries.

In the case of the United States, its export prominence in grains is the result of its long history of protectionism and farm subsidies, while its technological superiority and marketing skills account for its dominance of the processed food trade. In contrast, Mexico's agroexport sector did not emerge as a result of a coherent national food strategy and is the product neither of technological competitiveness nor of surplus production. Rather, it depends on low-cost labor and responds primarily to foreign market fluctuations.[3]

Shaped by Foreign Investment and Trade

Another major distinction between the export sectors of the United States and Mexico is that U.S. foreign investment has for more than 100 years shaped and maintained an important presence in the agroexport sector in Mexico.[4] In the late 1800s the U.S. expansion into Mexico paralleled the development of the West, and agroexports increased at the rate of 6 percent annually until shortly before the Mexican Revolution. Attracted to Mexico by the vast land concessions granted by the Díaz regime and the country's new railroad network, U.S. investors along with a small Mexican elite enriched themselves at the expense of the impoverished peasantry.

In the northern states, land companies and individual robber barons from the western United States invested in modern cattle and mining operations, laying the foundations for the anti-gringo nationalism of the

Mexican Revolution. Land concessions also attracted U.S. investors to the rich Sonoran and Sinaloan river valleys, which were converted into fruit and vegetable farms.[5] In the Southeast, U.S. investors were the leading forces in the *chicle* (gum), banana, and timber industries.

But the instability of the Mexican Revolution dampened enthusiasm for investment opportunities in Mexican agriculture, and later the Great Depression caused U.S. investors to regroup at home. It was not until after World War II that U.S. investors again began to look to Mexican agriculture. Actually the demand for Mexican produce, especially tomatoes, began during the war when U.S. farm production proved unable to meet both the food demands of the troops and domestic consumption.[6] Since the 1940s, nontraditional exports, mainly fruit and vegetables, have occupied a rising share of Mexico's export offering, although more traditional exports such as coffee still dominate the agroexport economy.

Mexico's agricultural exports surged in the 1940-60 period, expanding at an annual rate of more than 10 percent. Reflecting the generalized stagnation of the agricultural economy and as commercial growers began producing feedgrains and other crops that satisfied the demands of the expanding middle class, agroexport growth slowed in the 1960s. The contribution of agroexports to total exports rose from 25 percent in 1940 to 51 percent in 1960, and then began declining to 44 percent by 1970, 10 percent by 1980, and 6 percent in 1990.[7] The declining share of the export sector since 1970 is due largely to the increase of petroleum and *maquila* exports. The decline in proportional share of agroexports is not in itself a sign of ill health. Rather the problems are that agroexport income has not kept up with volume as the terms of trade decline for Mexico's exports and that agricultural imports have outpaced agroexport growth, thereby contributing to Mexico's increasingly problematic trade deficts.

Mexico's legal prohibition against foreign land ownership never proved a major obstacle to TNCs and other smaller foreign investors. Both agroexporters and those foreign investors targeting the national market actually prefer contracts rather than direct ownership of land and production.[8] This trend parallels patterns of foreign investment throughout the world, as investors have found that contracting production rather than directly owning and managing large estates is more cost effective. Investors regard land more as a factor of production than one of control or of market influence. Because land is considered more of as an input than as capital, foreign firms gain "effective" control in agricultural land through their ownership of nonland equity capital. By reducing the fixed costs of foreign investors, this system ensures that individual growers bear most of the risk of crop failure. Also, by not owning land and not directly managing farm labor, contracting corporations distance themselves from potential political conflicts.

Generally, U.S. agribusiness contracts to purchase that part of the harvest that meets specified quality standards, while providing growers with financing, technical assistance, seeds, and agrochemicals.[9] Even when foreign investors are not involved, there is a strong foreign foundation to agroexport production in Mexico formed by imported agricultural inputs. Virtually all the seed used in horticultural export production come from the United States, and only thirteen of the forty-one main pesticides used in Mexico are domestically supplied active ingredients.[10]

Although they usually do not own or cultivate the land, foreign agribusinesses exercise substantial control over the production process through their buying power, technology, and market links. Often the contracting corporations are so involved in the production process that they even direct soil preparation and cultivation schedules to ensure the quantity and quality needed to stock U.S. produce counters. Government cutbacks in its agricultural budget and the lack of any serious commitment to improve its agricultural research capabilities also make Mexican growers dependent on the flow of agricultural "know-how" from the United States. The penetration and control of foreign contractors have risen as the Mexican government has encouraged foreign investment as a means of financing rural development, especially in agroexport agriculture.

In the 1970s the government worked closely with the National Union of Fruit and Vegetable Producers (UNPH) to regulate the production and export of horticultural products in an effort to keep prices high, maintain quality control, and control marketing.[11] The corporatist oligopoly that the UNPH represented clearly benefited associated growers, but it also kept others from entering the agroexport economy while serving as a vehicle of political control for the PRI. With the termination of the system of export licenses and the PRI's embrace of a neoliberal program, the control exercised by corporatist organizations such as the UNPH faded while the influence of private exporting houses and foreign contractors increased.[12]

Although contract farming diminishes control by farmers and increases their exposure to risk, the contract does give Mexican growers access to credit, technology, and a market that they otherwise might not have. From Baja California to Michoacán, the contract system is common, but small growers often have difficulties entering it. Instead, U.S. brokers and produce companies generally prefer to deal with only larger growers, landowners, and entrepreneurs. Contract farming is emblematic of the penetration of the agrofood system not only in Mexico but also in the United States, where the remaining family farms supply oligopolistic food distributors and processors like Cargill, Archer-Daniels-Midland, and Continental Grain.[13]

Contract production facilitates global sourcing of agricultural products. The increased availability of fruits and vegetables in U.S. supermarkets testifies to the internationalization of agricultural production. No longer limited by seasonal availability, U.S. firms source their horticultural products throughout the world but mainly in Mexico, which supplies more than 80 percent of all fresh vegetables imported by the United States.[14]

Industry analysts predict that in the near future melons and most other fruits and vegetables in the produce section will have equal sales every month of the year.[15] More than agricultural sectors that produce primarily for the domestic market, the nontraditional export sector has attracted foreign participation, mostly in the form of credit, contract production, and technology rather than direct investment.

This profitable farm sector has also been a focus for Mexican investors who, like their U.S. counterparts, also engage in contract farming. In many cases Mexican investors have also established warehousing and distribution firms across the U.S. border, but only a narrow stratum of Mexican growers participate in the fruit and vegetable export business. A few dozen growers, for example, control the bulk of the fresh tomato export business.[16] Because of the high production costs — an estimated $2,600 per hectare for broccoli and $8,800 per hectare for strawberry production—small farmers are effectively excluded from the agroexport economy. As government support for *ejidatarios* and other small farmers decreases, the prospects for the campesino population to diversify into nontraditional export productions have further diminished.[17]

Looking North for Markets

Until 1979 Mexico experienced a steady surplus in agricultural trade, but now it is only the rare year in which Mexico exports more agricultural commodities than it imports. Mexico sends more than 80 percent of its agroexports to the United States, but only 10 percent of U.S. agricultural imports come from Mexico.

U.S.-Mexico agricultural trade is highly complementary. Of U.S. exports, 85 percent come from three product groups: animal products, grains (principally sorghum and corn), and oilseeds and oilseed products (principally soybeans, soybean meal, and oil). Similarly, 85 percent of Mexico's agricultural exports to the United States come from three product groups: fresh and processed fruits and vegetables, coffee, and live cattle. Large farmers dominate the fruit and vegetable export business, while both small- and large-scale farmers and ranchers participate in the coffee and cattle trade.

Horticultural products constitute the largest category of all Mexico's agroexports, accounting for approximately 50 percent of the total value of agricultural exports.[18] However, coffee is by far the single leading agricultural product, accounting for nearly 15 percent of Mexico's agricultural exports. Climate differences, which produce counter-cyclical growing seasons for many products, shape U.S.-Mexico horticultural trade. Roughly half of Mexico's agroexports to the United States are horticultural products. Although there is a clear pattern of complementary production, to a limited degree Mexican exports of tomatoes, cucumbers, bell peppers, and strawberries do overlap with U.S. growing seasons, especially in Florida.

The international division of labor, so evident in the export-oriented *maquila* sector, can also be seen in Mexican agriculture.[19] With labor costs lower in Baja California, many California growers have moved their labor-intensive operations south. Migrant families from Oaxaca pick strawberries and tomatoes and then place them in crates with English marketing labels.[20] Wage and technology differentials explain why the production of vine-ripened tomatoes is shifting to Mexico while the hardier, machine-friendly tomatoes are found in the fields of Florida and California. Although it is generally true that Mexican production is more labor-intensive, the country's horticultural sector, like most other parts of the economy, is becoming more capital-intensive and technologically sophisticated.

It is unlikely that the lowering of tariffs as a result of NAFTA will result in a surge of Mexican horticultural products into the United States. That is because the main patterns of horticultural production have been determined less by tariff barriers than by the complementary growing seasons, the longer producing season in Mexico, and the lower cost of production because of cheap labor and land.[21] However, some shifts in U.S. production to Mexico are likely as a result of the country's improved investment climate and because of rising land, water, and regulatory costs in the United States.

Too much can be made of Mexico's comparative advantage in fruit and vegetable production. Cheap land and labor together with the lack of occasional freezes do favor Mexican production. But the lack of adequate postharvest holding facilities, agricultural research and extension services, and an adequate transportation infrastructure keeps Mexico less competitive. Official corruption and delays entering the United States are other factors that make agroexport production in Mexico a logistical nightmare. Growers and contractors in Baja California also find that their most experienced workers and the ones who might make good managers are lost to the more attractive U.S. labor market. Although Mexican yields have improved, they commonly still fall below the yields enjoyed by U.S. growers. A looming problem for horticultural production in Mexico is lack of water and the salinization of irrigated lands, which are the environmental consequences of excessive groundwater pumping and deteriorating watersheds. This is also a rising problem in the United States, but it is more severe in Mexico because of its regular droughts, scarcity of arable land, and lack of adequate land-use and water planning

Looking Every Day for Work

Misery and economic desperation seem invariably to accompany the internationalization of agriculture in Mexico. The areas of Mexico where modernized cash-crop and agroexport is most advanced are also the areas where rural poverty is most dehumanizing. The farmworkers who weed the fields and pick the produce for the international market are part of an expanding rural underclass of the landless and land-poor who look to seasonal farm labor for their economic salvation.

It is a salvation that comes day to day, since there is never any security that there will be work tomorrow. The *jornaleros* are commonly hired only for a day's work. If the market is good and work available, there might be work tomorrow. If not, the farmworker families pack their *morrales* to join the migrant flow to another state where they hear that work is available picking melons, strawberries, tomatoes, or other cash crops. They are the *golondrinas* of the agroexport economy who follow the crops and the seasons throughout Mexico, hoping only that there will be enough work to ensure that their families survive another day, another season.

The small farmer and the farmworker are frequently one and the same person. For most campesinos—an estimated 80 percent—the family *minifundio* or ejido parcel provides only a home base and a declining part of their survival needs. While their personal identity and dignity are commonly closely associated with their own cropping, most peasants are in fact rural proletarians who depend on seasonal planting, weeding, and harvesting work on estates that are sometimes far away from their villages. As land becomes more scarce, the *campesinado* and the *jornalero* population is becoming increasingly differentiated. A rural proletariat that has little or no connection to traditional campesino agriculture has become a permanent presence, especially in the northwestern states.

Coffee, vegetable, fruit, cotton, and sugarcane harvesting requires at least one million *jornaleros*. Other cash crops, including the commercial production of basic grains, depend on hundreds of thousands more temporary workers. The number of landless and land-poor peasants looking for seasonal work has been estimated between 4.5 million and 5.6 million.[22] But these estimates are not based on any comprehensive surveys, and because of the absence of good employment data it is difficult to determine the extent to which the women and children involved in farm labor are considered in the estimates. In fact, as the traditional rural economy fractures and disintegrates, women and children constitute an ever-increasing part of the farmworker population.

Although many of these migrant families have never seen a map, they have their own mental maps, a geography defined by growing seasons that takes them from their peasant villages to Chiapas for coffee, Morelos and Veracruz for sugar, and the great Northwest for the fruit and vegetable harvests. The young and more ambitious move on to the United States. Their world visions expand to include the grape fields of California and the berry bushes of Oregon and Washington. Migrant farmworkers personally experience the vagaries of internationalized agriculture. They know that a freeze in Florida means more work in the fields of Sinaloa or that an economic slowdown in the United States probably means less farm work that year.

Things are much the same no matter what crops they pick or what part of the cash-crop world they find themselves in: too many workers and not enough cash. Entire extended families join the migrant stream, competing for jobs with other migrant families and with the local farmworker population. Unable to provide for themselves, the *ejidatarios* and *minifundistas* living near the agroexport estates also look for jobs in the fields and packing sheds. This local farmworker community grows each year as some of the *golondrinas* tire of following the seasons and drop out of the migrant stream.

The *enganchadores* (contractors), euphemistically also called *habilidatores* (enablers), deal in human merchandise. The workers are contracted in their villages and then transported long distances—"packed like cigarettes," complained one woman—in the back of trucks to the agribusinesses. In other cases, the contractors simply select crews from crowds of unemployed waiting in the early mornings in the towns near the estates. The young and strong are the ones who have the best chance of getting the $5 a day jobs. Left behind are those who look weak or too old for the rigors of slaving all day in the hot sun. The cut-off age in citrus, which requires climbing trees, is about 30-32 years, while the mid-40s is the effective retirement age in most field crops. It is a free labor market with no social security, and the abundant reserves of unemployed peasant youth mean that the prematurely aged are turned away, forgotten, and left to their own despair. The cruelty of the labor market is also evident in the early mornings when men and women gather in the dark around the pick-up trucks of *enganchadores*, bidding down their daily wages in desperation for pesos to feed themselves and their families.

The large supply of farm labor keeps the living and working conditions of agroexport workers among the most deplorable in Mexico. Employers often do not comply with minimum wage or overtime requirements.[23] At the peak of the harvest season in Sonora and Sinaloa the migrant population booms. In cities like Culiacán and Ciudad Obregón, migrant families who have no housing bed down at night along the sidewalks, plazas, railroad stations, and bus terminals. At the heart of the harvest season, from July to September, sleeping bodies are strewn throughout the most well-do-towns of northwestern Mexico. In the morning, as early as 3:00 a.m., the workers start their days with a breakfast of rice water and a couple of tortillas.

When housing is provided, it is the worst imaginable sort. Surrounded by fences and patrolled by company guards, the rows of sheds where migrant families live look and feel like concentration camps in some areas. In other cases, workers erect their own tar-paper and cardboard shacks on the outskirts of the agroexport farms. Exhausted after a day's work, workers return to their migrant camps in the blazing afternoon heat, but they have no running water, electricity, or toilets.

Most farmworkers in Mexico are not organized. When they are part of a labor union they often do not even know it.[24] The Mexican government and agroexporters have discouraged farm labor organizing by harassing and repressing independent organizers. The National Campesino Federation (CNC) has, as part of its pact with the government, ignored the plight of farmworkers, even though most campesinos leave their villages to seek seasonal work on commercial farms. The Mexican Workers Federation (CTM) does have some union contracts with agroexporters, but the workers rarely benefit or are even aware that these "unions" exist. For the growers, an official union contract serves as protection against independent labor organizing, while the CTM bureaucracy gets a cut of the workers' daily wages without having to represent their interests. The Independent Central of Campesino and Agricultural Workers (CIOAC) has been involved in the most important independent unionizing efforts, which take place mainly in Baja California and Sinaloa but also in Chiapas.

Factories of the Fields

Although cash crops, particularly agroexports, offer better income potential than the traditional *milpa* cropping of corn and beans, increased agroexport production for the world market will not necessarily improve the lot of the rural population. Mexico has a long history of agroexport production, and the peasantry has learned that the cultivation of agroexports does not hold the key to unlocking rural development.

For the most part, campesinos participate in the international agricultural economy mainly as seasonal labor. Only a small percentage of Mexican peasants who work as wage laborers in the farm economy find full-time jobs. Aside from the foremen and mechanics, most farmworkers only find temporary jobs, which commonly pay only the minimum wage and do not offer social security or other benefits. Because of the seasonal and migratory character of the agroexport workforce, increased exports to the United States are unlikely to slow northbound immigration flows. In fact, by encouraging more workers to enter the internal migratory stream, increased agroexport production may even spark new international migration.[25]

Even when horticultural production is directly linked to agroindustry, it fails to offer steady employment. El Bajío, a fertile agricultural region located northwest of Mexico City, has become a center of U.S. agroindustry, attracting such companies as Del Monte, Anderson Clayton, Campbell, Green Giant, and Bird's Eye. Since 1960 irrigated land and crop yields have increased dramatically, but the region has experienced a substantial loss in employment opportunities.[26] As land has shifted away from labor-intensive corn cultivation to more automated, single-harvest feedgrains like sorghum and to horticultural production, the need for farm labor has decreased. One problem is the increasing mechanization in the production of feedgrains, another is that the new horticultural crops only require intensive farm labor during harvesting. The factories that freeze and can fruits and vegetables for the U.S. and Mexican markets are a new source of jobs. But like production, food processing is highly seasonal. Because about three-quarters of those employed in the processing plants are women who are usually young and have never previously been employed, the agroindustries do not cut unemployment among men or stem migration.[27]

Agroexport production, like cash crops in general, largely bypasses the small farm sector. One obvious way to bolster this sector would be to combine corn production, which has a long growing season, with horticultural products, which usually have growing seasons of only a few months. In this way, campesinos would be employed throughout the year and have a source of cash income while maintaining their self-provisioning capabilities. But agroindustries and U.S. contractors rarely work with small farmers, preferring instead to contract production with large local landowners and entrepreneurs.[28]

In areas where *ejidatarios* have had a stake in horticultural production, they are losing their access to the U.S. market as the Mexican government shifts from state-suppported to full-blown capitalist development. This has been the case in the Valley of Apatzingán in Michoacán, where *ejidatarios* have since the late 1980s been pushed out of the melon market as a result of shifting relations among U.S. contractors, the Mexican government, and local entrepreneurs.[29] Under the old trading system under which the government granted export permits, the local union of *ejidatarios* could count on a certain share of the melon export market. The ejido union also formerly benefited from state support in the form of low-interest credit and subsidized fertilizers and irrigation.

No longer having to work within the Mexican government's export commodity system, U.S. contractors canceled their agreements with the ejido union and began to work with a small group of commercial entrepreneurs. As a result, the valley's *ejidatarios* no longer participate in the export system as producers but work as hired farmworkers or in the local packing sheds. With the government having dramatically reduced its farm support programs for ejido production, *ejidatarios* lack the capital and technical capacity to gain access to the international horticultural market.

The 1992 revision of Mexico's agrarian law opens the possibility that *ejidatarios* can enter into joint ventures with private capital, including foreign investment. However, in the absence of government support, it is unlikely that such associations will be business partnerships. It is more likely that current patterns of land rental will continue and expand under their new legalized status. Given the widespread prejudice against campesinos, the unwillingness of private investors to share their profits, and the *ejidatarios'* lack of capital to invest, it is also doubtful that national or foreign investors will be willing to enter into direct relationships with ejido cooperatives. Rather than becoming a new class of entrepreneurs, most *ejidatarios* participating in the international agricultural economy may end up working as *jornaleros* on their own land.

Options for Increasing Exports

Increasing the amount of land dedicated to agroexport production is one option for improving Mexico's agricultural trade balance and creating more employment. If all the irrigable land in the eleven states that produce horticultural agroexports were irrigated and all the irrigated land in those states currently dedicated to corn production were put into horticultural production, Mexico could increase the acreage in fruit and vegetable production by nearly 80 percent. Assuming that all new horticultural production was for the export market, fruit and vegetable exports could quintuple.[30]

Although at first glance this option seems a good one, especially if corn production were transfered to arable land now left untilled or in pasture, its implementation will be difficult. Already rapid economic development in northern Mexico is leading to water shortages as industrialization and urbanization compete for limited land and water. As it is, most irrigation projects have only enough water for one crop. Another obstacle is the falling rate of public-sector investment in agriculture, which makes large government spending in new irrigation projects unlikely.[31] Even if Mexico were to double its irrigated land in horticultural production from 2.5 to five million acres, it would still face tough competition in the U.S. market. California alone has more than nine million acres under irrigation, and new technological advances continue to increase its competitiveness. Other Latin American and Caribbean nations are also increasing their agroexports to the United States.

Another option would be to increase Mexico's ability to compete by improving its agricultural technologies. But Mexico has a long way to go to reach the U.S. level, and cutbacks in government spending have reduced its capability to provide growers with seeds, fertilizer, pesticides, and other inputs. Perhaps more important, Mexico lacks an agricultural research and development infrastructure. As it is, Mexico depends on seeds, agrochemicals, and cultivation practices largely developed for conditions in the United States. Little research is being done in Mexico to develop agricultural inputs and farming practices appropriate for the varied microclimates in mostly arid and mountainous Mexico.[32] In contrast, U.S. growers count on significant advantages, largely because of superior agricultural research and technology assistance offered by the country's universities and extension services. Plant and livestock varieties and cultivation practices developed for local conditions in the United States result in higher U.S. yields and productivity margins that offset Mexico's low labor costs.

Looking South for Markets

Mexico is the third largest market for U.S. farm exports, following Japan and the former Soviet Union. Since Mexico's trade liberalization began in the mid-1980s, U.S. agricultural and food exports to Mexico have increased by 150 percent. The result has been a widening trade imbalance for Mexico, which imported $1.5 billion more in agricultural and food products than it exported to the United States in 1994.

U.S. growers and food exporters find positive indicators for increased trade when looking at Mexico's demographics. Population and economic growth in rural areas, where there is the least demand for imported food, is far outpaced by that of urban Mexico. In urban Mexico 42 percent of personal spending is for food and beverages, in contrast to 37 percent in rural areas. With population increases and economic growth concentrated in urban Mexico, U.S. agroindustries see an expanding market for their packaged and processed foods.[33]

Also encouraging U.S. food exporters is the youthfulness of the Mexican population. Forty percent of the population is age 15 or younger. According to a promotional report published by the U.S. Foreign Agricultural Service, "Mexican youth has a more worldly view than older, more conservative generations and wants to consume products available from the global marketplace."[34] Trade liberalization along with urban growth sent the demand for high-value food imports soaring, increasing at an annual rate of 22 percent through 1994. The U.S. share of these imports has exceeded 90 percent.[35]

Shopping for food, a Mexican consumer knows he or she is living in a globalized economy. There is little to distinguish Mexican supermarkets and the mushrooming convenience stores from U.S. ones, either in style of marketing or the products they offer. U.S. apples, pears, breakfast cereals, ice cream, yogurt, beef, poultry products, delicatessen meats, fresh vegetables, microwave foods, diet products, kosher foods, and pet foods are all found in Mexico. Not only do the same products exist but also the same companies. All three nationwide supermarket chains in

Mexico have entered into joint ventures with major U.S. retailers and now operate discount cash and carry outlets.

To promote U.S. products, companies are storming through the country with in-store promotions and advertising campaigns. Food manufacturers and distributors have unabashedly brought U.S.-style marketing into the heart of Mexico. Attracting new customers with promotional events offering prizes, bargain prices, loss leaders, and appearances of entertainment figures (especially clowns to perk children's interests) is now common. Between 1986 and 1992, sales of imported snack food from the United States increased about 3,000 percent, and pet food sales rose 200 percent.[36] With respect to fast-food restuarants, nearly all the U.S. hamburger, chicken, and pizza franchises are operating throughout Mexico to the delight of Mexican consumers.

Mexico is also becoming a major market for U.S. horticultural products. With the elimination of import licensing, U.S. pears have flooded into Mexico, which is now the second largest foreign market for U.S. pear growers. Like other U.S. exporters, pear growers count on U.S. government financial assistance to expand their market share in Mexico. The U.S. government's Market Promotion Program helps pay for a Pear Bureau representative in Mexico, promotional literature in Spanish, consumer-tasting programs, supermarket ads, and market research. Today, Mexico is the largest foreign market for Pear Bureau producers—accounting for 40 percent of its foreign sales, up from zero in 1987.[37]

Complementary growing seasons in the two countries not only create a marketing opening for horticultural exports from Mexico but also from the United States. In the summer and early fall, heavy rains in Mexico curb domestic production of such produce as cauliflower, broccoli, lettuce, melons, onions, potatoes, and tomatoes.

Despite rising Mexican production and a seasonal overlap for about 50 percent of traded horticultural products, U.S. horticultural production is steadily rising. Technological advances that reduce labor and irrigation costs have allowed U.S. growers to spur production to satisfy increasing U.S. percapita demand for fresh fruit and vegetables. Greater water availability, superior technology, more resources for research and development, lower transportation costs, and lower capital costs give U.S. growers a competitive advantage over their Mexican counterparts. However, as U.S. growers and investors increase their stake in Mexican agriculture they bring the technology, access to credit, and research capabilities that have helped give U.S. production a competitive edge.

Elusive Benefits of Export Economy

Trade asymmetries are likely to accentuate under free trade and as the internationalization of agriculture increases. Mexico's comparative advantage depends on cheap labor, land, and water. To maintain this advantage means continuing with a dubious development strategy that is largely based on the exploitation and repression of the rural workforce and on the degradation of its environment.

Another problem with Mexico's agroexport economy is the lack of linkages with the domestic economy. To a large and increasing degree, foreign companies provide the credit, technical assistance, and inputs for agroexport production. One hopeful sign has been the rise of agroindustrial exports, which have greater linkages with the domestic economy. Mexico is becoming an important supplier of processed foods, including tomato sauce and paste, fruit juices, and beer. In fact, the increase in processed food exports has far outpaced that of fresh food exports in recent years. Production by national capital generally does mean greater linkages with domestic consumption and other economic sectors (services and supplies, for example). Linkage benefits are reduced by the easy flow of capital across national borders and the likelihood that a relatively high proportion of income resulting from agroexport production is transfered to U.S. banks and spent on luxury goods.

An underlying problem with agroexports is the declining terms of trade of agricultural commodities.[38] Saturated world markets, low prices, and the creation of substitute foods have hurt traditional agroexports, such as coffee, cocoa, and coconuts. As more growers inside and outside Mexico switch to fruit and vegetable production, the relatively high prices and secure markets of these agroexports will also be undermined. Already, growers of melons and other fruits and vegetables have seen border prices fall as Mexican exports increase. Another weakness in the nontraditional export sector is the high dependence on imported agricultural inputs, the cost of which increases as the Mexican peso loses value against the dollar. At the same time, however, a devalued peso increases the competitiveness of Mexican exports.

But Mexico was ill-prepared to take advantage of its increased competitiveness as a result of the devaluation. The scarcity of credit and domestic capital precluded major investment in fruit and vegetable production, and the lack of previous investment in coffee, citrus, and other crops requiring long lead periods also prevented Mexico from cashing in on new export production. Although the lower costs of production—mainly in the form of reduced wages—will probably increase foreign investment in winter vegetable production, it is likely that increased exports in this sector will probably result from declining domestic demand for nonessential foods. In other words, most of the increased export income resulting from the devalued peso will not come from rising production but rather from reduced domestic consumption and still lower wage levels for Mexican farmworkers.

Only Game in Town

The export solution, locked within a neoliberal framework, is the only game in town for less-industrialized countries that have accepted the logic of comparative advantage and free trade. There are, however, other development alternatives shaped by more inward-looking strategies of development.

Such alternative strategies commonly advocate domestic demand-led development based on support for small-scale farm production not the export-led development currently in vogue. The idea is to encourage mass consumption by improving agricultural production and ensuring that the peasantry and landless farmworkers share in the benefits of increased production. Rather than concentrating on commercial agriculture, such development plans advocate government support for increased and more diversified production by small- and medium-scale farmers, whose improved income would immediately translate into increased spending on food, shelter, and other basic goods that could be easily supplied by domestic producers.[39]

In all cases, alternative rural development planning would require that the government focus its technical and financial support for agriculture on sustainable production by the peasantry and protections against the influx of cheap imported grains. In the era of trade liberalization and privatization of government services, such solutions are quickly dismissed as overly interventionist by multilateral institutions and by government planners—even though this was the growth model successfuly followed by most of the industrialized countries of Europe and North America and the newly industrializing countries of Asia.

Other strategies stress the need for more balance between export production and cropping for domestic food needs. The issue is not whether agroexports and other cash crops should be promoted, but which crops should be encouraged, under what conditions, in which regions, and how much government support should be offered.[40] In making such decisions, farmers and policymakers will need to consider such issues as the varying impacts on land, labor, and income; potential for linkages with production and consumption; long-term comparative advantages; political and economic consequences of increased or decreased food sufficiency; and the impact on the distribution of wealth and power.

As it is, Mexico's agricultural economy is in deep crisis. Trade deficits are accumulating, large commercial production is facing new environmental limits, rural poverty is worsening, and agroexport production is proving unable to generate the kinds of jobs and income being lost in basic foods cropping. If free trade and prioritizing agroexports prove unable to provide at least part of the solution to the rural development crisis in Mexico, campesino-based rural development strategies and more coherent government agricultural policies may eventually receive more favorable consideration.

S i x

———

FEEDING MEXICO

"If the community loses corn, it means that the indian campesino loses dignity. Corn is our food, and the life of our culture."

—Joel Aquino, Zapotec leader from the
Oaxacan community of Yalaag, Oaxaca, October 1994.

Food is the most basic of needs. At an individual or family level, access to food is essential to survival and the main indicator of well-being. This is also true for communities and nations, whose welfare is also largely determined by their capacity to feed their members. Either food is self-provided by interacting directly with the environment (farming, hunting, fishing, and animal husbandry), or it is supplied by transactions with those who do. In most cases, this means purchasing food on the market. But these transactions can also include barter, mutual support, and charity.

Over time, as markets have come to shape society's relationship with nature, food provisioning has become more complex, as fewer people provide their own food and more agricultural products come from the international market. Before the widespread penetration of markets, a family or community's access to food was largely determined by the weather and the state of the surrounding environment. No longer, however, do families, communities, and nations need to rely solely on their own harvests. They can look to other regions and nations for agricultural commodities.

As markets have become increasingly internationalized, the issue of how Mexico feeds itself has become increasingly complex. It involves not only the condition of its basic foods sector but also an evaluation of the country's ability to purchase the food it needs on the world market.

An examination of food provisioning necessarily concerns production, pricing, and markets. But it also raises questions about the trade-offs involved in relying primarily on markets to determine access to food. Some of these trade-offs, such as imported vs. domestically produced foods and campesino vs. capitalist agriculture, lend themselves easily to economic evaluations of comparative costs and benefits.

But there are other trade-offs that cannot adequately be addressed by narrow economic evaluations of the bottom line of international market transactions. Overdependence on market forces has adverse long-range implications for the environment, the survival of indigenous peoples, nutrition, quality of life, and the political and economic stability of the nation. Questions about feeding Mexico go to the heart of such broader development issues as the relations among markets, the state, and communities and how food-deficit countries like Mexico should best integrate into the world trading system. Also important to remember in a country like Mexico where corn production is not only linked to food provisioning but is central to rural livelihood strategies is the role of small farm agriculture in providing substantial employment in a nation with such a large labor surplus.

Unable to meet food demands with domestic production, Mexico imports increasing quantities of staple foods as well as an expanding range of processed foods.[1] Imported food products in 1992 cost Mexico about $5.8 billion, resulting in a worldwide agricultural trade deficit of $3.1 billion or roughly 15 percent of the total trade deficit.[2] Mexico's agricultural trade deficit is increasing in all categories, but the most dramatic increases in imports are in intermediate goods and consumer foods (Table 7). Between 1980 and 1993, U.S. exports of pet food to Mexico increased by twelve times, snack foods by twenty-two times, and breakfast foods by eleven times.[3] As trade barriers fall and neoliberal policies take effect, this reliance on imported food is likely to increase. The U.S. Department of Agriculture in 1994 predicted that "over the next three to five years U.S. grain exports could increase significantly if Mexico does not increase production rapidly enough to meet domestic demand"—an unlikely prospect given the continuing stagnation of agricultural production.[4]

Table 7

Mexico's Balance of Trade

in Food and Agricultural Products (US$)

	1980	1985	1990	1992
Bulk*	-1,377,622	-545,666	-1,395,475	-1,582,559
Intermediate	-286,507	-447,786	-913,608	-879,736
Consumer	334,109	392,702	223,906	635,611
Total **	-1,330, 020	-600,750	-2,085,177	-3,097,906

* Bulk includes unprocessed grains; intermediate includes flour, live animals and oilseeds; and consumer includes fresh fruits, snack foods and packaged goods.
** Does not include fish and forestry products.
Source: *FAO*. "Global Imports and Exports of Agricultural Products by Country," 1980-1992.

Concern about adequate food for the world's rising population dates back at least two centuries. In his 1798 book, *Essay on the Principle of Population*, Thomas Malthus gave voice to the fears of the British elite who believed that social unrest would increase as food production declined relative to the expanding working class. The Malthusian contention that population would increase exponentially while food production would increase only arithmetically proved false. Technological advances constantly improved the productivity of agriculture, allowing global food supplies to keep pace with or even surpass population advances.

In the 1970s, however, concerns about access to adequate food increased, especially among less-industrialized and increasingly food-deficit nations like Mexico. These concerns deepened following the "shortage crisis" of the 1972-74 period, resulting in part from a massive and unprecedented U.S. grain sale to the Soviet Union, which was manipulated by the giant grain traders to raise world market prices. In Mexico, this global grain crisis coincided with the increasing severity of the nation's agricultural crisis. Just when Mexico found that it needed to import more grains, global supplies had become scarce and more expensive.

The calls heard around the world in the 1970s for national food security were not the reflection of a new acceptance of the Malthusian view of production and population growth. Instead, the rising concerns about food availability had more to do with how global grain production was distributed. Increased dependency on food imports had made importing countries especially vulnerable to the sudden price and supply variations of the volatile global market. There was also deepening concern in Mexico and throughout the third world that the allocation of food surpluses of the industrial nations was often politically motivated, meaning that the decision to sell or otherwise transfer grains to deficit countries was sometimes influenced by the political relations between the two countries.

According to the United Nations, the main attributes of food security are the following:

* Capacity to produce, store, and import sufficient food to meet ·basic food needs for all groups.

* Maximum autonomy and self-determination, reducing vulnerability to international market fluctuations and political pressures.

* Reliability such that seasonal, cyclical, and other variations in access to food are minimal.

* Sustainability of agricultural production systems.

* Dependable access to adequate food.[5]

National food security programs generally have two thrusts—one to promote farm production and the other to support more equitable distribution. For the most part, however, food security efforts focus more on supplying cheap food to mainly urban consumers than on assisting the farmers who produce for the domestic market. Overlaying national food security programs are international initiatives by food-surplus nations to expand markets, support friendly governments, and dispose of unmarketable inventories.

The economics of food production have inescapable political implications. Humanitarian considerations are not the only reason why food security is important. A close correspondence exists between political stability and food security. The lack of access to affordable food invariably results in domestic political turmoil and can lead to international conflict, which helps explain why food distribution programs are found in both developed and less-developed nations.

Markets and the Environment

The existence of sufficient grain supplies to meet the needs of the world population does not mean that those needs are met. On an international level, the lack of foreign exchange or political differences often means that a country is not supplied with all the grains it needs. Commonly, even when a country does have access to global surpluses, grain is distributed to meet only effective demand not real demand. Those without enough income go hungry. Government food programs sometimes fill this gap, but such programs are usually concentrated in urban centers. In rural areas grain prices are often much higher than in the cities because of transportation and commericalization obstacles.

Free markets are obviously a less-than -adequate mechanism for the distribution of basic foodstuffs. Production seasons and changing weather patterns mean that it is necessary to intervene in the market both to ensure that grains are available throughout the year and in the event that crops fail for a year or two. Supply and demand may be appropriate for the distribution of cars, stereos, and other luxury consumer goods but not for basic food items. If the market were allowed to govern food production and distribution without any government intervention, agricultural production would become ever more chaotic and more of the world would go hungry.

Underlying the logic of free trade in agricultural goods is the assumption that the world's large grain producers will be willing and able to continue producing surplus quantities of cheap grains. In the United States, a combination of fertile land, intensive technology use, and a support network of government agencies results in high productivity. Doubts about the sustainability of the U.S. agricultural system surfaced during the oil crisis as the costs of mechanization and agrochemicals increased. But as the crisis eased and supplies of inexpensive petroleum increased in the 1980s, concerns about the high energy-dependence of U.S. agriculture correspondingly diminished.

Especially within the environmental community, however, concerns about sustainable agricultural development lingered. In the 1980s, these fears broadened as environmentalists warned that the global community was reaching the earth's natural resource limits because of overpopulation, patterns of excessive consumption, and unsustainable technological systems of production. Environmental security is a precondition for food security.

Although global grain production has increased faster than population growth over the past several decades, it appears to be slowing down. According to estimates of the Worldwatch Institute, percapita output of rice, corn, and wheat have fallen 11 percent since 1984.[6] Economic, technological, and environmental factors all contribute to a slower rate of productivity growth. Farmers can no longer afford to keep increasing fertilizer use because of increasing costs, and there have been no major advances in technology that would increase productivity. As the population expands and environmental degradation increases, cropland is not expanding as it once did, and in many countries it is shrinking.

In the past, the capacity of global food production to meet food needs was evaluated largely in terms of the potential and limits of technology to increase productivity. Today, any serious evaluation of global food production also acknowledges the environmental limits to increasing production to meet the demands of a rising population. Those limits already appear to have been reached in rangelands and oceanic fisheries.

Overgrazed pasture land and overharvested seas have resulted in declining yields of beef and seafood. More cattle could be fed in feedlots and fish bred in inland ponds. But to provide the needed feed for increased meat and fish would require more grain production at a time when grain yields have reached a plateau. Technological advances and higher prices could increase grain production, but previous growth rates will be hard to duplicate. Limits to available fuel, water, and croplands will also make increased production hard to sustain.

Food Sufficiency, Security, and Sovereignty in Mexico

A surge of concern about food dependency arose during the López Portillo presidency. Nationalists within the government complained that by using oil revenues to import food the country was squandering its national patrimony. They successfully argued that the oil dollars would be better spent on the creation of a national food system that increased production incentives while at the same time improving food distribution networks.[7]

The establishment of the National Food System (SAM) in early 1980 represented a renewed national committment to food security. But it was short-lived. SAM achieved moderate success in increasing grain production, mainly because of the response of larger growers. Campesinos also had begun to respond to the production supports, but SAM was shut down before the potential for increased production by small growers was realized.[8]

After 1982 neoliberalism increasingly won out over populism and nationalism. A sharp drop in oil prices and the associated debt crisis caused revenues to shrink, forcing the government to cut back on SAM and other programs. The De la Madrid and Salinas administrations insisted on their continued commitment to guaranteeing Mexicans an adequate food supply. Instead of food security, they called this commitment one of *food sovereignty.* In the past, Mexico, concerned that rising food imports from the United States increased dependency and undermined national sovereignty, had stressed the importance of achieving *food self-sufficiency* as the best way to ensure food security. The new vision of food sovereignty, however, arose from the conviction that trade liberalization and increased market integration with the United States would increase agricultural productivity in Mexico, attract new investment to the agroexport sector, and provide the country with a cheap source of basic grains.

Imported grains were not only priced much lower than those produced domestically, but they came with attractive credit guarantees and terms of payment. The United States, in its effort to expand agricultural markets and to dispose of excess supplies, offered Mexico grains and other food commodities at subsidized prices, low rates of interest, and long pay-back schedules.[9]

The U.S. government was so eager to open up the Mexican market to U.S. agricultural commodities that it also supplied Mexico with vast quantities of food aid in the 1980s and early 1990s.[10] The export subsidies offered to U.S. grain exporters and the credit offered to Mexico for grain purchases served the dual purpose of shoring up the Mexican peso after the 1982 financial crisis and of demonstrating the inefficiency of Mexican agricultural production. This paved the way for more liberalized agricultural trading relations by 1990. Following the December 1994 devaluation, there were reports that Washington was considering increasing its already considerable credit guarantee program for

Mexico as part of its financial bailout program and to ensure that U.S. food exports would continue to flow to Mexico.

The cheap foodstuffs, mainly wheat and dairy products from the United States, were critical to Mexico's efforts to regain economic stability in the 1980s. By easing the impact of structural adjustment, the imported food also helped maintain the country's tenuous political stability, especially among urban consumers. The availability of basic foods at bargain prices meant that Mexico could proceed with its macroeconomic policies with little attention to developing a separate sectoral policy for agriculture. The fact that countries could import food at prices substantially below domestic production costs bolstered the arguments of free trade advocates by demonstrating the logic of trade governed by market forces and comparative advantage.

By supplying low-cost grains to urban consumers and food processing industries, cheap grain imports have given the government the political space and economic opportunity to reduce its subsidies to domestic producers and its subsidies to consumers. These benefits, however, must be weighed against the risks associated with overdependence on food imports, such as the possibility that at some point the availability of grains on the world market might diminish and the price of imported staples correspondingly increase. Also important to consider are the many benefits of domestic grain production, especially corn. These include the extensive linkages with the local economy, the large labor-absorption capacity, and the better access of corn to poor and remote populations.

Basic Grains and Basic Needs

Evaluations of a nation's food security commonly focus on its ability to produce or purchase basic grains, a term that is commonly used to refer to maize, wheat, rice, and sorghum, as well as to dry edible beans. This is because basic grains are the foundation of the diet of most nations, just as corn and beans form the basis of Mexican nourishment, although wheat and rice to a lesser extent are also important. Sorghum, consumed in some poor countries as a substitute for corn, is used almost exclusively for animal feed and to a lesser extend for food processing in Mexico.

The production of basic grains in Mexico reflects the agricultural sector's highly stratified structure. On the one side is the large-surplus producing sector that encompasses medium- and large-scale producers, whose farms are generally mechanized and often irrigated. This sector produces not only most of the country's agroexports but also dominates the production of feedgrains and higher-value foodgrains (wheat and rice). These commercial farms also produce about 20 percent to 30 percent of the nation's corn, a proportion that rises in times of relatively high guarantee prices, such as in 1980-82 and the last years of the Salinas administration. On the other side are the limited-surplus producing growers and the subsistence and infrasubsistence farmers, who produce corn and beans on small plots (five hectares or less) of marginal land with extremely low yields and in some cases exclusively for self-provisioning. Even so, these marginal producers have played an important role in providing Mexico with corn. Not only have these roughly 2.2 million marginal producers provided their families with corn, but they have also supplied the domestic market with about 3.5 million tons of corn or about one-fourth of national production in most years. Completing the corn production picture are mid-sized producers, both private farmers and *ejidatarios*, who commonly have between five and forty hectares, good rainfed lands, or irrigated farms.

The increased use of hybrid seeds and fertilizer that came with the Green Revolution, which started to take hold in the late 1940s, widened the gap between the large- and medium-scale commercial producers and the small farm sector. Wheat yields in the Northwest and in the Bajío region increased dramatically, but corn and bean production experienced less dramatic rises in yield per hectare. A sector of medium- and large-scale farmers were able, however, to continue profitable commercial production of these crops with the help of guarantee prices that covered their costs and profit margins. They also counted on massive government subsidies for such agricultural inputs as tractors, pesticides, seeds, and fertilizer and for warehousing and distribution services. In some cases, the productivity gains resulting from subsidized inputs even encouraged commercial growers with irrigated land to cultivate corn instead of less profitable cash crops such as cotton.

In the late 1960s and 1970s Mexican agriculture experienced its "Second Agricultural Revolution."[11] Like the Green Revolution that preceded it, this new revolution in agricultural production skirted the peasantry. There was a boom in sorghum production aided by the introduction of high-yielding varieties and driven by the exploding demand for feedgrains by the livestock industry. The expanding middle class and affluent population were consuming more meat products, which encouraged medium-scale farmers located primarily in the northeastern and north-central regions to switch from corn to higher-priced, less labor-intensive, and more drought-resistant sorghum.[12]

Along with the failure of the government to promote campesino agriculture and to raise the guarantee prices for corn and beans to the levels for feedgrains, this substitution of grains was a major reason why Mexico lost its high degree of grain self-sufficiency in the 1970s. Mexico's bimodal structure gained another dimension. Livestock production was promoted for the benefit of the more privileged consumers, while the lack of attention to the foodgrains sector resulted in rising volumes of imported corn.

At the same time, drylands and jungles throughout Mexico, from Chihuahua to Hidalgo and down to Chiapas, were cleared or converted from corn *milpas* to pastures. Cattle took over much of the Mexican countryside. In the north, landowners found a market in the United States for range-bred calves to be fattened in U.S. feedlots, while the forests and tropical jungles of the Southeast gave way to grazing grounds for cattle to feed the ever-rising demand for meat in the cities.

Generally, the new cattlemen of Mexico were large landowners and the local economic elites. But the peasantry also shared in the cattle boom as campesino families tried to cash in on the meat market. For both large and small landholders, the cow was a symbol of economic security and personal prestige. Ranching represented a step away from labor-intensive, back-breaking farming.

The booming urban demand for meat and poultry products had a devastating impact on Mexico's food security. As more farmers switched to feedgrains and more land turned over to pasture, there was less land to produce food grains for the market and for self-provisioning. The process of grain substitution together with the spread of pasture lands increased the social and economic polarization in the countryside. Many campesino families, particularly in the Southeast, were pushed off their lands by cattlemen protected by the army and their own paramilitary bands. In the central and northern states, those families without the resources or the land to take advantage of the sorghum boom were also forced to sell or rent their lands to wealthier neighbors.[13]

From being a food-surplus country, Mexico had by the 1970s become a net importer of agricultural commodities.[14] The negative per-capita growth in corn production meant that the volume of corn imports rose to nearly 20 percent of annual production in the 1970s and as high as 25 percent in the 1980s. Wheat imports also increased dramatically, and reliance on imported beans became more common. Unable to meet domestic needs, Mexico has been increasing imports of feed and fodders.

Corn is central to Mexico's rural economy and society (Table 8). About 45 percent of the country's arable land is dedicated to corn, a crop that has accounted for about 40 percent of the government's price supports. The traditional *milpa* system involves shifting corn production and diversified production usually for self-provisioning, but as the use of chemical fertilizers increased and land became more scarce *milpa* agriculture has become less common.[15] Although most campesinos rely on corn cropping for some degree of self-provisioning, it is the rare campesino who depends solely on what he

Table 8

Corn and Mexico's Farm Sector

* 85% of cropping on rainfed land and 15% on irrigated land. Of rainfed cropping, 30% is categorized as good, 53% as fair, and 17% as marginal.

* 2.7 million corn growers, accounting for 68% of total population employed in agriculture.

* Corn cropping occupies 45 percent of cultivated land and 6% of total irrigated land.

* Only one-third of corn producers are net surplus producers but most net deficit producers market portions of their harvest.

* 78% of *ejidatarios* grow corn.

* Corn accounts for two-thirds of total grain consumed and one-third of total agricultural production in 1990.

* Average corn yields in Mexico are 1.4 tons/hectare for those farming one hectare, 1.6 tons/hectare for those with one to five hectares, and 2.4 tons/hectare for those with more than five hectares far below U.S. yields of more than eight tons/hectare.

Sources: INEGI, *Encuesta nacional agropecuaria ejidal, 1988;* Raúl Salinas de Gortari, "El campo méxicano ante el reto de la modernización," Comercio Exterior, September 1990; CESPA-SAR-ONU/CEPAL, El desarrollo *agropecuario de México,* 1982.

or she harvests. As central as it is to campesino society and economy, corn production, even before recent agricultural restructuring, only infrequently covers the subsistence needs of campesinos. An estimated 85 percent of corn growers depend on other economic activities on or off the farm to ensure family survival.[16]

Most corn producers are also corn consumers, either because they do not produce enough corn for self-provisioning or because they sell most of their corn immediately after harvest and are thereby forced to buy corn when their reserves run out. Because they are often far removed from government stores and warehouses, this puts campesino corn farmers in the position of selling when prices are the lowest and buying when they are usually at their height. Although most of Mexico's corn farmers purchase corn, they are also commonly sellers of corn. Small farmers with five hectares or less market nearly one-half of the total corn they produce.[17] This means that even though most of campesino farmers who cultivate corn may be net-deficit producers they will be adversely affected by falling corn prices resulting from trade liberalization.

Domestic price levels and weather conditions can cause grain production and imports to vary greatly from one year to another. Government-guarantee corn prices, for example, resulted in dramatic production increases in the 1990-93 period as farmers switched from sorghum and other crops with no guarantee prices and that were less protected from cheap imports.[18] Increasing imports of sorghum, wheat, soybeans, rice, and processed foods resulted in a deepening agricultural trade deficit, however. The overall trend, however, is toward declining percapita corn production and increased imports—a pattern that will accelerate as the provisions of the free trade accord take effect and as Mexico eliminates its system of guarantee prices.

Prices and Subsidies

The level and the type of basic grain production for the market have been largely determined by the government price and subsidy policies. These have taken the form of guarantee prices for producers and below-cost prices for consumers with access to government outlet stores. Although the balance of these subsidies changed over time, most government intervention has benefited urban consumers more than producers.[19]

As restructuring deepened during the Salinas administration, the government lifted guarantee prices in 1990 for all agricultural commodities except corn and beans. The government also gradually reduced indirect subsidies to producers in the form of low-cost agricultural inputs and low-interest credit. Changing price and subsidy policies, as well as the new productivist (as opposed to agrarian) focus of the campesino movement, gave rise in the 1980s to new conflicts between the government and the farm sector. In some states, notably Chihuahua, producer organizations successfully challenged the guarantee price for corn set by the government, although demands for higher prices by producers in other states like Chiapas were met only with increased government repression.[20]

In 1993 a militant movement composed largely of medium- to large-scale private farmers who produced mainly basic grains emerged in Jalisco. Called the Barzón Movement, these growers complained that they were unable to pay their farm loans because of cutbacks in government subsidies for inputs, dropping commodity prices, and especially because of rising interest rates. High interest rates, which proved a boon to the financial sector, were driving commercial producers into bankruptcy and into taking increasingly militant stands, even to the extent of opportunistically allying themselves with the *zapatistas.*

The impact of price liberalization and free trade on basic grain production is highly differentiated. Not all producers are affected equally by falling prices, reduced input subsidies, and the increased availability of U.S. grain. Ironically, those most directly affected are the medium- and large-scale producers whose productivity permitted them to profit under a system of guarantee prices and subsidized inputs. The impact of falling prices on the production decisions of subsistence and infrasubsistence is not as direct, since this sector either does not market its produce or has never benefited from guarantee prices because of its remote locations and the corresponding control by private intermediaries over grain purchases and sales. Nonetheless, the entire rural society and economy is being victimized by liberalized prices since guarantee prices did serve to boost corn prices well above the international level for even those farmers who sold their surplus to intermediaries. Also, as corn production declines by surplus-producing farmers there will be less temporary work for landless and land-poor campesinos.

Less than one-third of corn growers have had access to credit, less than one-half have received technical assistance, and only seven in ten have used chemical fertilizers.[21] Even guarantee prices are often not of direct benefit to corn producers who did not sell to Conasupo because of their isolation. Market prices, however, bear some relation to guarantee prices, although they have functioned more as a ceiling than a floor. Commonly, the prices paid to campesinos selling corn has been lower than the guarantee price while the prices for those buying corn in rural areas have been higher than the national average. In other words, even when campesinos do have surplus corn, they often sell below the guarantee prices to intermediaries since they themselves had no way of transporting the grain to government warehouses.[22]

Following closely on the heels of changes to the agrarian reform law, President Salinas in 1993 announced a new farm policy called Procampo (Program of Direct Support Payments to the Countryside) that revamped the government's price and subsidy structures. Akin to the decoupling measures advocated by free trade proponents in the industrialized nations, the Procampo plan separates or decouples farmer subsidies from commodity prices. In other words, farm support programs assist farmers with direct payments, not through subsidies that skew market prices or reward inefficient production. This is not to say that the government does not affect market prices in other ways, including policies that shape interest rates, exchange rates, inflation, and trade barriers.

Rather than setting a guarantee price for a particular commodity, Procampo provides a small direct income subsidy to farmers in the form of an annual payment. The more hectares in production, the more a grower will receive. Since farmers themselves can decide each year what crop is more profitable to plant, the subsidy program does not directly influence production levels or prices for any one commodity.[23] The subsidy program will (if continued by Zedillo and subsequent presidents) extend through the entire fifteen-year phase-out period for agricultural tariffs under NAFTA.[24]

Initial response to the program differed according to production levels. Larger growers who produce for the market complained that the small payments per hectare (approximately $105 per hectare) would not begin to cover the losses they faced because of low prices and high production costs (resulting from high interest rates and reduced or eliminated government subsidies for agricultural inputs). In 1994, the reduced guarantee price for corn meant that corn farmers were really only receiving an additional $40 per hectare. Many argued that the subsidy payments should be tied to production, not land cultivated, thereby rewarding farmers with higher productivity and encouraging others to increase their competitiveness. In contrast, self-provisioning campesinos welcomed the subsidy program, although still complaining about the overall negative impact of the government's agricultural policies. There was also widespread dissatisfaction that the government did not consult with farm organizations before announcing the program.[25]

In the short-run, Procampo functions more as a patronage and welfare program than as the foundation for a new farm policy in the NAFTA era. For those campesino farmers who received their first payments only a couple of weeks before the August 1994 presidential election, it affirmed the political wisdom that it was the PRI and not the opposition parties that put beans on their tortillas. The message was that the PRI government had not forgotten its special responsibilities to the peasantry, and here was a check to prove it. Denise Dresser, professor of politics at the Autonomous Technological Institute in Mexico City, called Procampo "a neopopulist solution to a neoliberal problem" that provides "political slush to those negatively affected by the Salinas economic reforms."[26]

The other component of Procampo—the total liberalization of corn—was not scheduled to take effect until 1995. Until corn growers feel the impact of the elimination of guarantee prices, the economic and social consequences of Procampo will not be known. For some, especially the self-provisioning sector, the small payments may be enough to keep them on the farm. But for others, the annual Procampo checks will be too small of an incentive to keep them producing and will be used instead to pay for bus tickets to the city or the northern border.

Food production responds not only to prices and subsidies but also to climate. With 85 percent of Mexico's land being arid or semi-arid, most Mexican agriculture relies on low, seasonal, and variable rainfall. Drought is a constant in Mexican agriculture, usually hitting at least one region every year.[27] Approximately 20 percent of cropped land is irrigated, but many irrigation districts rely on small reservoirs and wells that deplete rapidly during dry years.

Drought, which causes 90 percent of production losses in Mexican agriculture, has a major impact on food security in Mexico. Less production results in more imports. But imports do not make up all of the shortfall, especially for those campesinos who rely on their own production for most of their consumption needs. For campesinos, a dry year increases the incidence of malnutrition and hunger and sparks new migration to the cities.

In the past, massive public-sector investment in irrigation projects reduced the impact of droughts on production. However, irrigation's ability to counterbalance the impact of drought is limited not only by its concentration in the Northwest but also by falling groundwater levels, salinization, and inadequate reservoir supplies.[28]

Consequences for Consumers

Just as the government has recognized the need to buffer food producers against imperfect markets and the competition of international grains, so too has it intervened to buffer the consumer against market forces that would threaten their access to basic foods. It has done this by keeping prices for most basic goods lower than the real costs of production, marketing, and distribution. It has set official prices and established an elaborate distribution and marketing network called Conasupo (National Food Staples Company) designed to serve low-income consumers.

Food subsidies together with cheap imports have protected consumers against falling wage levels and have played a critical role in the government's cheap food strategy of development. By keeping food prices low, employers in both the agricultural and industrial sectors felt less worker pressure to raise wages to cover the costs of basic foods.

It is too early to project the range of consequences of price liberalization on consumption. But it should be remembered that at the same time guarantee prices are being eliminated for producers so are most generalized food subsidies for consumers, although price controls on tortillas remain. Being swept away along with import barriers are many programs that have kept prices of basic foodstuffs low for consumers.

Despite its achievements, the consumer subsidy program that emerged in the 1960s began to be dismantled in the late 1980s because of its high fiscal cost. According to one estimate, consumer food subsidies in the early 1980s cost the government fifteen times more than producer subsidies.[29] Another problem was the generalized character of food subsidies. Poor and rich alike benefited from low prices for milk, beans, tortillas, and other foodstuffs. In fact, millers and feedgrain producers were among the main sectors to benefit from generalized subsidies. A continuing problem is that consumer subsidies have disproportionately benefited urban consumers, a problem that was at least partially remedied by an extensive rural distribution network created under the SAM program and managed by community food councils.

As part of its austerity program, the government has moved away from generalized consumer subsidies to more targeted programs designed to benefit the poorest of the poor. Such an approach cuts government costs while channeling the subsidized or free food to those who most need it. Targeted consumer subsidies certainly make more sense as part of a food policy that recognizes the sharp income difference among the Mexican population and the deepening pockets of severe malnutrition found in the *colonias perdidas* (forgotten neighborhoods) of urban Mexico and throughout rural Mexico. Despite targeting, it is still not the poorest of the poor who gain access to government distribution programs because of the difficulty of reaching the most needy. This is especially true in remote rural areas.

Clearly, consumer subsidies are an essential component of any serious food policy. The moving away from generalized subsidies and the availability of cheaper grains on the liberalized foreign market can help reduce the fiscal cost of consumer subsidies while at the same time making them more effective. But many problems remain, and new ones will emerge.

If grain imports increase and local production falls, as seems likely, the challenges of ensuring that the rural population has adequate access to basic foods will increase. With little purchasing power and the scattered population of rural Mexico, there will be little financial incentive for grain distributors to supply poor and remote areas. It is likely that unless the government intervenes in rural markets, a small number of distributors will be able to set high prices, especially as corn production declines in the countryside. As the government continues to withdraw from its role in distribution, private middlemen, transportation companies, and merchants will likely assume a more central role and have increased arbitrary power to set prices well above those in the cities.[30]

Malnutrition is widespread in Mexico and needs increased attention. Although targeting the poorest and most malnourished makes sense, it must be remembered the conditions of undernourishment and poverty affect half or more of Mexico's population. As trade liberalization sets in, it is likely that rural unemployment will increase, placing further down-ward pressure on wage levels in both urban and rural areas alike, thereby adversely affecting nutrition levels.

Malnutrition and Income

Average consumption figures for calories and protein indicate that Mexicans consume more than they need.[31] The average caloric consumption in Mexico is 130 percent of the required amount, roughly about the same level as industrial countries. (The U.S. rate is 138 percent.) Since the late 1960s percapita protein consumption has increased 19 percent, which means that the average Mexican consumes 23 percent more protein than she or he needs.[32]

But just as percapita income figures hide the degree of economic destitution, so too do average consumption statistics disguise the preva-lence of hunger and malnutrition in Mexico. The distribution of food, like income, is highly uneven. Although food availability in Mexico approxi-mates that in many industrialized nations, the country's poverty and malnutrition rates are comparable with those of countries with insufficient percapita supplies.[33] Moreover, caloric consumption alone is not an adequate measure of nutrition.

Poverty is the main cause of malnutrition. Without money, access to food is obstructed no matter how much food may be available in the marketplace. Income levels in Mexico have always been highly skewed, but government growth and income policies since the early 1980s have widened the gap between the very rich and the very poor while dramati-cally thinning the ranks of the middle class. In the 1984-92 period, 90 percent of Mexican families saw their share of national income decrease. During the same period the wealthiest 10 percent of the population saw their share of national income increase significantly. Between 1984 and 1992, the wealthiest 10 percent of Mexican farmers saw their income increase by 25 percent, while the poorest 10 percent saw their income fall by 3 percent. By 1992 the poorest 40 percent of the Mexican population accounted for only 13 percent of national income while the top 10 percent received 38 percent.

Generally, the poorer a family was in 1982, the greater proportional loss in its share of national income in the 1984-92 period. The proportional income share of the poorest 40 percent fell by 40 percent, while the middle 30 percent experienced only an 8 percent proportional drop in income share. [34]

Even these figures on declining income shares obscure the degree to which wealth has become concentrated within a small circle of companies and individuals. The country's eight largest private corporations or financial groups have a combined value that is equal to 25 percent of Mexico's GDP. The 1980s and early 1990s spelled doom for most of the population, but they have been boom times for the wealthy. According to the July 1994 *Forbes* magazine listing of the "World's Billionaires," Mexico, with twenty-four billionaires (up from the thirteen listed in 1993 and two in the early 1980s), ranked fourth among the countries spawning billionaires. [35]

Declining wage levels and rising underemployment have been the main factors behind the widening of poverty in Mexico. The fact that economic growth has failed to keep up with population increases has also contributed to the declining or stagnant percapita income levels of most of the population. [36] The deterioration of income levels and living standards was most severe in the 1982-89 period, but showed modest improvement between 1989 and 1992 according to one government report. [37]

The financial crisis and the peso devaluation that hit Mexico in the final days of 1994 resulted in new threats to the food security of Mexicans in the form of higher prices and massive layoffs and bankruptcies. It is likely that in coming years hunger and malnutrition will become even more widespread and severe in Mexico.

Low income levels mean that families cannot afford basic necessities. In the case of the poorest 10 percent, their income is not sufficient to buy even 60 percent of the basic food items they need. Although the lack of income is the fundamental cause of malnutrition in Mexico, it is not always the case that increased income results in improved nutrition.

Studies from both the southeastern lowlands of Tabasco and the Sierras of Sonora have shown that the conversion from subsistence to commercial agriculture has meant worse nutrition for campesinos, even if cash incomes have increased slightly. [38] Simply stated, the income obtained from selling cash crops is not enough to offset the loss of home-grown foods. Neither do campesinos who leave their farms for wage labor necessarily experience improved nutrition despite having

higher levels of cash income. This is especially true for migrant farmworkers, whose nutrition levels are among the worst of any sector.

The government's own agencies indicate that malnutrition is widespread and rising, ranging from roughly 40 percent to 65 percent of the
population. According to the National Solidarity Program, nearly 50
percent of the population was unable to meet basic nutritional requirements in 1990 because of income deficiencies, although a nutritional
survey by the same agency concluded that 39 percent of the population
was undernourished. According to the National Nutrition Commission,
66 percent of the population suffered from malnutrition, ranging from
relatively minor vitamin deficiencies to severe undernourishment. The
National Nutrition Institute estimated that 20 million Mexicans suffer
from health problems linked to malnutrition and that half of the rural
population is likely suffering from physical or mental deficiencies resulting from or exacerbated by inadequate nutrition.[39]

One of the reasons there are so many conflicting figures on the
levels of malnutrition is that there are many different ways to measure
nutritional status. Some of the highest estimates are based on purchasing
power calculations or include vitamin deficiencies.

While national-level statistics commonly report calories percapita
or annual consumption of various foods, many case studies and surveys
use anthropomorphic measures such as weight for age, height for age, or
weight for height. These measurements are then compared to norms
established by the World Health Organization (WHO) and rated Normal,
Malnourished I, II or III, Overweight, or Obese. Another index known as
the Waterlow method combines height for age with weight for height to
create four categories. These indicators are typically applied to young
children and women of childbearing age, since they are the populations
most impacted by nutritional deficiencies.[40] Nationally, 12 percent of
children suffer from low birthweight, 13.9 percent of children under five
years are underweight, and 22 percent of children under five years have
stunted growth.[41]

Another way to assess malnutrition is to look at income and the cost
of staple foods. The condition of "extreme poverty" is defined as a family
not having cnough income to afford basic food necessities or other
necessities such as housing and health care. An estimated 12 percent of
Mexican households, or about 13.6 million people, fall within this category of extreme poverty. Another 28 percent of the population are

categorized as poor, meaning they do not have sufficient income to pay for their food and other basic needs.[42] One of the great ironies in Mexico is that malnutrition and hunger are concentrated in rural areas—a reflection not just of rural/urban income disparities but also of the continuing government policies that give priority to cheap food for the cities. According to a 1990 report by the Health Ministry, the percentage of rural children affected by severe malnutrition doubled in the 1974-1989 period.[43]

Malnutrition is more severe in southern Mexico and in rural areas than in the northern states or in the cities. The incidence of malnutrition among preschool children in the Southeast is double that of the North. In Mexico City, just 3 percent of children under five suffer from malnutrition compared to 14 percent in the Southeast.[44]

Also important in describing the national variations in malnutrition is its prevalence among indigenous communities. The poorest and hungriest of the rural poor in Mexico are usually found in indian communities. The vast majority of indigenous peoples are malnourished, and conditions are deteriorating, not improving. A 1989 survey showed that in indigenous communities 70 percent of the population were below normal weight for age and 80 percent were below normal height, with over 30 percent exhibiting severe deficiencies in both categories. These levels were seven times higher than those found in nonindigenous communities. Furthermore, the survey found that while malnutrition had significantly declined in nonindigenous communities there was no improvement in indian communities during the 1980s.

Consumption of animal products compared to grains and vegetables reflects the economic condition of households. For example, during the crisis of the 1980s, consumption of all foods dropped, but meat consumption declined the most, as meat was practically eliminated from the diets of many Mexicans. For example, rural consumption of meat fell from 85 grams/person/day in 1979 to 77 grams in 1989, and in the rural South consumption was only 52 grams. In Mexico City, meat consumption fell from a high of 124 grams in 1981 to 82 grams in 1989.[45] Percapita consumption of basic grains also dropped as a result of declining incomes. A study of the 1982-88 period by the agricultural ministry found that wheat consumption had dropped by 30 percent, corn and rice by 9 percent, and beans by 5 percent.

The government does have programs to improve nutrition, but these programs are inadequate and beset with the same kind of bureaucratic corruption and inefficiency seen in other government agencies. One survey found that 90 percent of the food scheduled for distribution in one region spoiled, and that the remaining 10 percent did not go to the most undernourished strata of the population.[46]

Although inadequate supply because of low income is the main contributor to malnutrition, bad eating habits among all classes of Mexicans are becoming increasingly serious. Highly processed foods and sodas are replacing traditional diets of tortillas, beans, and chiles, pointing to the need for better nutrition education by the government in addition to improved distribution programs. It also points to a reexamination of policies that encourage international fast-food chains and processed foods into Mexico.

Farm and Food Needs

Mexico's economic restructuring to regain economic stability and to bolster its position in the integrating global economy has left it without a coherent food and farm policy. Trade liberalization, the reduction of government support, and the absence of an alternative farm policy have left corn producers extremely vulnerable to foreign competitors. A farm policy is needed that will give producers the stability they need to cover their costs and increase agricultural production. To be effective, such a policy should respond to the varying productive capabilities of the different strata of growers and to varying regional conditions and needs. The formulation of a farm policy in Mexico must be closely linked to a food policy, given the large rural population that both produces and buys corn. Locally produced corn plays an important role in sustaining most rural families (even-net deficit producers), a function that stands to be undermined by opening up national borders to cheap corn imports. The complexity of corn production and provisioning in rural areas makes reliance on the free market problematic if the government is committed to improving rural nutrition and staving off prolonged periods of scarcity and high prices.[47]

A successful food policy must incorporate measures that will ensure that enough food is available to satisfy the needs of a basic diet for all citizens and that basic foodstuffs are universally accessible. On the supply side, a food policy should stimulate national production and guarantee that revenues are available to cover shortfalls with imports. On the demand side, a food policy should shape distribution systems that provide food at affordable prices or at no cost to low-income sectors that are marginalized from the market because of their lack of effective demand or purchasing power.

In a country like Mexico,where a large sector of the food-producing population live in remote rural villages, a national food policy faces the additional challenges of creating distribution and marketing structures that address the problems arising from imperfect markets. Transportation obstacles; absence of storage facilities; lack of access to credit and agricultural inputs; the power of local intermediaries, moneylenders, and merchants to independently set prices are among problems that a food policy must confront. Working with the framework of international, national, and local markets, a food policy serves to buffer both consumers and producers from market forces that discourage consumption and disrupt desired production.

Food distribution programs must form part of the government's response to malnutrition. But at least as important is an income policy that increases minimum wage levels, encourages worker bargaining for higher wages, and supports development policies that generate jobs and distribute income more equitably.

The existence of a "safety net" that catches those whose basic food needs are not being met by the interplay of supply and demand is an essential part of a national food policy. However, Mexico's food policy will fall short and prove too expensive unless it is accompanied by redistributive and regulatory measures that narrow the widening gap between the rich and the poor and between the beneficiaries and the victims of free trade.

The financial crisis that broke out in Mexico at the end of 1994 cast new doubt about the wisdom of the government's claims that the neoliberal model of liberalized trade and reduced public-sector involvement in the economy would lead to food sovereignty. As dollars reserves dwindled, the country was faced with its inability to continue financing its trade deficit, which had risen to more than $23 billion in 1994. With the peso having lost about 40 percent of its former value, food and other imports would be considerably more expensive. Clearly, Mexico could no longer afford its large food import bill. Families, whose buying power had dramatically declined, would be forced to reduce their food purchases, and the government no longer had the foreign reserves to cover food imports.

Higher prices for imports provided a measure of protection for the domestic market. But that market had suddenly become smaller as effective demand diminished in the wake of the deepening economic crisis. Yet another threat to the country's food security was the prospect of a rapidly rising external debt burden, which would result in new limitations on the government's capacity and willingness to devote scarce revenues to designing an appropriate food production and distribution system.

Seven

THE END OF AGRARIAN REFORM

"Like the agrarian struggles of the past, the objective of the [reform of Article 27] is the broadening of justice and liberty."

—President Carlos Salinas de Gortari, November 1991.

Following closely on the heels of a series of dramatic changes that aimed to make Mexico's farm sector more compatible with the international market, President Salinas in late 1991 proceeded to amend the hallowed Article 27 of the constitution. The amendments terminated the government's historic commitment to provide land to petitioning campesinos and opened the doors to the privatization of the country's social sector. (The ejidos, along with the agrarian communities, are known as the *social sector*, which distinguishes it from the sector of private holders).[1]

The amendments included the termination of land redistribution; the granting to *ejidatarios* of the rights to sell, rent, sharecrop, or mortgage their individual parcels and to enter into joint ventures and contracts with private (including foreign) investors and stockholding companies; the collective right of *ejidatarios* to dissolve the ejido and distribute the property among members; and the elimination of the requirement that *ejidatarios* had to work their land to retain control.[2] Additionally, the reforms established a new decentralized government bureaucracy to certify ejido rights, title ejido parcels, and settle land disputes.[3] The language of Article 27 that established the government's dominion and eminent domain over land and natural resources remained. However, by eliminating the clause authorizing the *reparto agrario* (land distribution), the government took another important step away from *rectoría* or the arbitrating role of the state.[4]

President Salinas argued that the reforms were necessary to make the agricultural sector more productive by removing the fear of expropriation, attracting new investment to the countryside, and allowing the consolidation of *minifundios*. To those who claimed that the right to land was part of the country's revolutionary heritage, the government responded that there was no more land to distribute. Any attempt to continue agrarian reform by expropriating private property would only lead to the creation of more unproductive *minifundios*. Salinas also couched the reforms in the context of democratization and the end to government paternalism, pointing to the new freedom that *ejidatarios* would have to manage their individual parcels and common lands.

Opponents charged that the changes to Article 27 would accelerate land concentration, spark increased rural-to-urban migration, and increase class polarization in the countryside. They countered government claims that there was no more land to be distributed with assertions that neo-*latifundios*, which were protected by special exemptions from hectare limits and previous presidential land-distribution decrees or disguised by dividing estates among relatives and by the use of *prestanombres* (loaned names), could be found throughout the country, especially in states such as Chiapas where the local elites had successfully resisted the agrarian reform program. According to many critics, the government, by restricting its power of eminent domain, was abdicating its revolutionary obligation to supply land to the peasantry and to ensure that the country's natural resources were being used in socially responsible ways.[5]

Ejidos and Agrarian Communities

The ejido system was the central element in Mexico's agrarian reform program (Table 9).[6] Unlike agrarian reforms in other countries, the program in Mexico did not hand over property rights to campesinos but only the rights to use the expropriated private properties or national lands distributed to groups of petitioning campesinos. One benefit of this system of usufruct rights was that as long as an ejido and its members were using the land they could not lose it to banks or other private creditors, which has historically been one of the main factors worldwide in the disenfranchisement of small farmers. This protection, however, came at the high cost of making the reform sector dependent on the government, which intervened extensively in internal ejido affairs by controlling credit and internal ejidal politics. The indigenous agrarian communities retained more autonomy from the government.

A problem with the usufruct character of the social sector is that it blocked the possibility of using property as a guarantee for loans and thus hampered credit extension. Furthermore, it served as a disincentive for land improvements and restricted the market for land, leading in many cases to the inefficient use of land and the rise of *minifundios*.

Table 9

Ejido Facts

* 28,058 ejidos and agarian communities

* 49% of total land area in Mexico

* 3.1 million ejidatarios and members of agarian communities, accounting for 70 percent of Mexican farmers and some 15 million family members.

* 95 million hectares (21% of which is not considered arable).

* 73% of the social sector's land is not divided into parcels.

* 9.5 hectares is average parcel size of *ejidatarios*.

* 64% of *ejidatarios* have parcels of less than 5 hectares, a quantity generally not sufficient to support a family given quality of land, productivity, and unprofitable markets.

* 9% of *ejidatarios* have parcels larger than 20 hectares and constitute part of Mexico's commercial farm sector.

* 16% of ejido land is irrigated.

Sources: INEGI, *Encuesta nacional agropecuario ejidal,* 1988 (1990); Banamex, *Review of the Economic Situation in Mexico* (May 1992); Billie R. DeWalt and Martha W. Rees, *The End of Agararian Reform in Mexico* (San Diego: Center for U.S. Mexican Studies, 1994).

During the course of the agrarian reform, the quality of land distributed progressively worsened. Only about one-fifth of the land held by the social sector is considered arable, and much of this is highly eroded and rocky. Ejido land is held communally, although most arable land is divided into individual plots.[7] In the best of cases, the remaining communal land is often suitable only for pastures and forestry, while much of it is desert and mountainous terrain with no productive use.

Also part of the social sector are *comunidades agrarias*, which are mostly the holdings of indigenous communities whose claim on the land usually dates back to pre-Columbian and colonial eras. Traditionally, the roughly 1,200 agrarian communities have operated under a more communal structure than the ejidos. Over time, however, the laws regarding the communal character of the communites have been skirted, and plots have been treated more as private and transferable private property, although the renting or sale of arable land to outsiders is still rare. However, contracts granting outsiders rights to communal lands have become more frequent. Because of the lack of well-established boundaries, land conflicts between members of neighboring agrarian communities and ejidos are frequent and violent. Intra-community conflict, which also has become increasingly common, generally revolves around issues of the inheritance of land rights, the individual appropriation of communal lands, and the approval by corrupt leadership of grazing and forestry contracts of doubtful community value.

Ejidos have been governed by a democratic structure of a general assembly of *ejidatarios* and an elected three-member commision called the *comisariado ejidal* (president, secretary, and treasurer). The structure of agrarian communities has been less well-defined, although in most cases the leadership has come from a traditional civil-religious hierarchical structure sometimes referred to as the *cargo* system.

Ejido governance has reflected the paternalistic, clientelistic, and self-serving character of the national political system and is not an instance of direct democracy. The comisariados have often functioned as part of the PRI's agrarian electoral system and are commonly controlled by the ejido's economic elite and the most politically well-connected members. Only in isolated cases have the ejidal assemblies functioned as effective community forums. Social stratification and politics have also corrupted the integrity of the agrarian communities, a process that was largely associated with the control of all ejidal proceedings by government bureaucrats, who commonly had their own political and economic agendas.

The Article 27 reforms not only raise questions about the transfer of ejido lands but also about the future of the ejido structure. The creation of a more decentralized and less politicized agrarian bureaucracy will help undermine the power of corrupt *comisariados* while opening up new possibilities for broader participation. The approval of a majority of a community's *ejidatarios* at an assembly is needed before land can be sold to outsiders.[8] The new importance given to the assembly in deciding the fate of the ejido comes at a time, however, when the ejido has less responsibility over productive issues, such as credit and fertilizer distribution, which previously was managed by the traditional ejido leadership.

Although maintaining a formal existence, many ejidos will likely become little more than collections of private landholders as their social role diminishes. In many isolated areas, the ejidos have functioned as local governments in the absence of any other juridical unit on a village level. This points to the need either of reinforcing ejidal assemblies as the local base for democratic rule or of expanding local participation in municipal government.[9] By fostering individualism by facilitating privatization, the agrarian reforms will also adversely affect the role of campesino organizations that are linked to the ejido structure. The move to "individualize" will likely undermine collective forms of economic organization of *ejidatarios* that take advantage of economies of scale when small farmers cooperatively cultivate, purchase agricultural inputs, and market.

At least in the short term, the Article 27 revisions did not elicit the intense political reaction that many had predicted. The relative lack of opposition was due to a combination of factors. Probably the most important was that to a large degree the reforms only reflected the reality that the government had already stopped distributing land and that *ejidatarios* were already renting, sharecropping, and even selling their land, albeit somewhat clandestinely. This was true throughout Mexico but particularly common in urban and irrigated areas.

The muted reaction can also be explained by the way in which the proposal was quickly pushed through the national congress and state legislatures, leaving little room for popular debate. This was especially a problem for the peasantry, who because of geographical dispersion and isolation, has been traditionally slow to react to changes on the national level. The lack of unified opposition to the changes in Article 27, however, also reflected the differing positions of *ejidatarios* and campesino organizations. The approval by or at least acceptance of the reforms by the leadership of national campesino organizations created new schisms within the campesino movement and sharp divisions between the leadership and the base membership.[10] It was not until the explosion of the Chiapas rebellion that the depth of opposition to the reforms among many rural communities was really understood.

The ambivalent response of the campesino movement could also be related to the fact that the Article 27 amendment was itself the product of a compromise between the *campesinistas* and the neoliberal technocrats in government. Rather than dictating the privatization of the ejido, abolishing the social sector, and removing hectare limits on land ownership, as the neoliberal modernizers would have preferred, the amendment only opened the door to privatization and kept the hectare limits largely in place.[11] It is left up to the *ejidatarios* themselves to decide what they want to do with their own parcels and common lands. Common lands, except for forested lands, can be redistributed by the ejidal assembly to *ejidatarios*, family members, and the landless and eventually privatized. Control over common lands but not ownership (*dominio pleno*), including forested lands, can be transferred to production associations over which outside investors hold control, thereby effectively privatizing the common lands.[12]

President Salinas had promised as a candidate that campesinos would no longer be treated as children by a paternalistic and meddlesome government but rather as adults in a new context of "shared responsibility." The arguments of such *campesinista* government officials as Gustavo Gordillo and Arturo Warman were persuasive to many *ejidatarios* and leaders of independent and autonomous campesino organizations who had grown tired and frustrated with the government's agrarian bureaucracy.[13]

Even among ardent defenders of the social sector, it was clear that some type of overhaul of the ejido system was needed. Many regional differences make it hard to generalize about Mexico. Yet even before the changes to Article 27, the same dark shadow could be seen over ejido society and economy wherever one traveled in Mexico. Land parcels were becoming ever smaller with each generation, and the common lands were increasingly appropriated for private use and degraded by overuse. Individualism, corruption by ejido officials, and land grabbing and mercantilism by the most powerful had worn down the communal structure and led to increased social stratification. Young people saw no future in farming and regarded the ejido system as a dusty artifact incompatible with the modern world. Only among the middle-aged and elderly was there an enduring conviction that ejidos represented a step forward from peonage and landlessness. With or without changes to Article 27, the prospects for the social sector in Mexico looked dismal.[14]

At least in the short term, there were no signs that the revised Article 27 would either spark a new economic dynamism in the Mexican countryside or confirm the apocalyptic projections of its opponents. The official termination of land distribution and the opening up of ejido lands to private investment did not have an immediate impact on production and investment patterns. Neither did the amendment set off a flood of land transfers.

Private investment in agriculture showed no increase in the 1992-94 period, and the government was hard put to show that the reforms resulted in any significant rise in the number of associations between *ejidatarios* and private investors. The continued crisis of the agriculture sector created new doubts about the optimistic predictions of government officials that the policy changes would help revitalize the agricultural sector. The rental and sale of ejido lands to those outside the ejidos did increase but not on a massive scale. Generally, land transfers and rental agreements affected only those ejidos where such practices were already common, such as those located on the fringes of expanding urban areas and tourist centers and those that were irrigated.

There has never been a comprehensive survey of land ownership and use in Mexico. Without such a survey, government claims that there is no more land to distribute and opposition claims that neo-*latifundios* pervade the countryside are difficult to evaluate.[15] Before the government announced a definitive end to land distribution such a survey would have been appropriate. Although the government asserted that the end of land distribution did not mean that it was defending the existence of large estates, it was unwilling to mount an investigation into the extent to which many large growers and cattle ranchers had avoided the agrarian reform by hiding their holdings behind *prestanombres* and receiving special government exemptions from hectare limits.

Although in some states, such as Morelos, the lack of land to distribute is an accepted fact, in other states, such as Chiapas, it is just as obvious that the agrarian reform program was never fully implemented because of the resistance of local elites. The government's promise that although the land distribution program was over it would facilitate some land transfers to campesino groups by negotiating land sales did reduce some of the mounting opposition to the Article 27 reforms. Limited government resources, the government's apparent unwillingness to challenge the interests of large landholders and ranchers, and the inevitably selective character of such a program, however, make it a less than an adequate solution to the inequities in Mexico's pattern of land ownership.

The new Article 27 does maintain limits to private property, but there is little confidence that these limits will be enforced given the government's past history of protecting large landowners and its current commitment to market mechanisms.[16] Opponents cite the large loophole created by the revised Article 27 that allows land categorized as pasture to be converted to improved farmland, for which the allowable limit for private ownership is much smaller than for either grazing land or rainfed agricultural land. In this way, vast agricultural estates could legally be established because converted land would be covered under the higher hectare limit. Supporters of the reform argue that the previous system of acreage limits discouraged the conversion of arable land that was categorized as pasture land to more productive use, thereby potentially opens up new sources of farmland.

At least in the short term, the new Article 27 seemed more likely to lead to the consolidation of land within the ejidos than to give rise to neo-*latifundismo*. Within the ejidos, the wealthiest *ejidatarios* are free to expand their holdings to include up to 5 percent of the total ejido land. In the absence of an increased demand for agricultural land in Mexico, the upper stratum of *ejidatarios* can buy land at dirt-cheap prices from hard-pressed fellow ejido members. On the one hand, this consolidation of properties will cut down on the number of inefficient *minifundios*, thereby creating the possibility of higher productivity and increased yields. On the other hand, the transfers of land will accelerate class divisions in rural Mexico and thereby increase social tensions.

Risks of Land Titles

Closely associated with the Article 27 revisions was the launching by the government of the Land Rights Certification Program (Procede). A two-step program, Procede first grants certificates of rights to petitioning ejidos and *ejidatarios* that will facilitate the rental, mortgaging, or use of the land in association with outside investors.

Once granted their certificates of rights, *ejidatarios* can then petition for a clear title that will permit the sale of their parcels. Initial reactions to Procede demonstrated the complexity of sorting out land rights in Mexico. In areas such as Morelos or the Bajío where land transfers were already an accepted practice, *ejidatarios* welcomed Procede, hoping that it would clear up uncertainty over boundaries of parcels and common lands.[17] But in other areas such as in Chiapas and Hidalgo, more communities resisted Procede, believing that land titling was the first step toward losing their land.[18]

This resistance to Procede and the accompanying opposition to the new Article 27 was generally not associated with any philosophical defense of the social sector. Rather, poor campesinos feared that once certified their individual parcels would be vulnerable to confiscation if they could not pay their debts.[19] Under the new system, *ejidatarios* are free to sell their parcels (assuming prior approval by the ejido assembly), but they are also free to lose their parcels. For all its problems, the old system that guaranteed the "inalienability" of lands in the social sector at least ensured that the holdings of campesinos would not fall into the hands of the banks and the landed elite because a grower could not pay back his or her farm loan. In some close-knit ejidos, *ejidatarios* have also successfully resisted the surveying of individual parcels by Procede out of fear that land certification and the possibility of sale would pit family members and *ejidatarios* against one another. Another factor that slows the progress of Procede is the massive confusion and misunderstanding among the *campesinado* about the changes to Article 27 and how they relate to other government programs such as Procampo and to the overall restructuring of agricultural markets.

As a result of the government's macroeconomic policies and its decreasing involvement in agriculture, the farm sector had become increasingly decapitalized and indebted in the 1980s and early 1990s. Although the stability of campesino agriculture had certainly deteriorated, campesinos in Mexico had long become accustomed to and dependent on what was known as the *industria de siniestros* (crop disaster manipulation).[20] This refers to the government's programs of credit and insurance that propped up campesino agriculture with little expectation that it would prove profitable. Claiming they were victims of natural disasters, usually droughts or heavy rains, the recipients of government credit and insurance usually never paid back their loans, but they did have to pay off government investors. If they had been private landholders, their land would have been subject to expropriation. However, as holders of ejido land, their land was protected—a security they now were losing.

In many regions, the process of certifying ejido parcels also opened up the problem of conflicting land claims within and between ejidos. Family feuds and inter-ejido conflicts over land boundaries have become endemic. The government itself bears much of the responsibility for the confusion and conflict that pervade the social sector. Presidents announced expropriations and land transfers that were never implemented, and more often than not when ejidos were created the lands were not surveyed, leading to many overlapping boundaries. Compounding this sloppiness has been a long history of corruption within the agrarian bureaucracy. Commonly, technicians and surveyors working for the agrarian reform ministry demanded bribes of communities that were seeking land, which also contributed to the nightmare of overlapping boundaries.

In attempting to push the land-certification program forward, Procede agents were also confronted by the usual campesino suspicion of government programs, which exhibited itself in passive resistance to their efforts to convoke meetings and get information. There have also been complaints that Procede officials were pushing forward the land-certification program by creating the impression that incorporation in the program was a condition to receiving Procampo benefits.[21] Even if it could count on a receptive peasantry, Procede faced the mammoth task of registering and titling 4.6 million farm parcels and 4.3 million house plots claimed by the more than three million *ejidatarios* and *comuneros*.[22]

Production and Ownership

As the government itself has concluded, the problem of the Mexican countryside and the agricultural sector lies more in production than in ownership. It is doubtful, however, that this production problem will be solved simply by opening up the ejidos to private ownership and land transfers. On a small scale, land consolidation may lead to more productive farming, but there are few signs that the liberalized land market is attracting substantial amounts of new investment in land and production.

Foreign investors, seeing an expanded market for Mexican agro-exports, are looking for new opportunities in Mexico but are unlikely to invest directly in agricultural production.[23] More likely is a continuation, and perhaps an increase in, contract relationships with Mexican producers, which are considerably less risky than direct involvement in production. Given the lack of interest in investing in agricultural production, it is unlikely that the radical revamping of Article 27 will lead to a substantial change in land ownership patterns because of foreign investment.

Clearly, the relationship between the state and the social sector needed a major overhaul. Decades of paternalism and corruption combined with the lack of a real commitment to make the ejidos productive made reform necessary. But in the absence of other viable alternatives that would absorb the rural workforce and increase agricultural production, the rehabilitation of the sector, rather than creating the conditions for its disintegration, would have been a better choice. Such a rehabilitation could include many of the reforms that were incorporated in new Article 27 and accompanying agrarian law. An essential element, however, for rural development would be continued state involvement in the form of public-sector investment in collaboration with campesino organizations and some protection against cheap imports.

Also at issue with the changes to Article 27 is the more fundamental concern about the character of land and natural resources. By terminating land distribution and opening up the ejido sector to land transfers, the government has made land more of a commodity and less of a national resource to be used for socially productive purposes. By favoring the individual over the social or communal, and financial over moral considerations, the state released itself from its responsibility to promote the common good. If indeed this change eventually leads to increased investment, trade, and job creation in rural Mexico, this switch from social to individual values may prove worth the disappearance of the social sector and its communitarian structures. Otherwise, Mexico will at the same time have increased landlessness and insecurity in the countryside, accelerated the rate of rural-to-urban migration, and forever lost an established social base for integrated rural development. This move away from a social definition of land and other natural resources has implications for the ability and the commitment of the government to ensure that the agricultural economy develops in an environmentally sustainable manner.

The Article 27 revisions, while not having much immediate impact, do represent the dramatic change that is underway in the relations between the Mexican state and the peasantry. The changes came within the context of an array of neoliberal measures that put market forces in control, while pushing off to the side more social concerns such as maintaining food security, absorbing rural labor, halting out-migration, preserving cultural values, and fostering rural development. Bowing to rural pressure, the government might consider making minor changes to the new Article 27. But any substantial changes, such as a return to agrarian reform, are unlikely unless they come within the context of a major revamping of Mexico's entire economic development strategy.

Eight

THE PEOPLE OF THE LAND

"In today's world, the free market and the withdrawal of state support for the campesinos is a fact. There's no other alternative but to face this reality head on—and to take into our own hands our own destiny."

— Arturo García, leader of the Coalition of
Ejidos of Costa Grande, Guerrero, March 1992.

Mexico is an urbanizing nation but one with an enduring rural core. More than one-quarter of the population still lives and works outside of the cities, and many of those Mexicans who have found jobs in the cities have strong rural roots, returning to their villages for annual festivals, vacations, and family visits. When the struggle for daily survival becomes too difficult in the city, the daughters and sons of the *campo* often return to their ancestral homes. Although city dwellers now outnumber campesinos, there are today more Mexicans living and working the land than there were at the time of the Mexican Revolution.

The *zapatista* and *villista* armies ensured that the postrevolutionary government devoted special attention to the demands of the peasantry. Simply continuing the practice of exploiting peasants and ignoring their demands would have been a recipe for continued political instability that the newly constituted state could not risk. Land reform, although not in the form envisioned by Zapata, was written into the new constitution in

1917, and the government later established a multilayered bureaucracy to address campesino concerns. Even during the three decades of the counterreform (1940-70) and the recent neoliberal governments, government discourse has been laced with references to the official commitment to the welfare of the campesinos. Maintaining the support of the peasantry and control over its organizations were seen as essential to the state's legitimacy and political stability.

The future of these "chosen children of the regime" has always been a matter of debate in Mexico.[1] While the campesinos themselves focused on the battle for daily subsistence, the political and economic role of campesinos has been a source of contention among policymakers, academics, and activists.

Basically, the debate revolves around the question of whether these masses of small-scale growers have a positive role to play in the future economic and political development of Mexico. Do they ultimately act as a brake on development because of their backward ways and their adherence to small family plots? Or alternatively, does the peasantry have an integral role to play in feeding the nation, in maintaining cultural plurality, and in leading the way to sustainable agricultural development? Because of their status as landholders, are campesinos inherently conservative and therefore unable to identify with the interests of the working class? Or rather, as a poor sector left behind by economic progress, can the peasantry play a leading role in movements for social justice and democracy in Mexico? Underlying the contentious debate about the fate and function of the campesino population is the question of whether the state should help perpetuate the campesino sector by providing it with the assistance and market protections it needs to maintain its place in rural Mexico.

The class status of the peasantry has been a matter of sharp dispute. Some contend that the peasantry, despite the inroads of capitalism, remains a fundamentally distinct class that has adapted to external penetration in ways that ensure its survival. Others say that the peasantry has no future other than proletarianization. While some see the disintegration of the peasantry as an historical, cultural, and economic loss, others regard this process more favorably, arguing that campesinos will benefit from their incorporation into the logic of modern historical development.[2]

Discussions about the role of the peasantry and its future are not just a matter of academic conjecture but have had direct impact on the direction of government rural programs and on the organizing tactics of political activists. For those who, in the Liberal tradition, view the peasantry as an anachronism in history, ejidos and indigenous agrarian communities have been regarded as transitory forms of land tenure—necessary for political stability but restraining the creative forces of private property. In this view, the only viable base for economic progress is private property, while the "social" property of the ejidos and indigenous communities serve merely as holding areas for inefficient producers and a pacification zone for restive campesinos.

The debate about the fate of the peasantry has not, of course, been restricted to Mexico. The peasantry constitutes nearly one-third of Latin America's population and as much as half of the population of Africa and Asia. Analysts throughout the world have long reflected on the historical and economic role of campesino communities that have endured the transitions from feudal economies to capitalist and socialist ones. A review of the broad outlines of these discussions is helpful in understanding not only past and present agrarian policies but also in evaluating the future prospects of the peasantry and the development possibilities of Mexico.

Slowly But Surely Proletarians

The view that the peasantry is a retrograde element is shared by those on the left and the right who see history as constituting a forward movement of economic, social, and political forces. This materialist world view is common to classical liberals, neoliberals, economic modernizers, and Marxists. As the manifestation of precapitalist modes of production not guided by market considerations or driven by the need to create surplus, campesinos are considered artifacts of the past who will inevitably disappear. Eventually they will either become capitalist producers or merge into the proletariat.

The peasantry as part of the agricultural economy has come under attack by economic liberals and modernizers who regard the agrarian reform sector as an obstacle to capitalist development and who deprecate small-farm production while promoting the virtues of "economies-of-scale" agriculture. For both neoliberal ideologues and modernizers, economic progress and social welfare will result only when the forces of supply and demand can function without artificial constraints.

It is argued that the propping up of the peasantry with land distribution and production and marketing subsidies—while perhaps necessary in the past to guarantee political stability, a source of cheap food, and a ready reserve of seasonal labor for agribusiness—is counterproductive today because it wastes state revenues, keeps land out of the private market, and perpetuates the inefficient *minifundio*. Cheap grains are available from the United States, and there is now an abundant supply of rural labor willing to work for subsubsistence wages. With the free flow of capital and investment, production will increase and more jobs will be created. In the liberal and modernizing framework, Mexico's economy and society will then move forward to a higher level of development.

In the 1960s and 1970s, the debate on the left over the peasantry's future revolved around positions put forward by *proletaristas* or *descampesinistas*, who espoused a Marxist, class-based analysis, and the *campesinistas*, who were dedicated to promoting, protecting, and organizing the peasantry. The *descampesinistas* were critical of the agrarianism of the Mexican state and leftist intellectuals.[3] They charged that efforts by the *campesinistas* were misdirected, given that the peasantry was a class in the process of inevitable disintegration. Although orthodox Marxists modified earlier claims that the peasantry would soon disappear, they still maintained that the campesino economy was unviable, self-exploitative, and in a state of ruin. Furthermore, they argued that the populist policies of the state—its creation of the National Campesino Federation (CNC), land reform, and rural integration programs—were largely self-serving because they increased state control without substantially improving campesino conditions. The *descampesinistas* also refuted claims that campesino production is actually more efficient than agribusiness operations, noting that any higher productivity or reduced production costs come from the exploitation of unremunerated daily labor.

Labeling the *campesinista* views as romantic and unrealistic, the *descampesinistas* concluded that the campesino economy and the ejidal sector are sources of primitive capital accumulation by the dominant economy. They pointed out that campesino communities are highly stratified with local *caciques* and merchants taking advantage of the noncapitalist forms of production to bolster their own wealth and power.[4] One of the main contributions of the *proletarista* critique was its highlighting of the mixed identity of Mexico's campesinos. Although most campesinos have not yet assumed a clear identity as wage laborers, they at least can be safely categorized as semiproletarians because of their seasonal work on cash-crop farms. For whatever reason—whether because of their own primordial attachment to the land or the history of state agrarian populism—these semiproletarians often organize themselves more as campesinos than workers. It was this "false consciousness" that Marxist organizers and theorists wanted to see changed.

The still-thriving *campesinista* camp rejects notions by liberals and neoliberals that economic and political development follows from economic modernization. Nor does it share the conviction of Marxists that the peasantry is destined to disappear as it becomes proletarianized. Instead, *campesinistas* generally hold that the peasantry is an enduring social sector in a dependent capitalist country, a sector that can play a progressive economic and political role.[5] They acknowledge that the capitalist economy has penetrated traditional rural communities but argue that campesinos still struggle to maintain their rural identities.[6] Often this battle for survival takes the form of militant resistance to landowners, *caciques*, and the state, but it is also seen in a more passive, everyday effort to hold on to the land, labor, and capital of rural communities.[7]

Part of the *campesinista* thought is a spin-off of the *zapatista*, *cardenista*, and even *echeverrista* agrarianism, although there have also been strong class-based and dependency-theory components to *campesinista* analysis. Most *campesinistas* agree that if the Mexican economy could indeed supply decent jobs either in industry or capitalist agriculture, the peasantry would fade away as the *descampesinistas* predicted. But they argue that Mexico's status as a dependent capitalist country will keep it from developing a modern capitalist farm sector. Present-day *campesinistas* point to the economy's failure to generate jobs for campesinos. The current lack of investment in production bodes ill for future job generation. Campesinos, while most do seek cash income outside their villages, have not yet disappeared from the *campo* because they have no place else to go.

Rather than dismissing campesinos as a backward force, the *campesinistas* look to the peasantry to become the basis of a dynamic agricultural system capable of meeting Mexico's food needs and to serve as a leading force for social change. They advocate state support of the campesino economy and campesino organizations to enable them to put forward their own demands. These notions became an important current in the Mexican campesino movement led by the National Union of

Autonomous Campesino Organizations (UNORCA). In recent years, the *campesinista* camp of opinion has been bolstered by those who argue that campesino society and economy represent a viable alternative to the increasing problems resulting from rapid urbanization, unsustainable practices of capitalist agriculture, and overly centralized government.

In the absence of alternative strategies to provide jobs and food for Mexicans, a new sector of *campesinistas* propose the maintenance of small agricultural units for economic, cultural, agronomic, and environmental reasons.[8] The peasantry, while admittedly not as efficient as capitalist agribusiness, can absorb large quantities of labor and can provide the country with basic grains. Moreover, it is argued that the communitarian ethic of rural villages offers an alternative to the destructive individualistic ethos of modern urban society.

At the center of the debate is whether a viable campesino economy can exist free of state tutelage and cut off from major government services. While the *campesinistas* incorporated within the Salinas government envisioned a dynamic rural economy based on consolidated land holdings, a capitalistic ethic, and the end to state paternalism, others grouped within the autonomous campesino organizations stressed the importance of social organization, an autonomous relationship with the states, and significant government support and protection. Conspiciously absent from the *campesinista-descampesinista* debate has been a discussion of the issue of population growth and resource availability. Demographic pressures of a limited and deteriorating land base have forced many campesinos to become proletarians or to join the informal economy.

New Paradigms

Much of the debate about the fate of the peasantry has been shaped by changing anthropological paradigms and interpretations.[9] Initially, anthropologists in Mexico focused on indigenous communities that they thought were not affected by the surrounding economy and culture. But as anthropologists looked more closely at even the most "primitive" and remote communities, they usually found some degree of economic and cultural penetration by the dominant society. Similarly, economists who previously regarded campesino economies as operating outside or on the margin of the capitalist market found substantial integration.

Rather than simply describing the behavior and roles of indigenous peoples and campesinos, anthropologists in the 1960s began to look more critically at the interaction and integration between rural and urban communities. Anthropologists influenced by theories of dependency, historical stucturalism, and cultural ecology—all of which focused on the material or economic circumstances of societal relations—accented the exploitive character of rural-urban relations. Rejecting the cultural relativism and the functionalism of earlier anthropologists, they detailed a chain of exploitation originating in metropolitan areas.

Instead of conceiving rural communities as isolated vestiges of the past, anthropologists noted that the identity and functions of these communities were increasingly being defined by their inequitable interaction with regional, national, and international markets. As a result, the boundaries of anthropology became increasingly difficult to define as researchers started branching out from field studies to examine questions of political economy. To understand rural societies, many anthropologists looked beyond the campesino village to relations with the state and capitalism in Mexico.

Recognizing the subordinate position of the peasantry, some anthropologists placed greater emphasis on the mental or cultural traits that act as obstacles to economic advancement. Others stressed the economic barriers that keep campesinos poor.[10] But the debate did not end there. Depending on their position about the class status and contributions of the peasantry, some anthropologists favored programs and reforms that help remove cultural and economic barriers to rural development, while others argued that some economic barriers should be kept in place to preserve cultural pluralism and to protect the peasantry against unfair competition.

Insurgent Mexico

Historically, campesinos themselves have been sidelined in the theoretical debate about their future, but they have not been passive in the face of changing economic and political structures. Throughout Mexican history—from the *Porfiriato* and the revolutionary struggles of the *zapatistas* to the Chiapas rebellion—campesinos have acted to shape their own future. In recent years, the leaders of autonomous campesino organizations have also entered the theoretical and policy debate about the fate of the peasantry.

Access to land and water has been the central but not the only demand of campesino activists. Cultural survival, increased state support for production and marketing, and the right to self-determination and democracy are other important demands that have shaped campesino struggles since the early nineteenth century.[11] All the major forms of campesino rebellion—land invasions, village uprisings, caste wars, and guerrilla warfare—have been part of Mexico's tumultuous rural history. In some cases, campesinos and indians have acted alone, but in times of national political upheaval they have frequently formed tactical alliances with large landowners, the local bourgeoisie, and political elites to advance their demands.

During the colonial era most rural revolts were struggles to preserve local autonomy or protests by indigenous communities against the tribute imposed by the Catholic Church and the colonial government. Genocidal wars against indian communities, especially by frontier colonialists in the North, incited defensive violence by embattled communities. In both colonial and postcolonial times, the lack of a common language and history among the many indigenous groups kept peasant revolts localized and easier to crush.[12] The decimation of the indian people—from some twenty million to an estimated two million—by conquest and disease facilitated dominance over the indigenous peasantry by the Spanish and local creole elites.[13]

For the most part, campesino and indian uprisings have been regional or local insurgencies. Yet, unlike in many other Latin American nations, in Mexico campesinos have also played key roles in national political movements as they joined with emerging political elites in uneasy alliances. History memorializes Miguel Hidalgo, José María Morelos, and Ignacio Allende for their independence fight against the *peninsulares* or Spaniards. Yet it was the peasantry, mostly dispossessed indians, who constituted the backbone of the War of Independence (1810-21). Responding to Padre Hidalgo's fiery declaration against the Spanish, known as Grito de Dolores, they raised their machetes against the Spanish, hoping that their support would be rewarded with the return of lands stolen by the colonizers. The decisive battles, however, were fought by the conservatives who were intent on preventing such an outcome of the independence struggles.

Postindependence rule by the Conservatives brought no improvement for the peasantry, and localized rebellion continued for most of the century. Organized rural violence in the mid-nineteenth century aggravated the political and ideological fragmentation of the nation's weak ruling class.[14] This obstructed the consolidation of conservative rule while creating the political space needed by the liberals, who became the new political elite in the late 1850s and 1860s. The lack of a strong national state and the liberal property reforms of the 1850s contributed to frequent rural rebellions in the pre-*Porfiriato* period. Major regional uprisings occurred in central Mexico in which indian and *mestizo* campesinos joined together. But the broadest rebellion was the mid-century War of the Castes in which Maya indians launched a messianic crusade against all nonindians in the remote Yucatán province. A stronger and more repressive government after 1876 together with the system of debt peonage by the *hacendados* kept campesino resistance localized, sporadic, and of limited scale until the revolutionary period.

Diego Rivera and other postrevolutionary muralists created lasting images of brutally exploited peons rising to revolutionary heroics. Although there is no doubt that campesino armies played a major role in the unfolding of the revolution, the Rivera murals and some early scholarship gave rise to the mistaken impression that the Mexican Revolution was at its heart an agrarian revolution.[15]

The rise of campesino armies in the North and the South did add a decisively social element to what was essentially a dispute among national elites. Yet in many regions there was no independent campesino militancy, and only in rare cases did the peons of the *haciendas* join the campesino and constitutionalist revolutionary armies. In the end, as in the beginning of the revolution, it was the emerging political and economic elites of northern Mexico that retained control of the political transition. At the same time, however, in no other country of Latin America did the peasantry assume such a substantial role in the major national political movements of the nineteenth and twentieth centuries.

Generally, the campesinos who joined Mexico's revolutionary armies either felt threatened by advancing capitalist modernization or were affected by the economic stagnation that set in during the last years of the *Porfiriato*. Especially in the South, the campesinos who became revolutionaries were driven by local land and water issues. Like those campesinos who joined the independence struggle, they hoped that a new government would help them recover lost lands. By contrast, most of the campesinos who joined Villa or the constitutionalist armies were reacting more to rising joblessness and falling agricultural wages than to *zapatista*-like promises to win back stolen lands.

In some cases, the campesino warriors had no political agenda and degenerated into bandit cavalries. However, as much as the reactionary constitutionalist elites tried to characterize the *zapatistas* as thieves and barbarians who thrived on violence, the Liberation Army of the South was as much a political force as a military one. In fact, Zapata's Liberation Army of the South was the only revolutionary armed force that insisted the military be subordinated to civilian society.[16] Although firmly based in Morelos, the *zapatistas* formulated a national political agenda that, while mostly ignored by the postrevolutionary governments, did help ensure that land distribution was included in the nation's constitution. Their insistence on local democracy and control over natural resources also remains part of their enduring legacy.

Despite their failure to meet fully their immediate goals of recovering land, regaining autonomy, or halting capitalist modernization, campesino rebels have had a lasting impact on Mexican history.[17] In the case of the major political revolutions in Mexico's history—the War of Independence, the Liberal victory over the Conservatives and Maximilian, and the Mexican Revolution—campesino rebellions and alliances with other insurgent forces proved critical to the development of new economic and political structures. As a result of campesino militancy, the old-style *latifundios* largely disappeared and land distribution became an integral element in guiding economic progress and ensuring political stability in the twentieth century. More recently, the campesino uprising in Chiapas, while not successful in reversing the free trade accord and neoliberal restructuring of the agricultural sector, did give a new impetus to the democratization movement, both locally and nationally.

Corporatist Framework

The murders of the two revolutionary *caudillos*, Emiliano Zapata (1919) and Francisco Villa (1923), signaled the defeat of the peasantry as an independent social force within the Mexican Revolution. Land reform did become law, but it was enforced selectively and sporadically in the

1920-34 period, mainly to pacify and co-opt armed peasant groups and the radical or leftist ones commited to *agrarismo rojo* (red agrarianism). Mexico's agrarian reform worked to subordinate campesino communities and organizations to the state by obligating them to apply to the government for usufruct rights on land that in many cases historically belonged to them, as was the case with the *zapatistas* in Morelos. By holding out the promise of new land distribution, the government discouraged campesinos from joining organizations that had a hostile relationship with the government.[18]

The revolution effectively shattered the political power of the old *latifundio* class, but the economic power of the landed oligarchy remained largely intact until the Cárdenas presidency. During the early postrevolutionary years, local warlords suppressed campesino uprisings and largely succeeded in blocking their demands for land distribution.

By the 1930s, however, rural rebellion was becoming increasingly widespread as campesinos fell victim to the deepening economic recession and as their dissatisfaction with the revolutionary government increased. President Cárdenas encouraged rural mobilization in his efforts to fortify a progressive alliance that would lay the base for political stability and economic development. Although he initially promoted the formation of peasant leagues to push forward agrarian reform, even to the extent of arming them, Cárdenas later incorporated those and other campesino organizations into the government-controlled CNC, while suppressing campesino organizations that were considered too radical or beyond the control of the government's corporatist structures.[19]

The CNC initially served as a vehicle to mobilize campesinos, but it soon degenerated into an instrument for maintaining state control. Except for its first few years, the CNC has functioned largely as an agrarian electoral machine. All *ejidatarios* automatically became members of the CNC, which in turn was part of the PRI's corporatist network, which included regional and state-level organizations as well as the national-level CNC. The local representatives of the CNC—and hence the PRI—were the *comisariados* or ejido presidents, who responded to the CNC bureaucracy. A local campesino leader's influence rested on his power of *picaporte* or access to government agencies. Hopes of landless campesinos that the government would grant them land depended largely on their association with the CNC.

For more than three decades, the agrarian reform program together with the CNC kept the peasantry dependent on the government, thereby obstructing the rise of independent national campesino organizations.[20] But struggles over land persisted as the landless and land-poor demanded that the agrarian reform be fully implemented in states with concentrations of large estates and agribusnesses such as Sonora and Chihuahua. Out of the militant struggles of collectivized ejidos in the region of La Laguna and in the Northwest arose other independent campesino movements. Frequently, these independent campesino organizations became associated with communist and socialist parties eager to expand their base and challenge the coalescing of state capitalism in Mexico.

The fading of the CNC as the main constitutive rural force in the 1970s paralleled the withering of the government land distribution program and the rising emphasis on productivist objectives. Although there have long been productivist currents and affiliates within the CNC, dependent agrarianism was the dominant tendency. With no more land being distributed and the state playing a new role in supplying inputs and marketing assistance, the CNC's function as a corporatist institution that pacified and coordinated land solicitors was becoming obsolete by the 1970s. But the CNC did manage to win control of most of the new service and credit associations established by President Echeverría, and by the late 1980s the CNC had switched to a more productivist orientation that complemented the neoliberalism of the De la Madrid and Salinas governments.

The CNC—even more than the Mexican Workers Federation (CTM)— has functioned as a passive instrument of the state, as seen in its failures to represent the most basic interests of campesinos and farmworkers. It has a sordid history of collaborating with the PRI to co-opt, divide, and repress independent organizing efforts. Its failure to maintain principled positions on food security, land distribution, and the continued need for government support of campesino agriculture, as well as its subservient position with regard to ejidio reform and trade liberalization, further reinforced the CNC's identity as a pawn of the government.

The New Campesino Movement

Nongovernmental campesino organizations did spring up peri-
odically in the 1940s and 1950s, but it was not until the late 1960s and
early 1970s that the government was again confronted with widespread
campesino militancy. Decades of control by the ruling party, the superfi-
ciality of the government's populist commitments, and the exclusive
character of state capitalism in Mexico contributed to widening disenchantment with the government. Increasingly, the government's legitimacy was questioned not just by workers and campesinos but also by
rising numbers of middle-class Mexicans, especially students and
teachers.

The Tlatelolco massacre in October 1968 of hundreds of protesting
students sharpened this deepening legitimacy crisis. It sparked an outburst
of antigovernment organizing by leftist students and intellectuals, who
recognized the limitations of working within the system. The massacre
also pushed the political pendulum to the left. Attempting to recover its
legitimacy, the new government of President Echeverría (1970-76)
adopted a pronounced populist tone.

The 1968 massacre forced the left to reevaluate its strategies for
reform and revolution. Some decided to leave the university and the leftist
parties to form terrorist and guerrilla opposition groups. Others, recognizing the large gap that existed between the left and the masses whose
interests they supposedly represented, resolved to insert themselves directly into the world of the urban and rural poor. Yet another group of the
"generation of 1968" joined the government and were largely responsible
for the new populism of the Echeverría and López Portillo governments,
later going on to shape the social liberalism and campesino policies of the
Salinas administration. This burst of leftist energy helped shape the
campesino movement of the 1970s and 1980s.

At least as important as the post-1968 ideological shake-up in
reshaping the campesino movement were the deteriorating social and
economic conditions in the *campo*. The expansion of the cattle industry,
shrinking of the agricultural frontier, the mounting population pressures,
the mechanization of northwest agribusiness, the switch to less labor-intensive crops such as sorghum, and the deteriorating terms of trade for

campesino agriculture were among the main reasons for the explosion of land invasions and conflicts with local elites in the early 1970s.[21]

Reacting to the explosion in agrarian organizing in the 1970-73 period, President Echeverría heightened his own populist rhetoric. Although he did attempt to bolster his own agrarian credentials by authorizing land expropriations in the Northwest in 1975-76, he was more concerned about renewing the productive capacity of the ejido and small farm sector. He did this by increasing government services and by encouraging the formation of Ejido Unions (UEs) and the Rural Collective Interest Associations (ARICs), which were unions of two or more UEs. In addition to ejidos, these new production and market-oriented associations could include the indigenous agrarian communities as well as groupings of small private farmers.

Another important change in this period was the rise of local and regional campesino organizations that were associated with neither the government nor leftist political parties. The importance of the Mexico City-based *centrales* diminished as local groups asserted their independence and own agendas. By the late 1970s and early 1980s these local organizations began coming together in national networks, the two most important of which were the National Network of the Plan of Ayala (CNPA), founded in 1979, and UNORCA, founded in 1985. Other than the CNC, the only other important campesino centrally structured organization that remained active in the 1990s was the Independent Central of Campesinos and Farmworkers (CIOAC).[22]

The CNPA and UNORCA represented two different tendencies within the campesino sector: the radical agrarians and the pragmatic productivists. The former, whose presence faded as that of UNORCA expanded, represented the agrarian demands of landless and semi-subsistence *ejidatarios*, while the latter incorporated a new crop of organizations of mostly small- and medium-sized, surplus-producing *ejidatarios* based mainly in the UEs and whose concerns revolved around production, prices, services, and marketing.[23]

While the CNPA stressed the importance of campesino mobilization and defense of human rights, UNORCA focused more on proposing policy changes and negotiating solutions with the government, although it also recognized the necessity of popular mobilization. CNPA played a leading role in incorporating indian communities from the South and Southeast into the national campesino movement and raising national awareness about human rights abuses by government security forces and the vigilante squads operated by local *caciques*, landowners, and the CNC. By associating itself with the Plan of Ayala, the CNPA succeeded in reviving the legacy of Zapata while calling attention to the degree to which the state had failed to meet the revolution's commitments to the peasantry. In contrast, UNORCA's leaders made little attempt to situate themselves within the country's agrarian traditions. Instead, they wanted to be respected as important actors in the national economy who should be included in agricultural policy discussions. These different orientations toward agrarian and agricultural policies were driven by the different constituencies. While the CNPA represented mostly subsistence and sub-subsistence peasants, UNORCA found its base mostly among surplus-producing *ejidatarios*.

The terms *agrarian* and *productivist* described the economic orientations of these two tendencies, while *independent* and *autonomous* were the labels used to describe their relations with the government. Given the long history of domination of campesino groups by the government and political parties, most campesino organizations formed in Mexico during the past fifteen years generally have taken care to assert their independence from the government and political parties. The more radical and usually more agrarian-oriented groups, such as the CNPA, have defined themselves as being completely independent of the government. But more than independent, these organizations were usually vehemently antigovernment as well and had close connections with leftist groups. In contrast, other organizations, such as UNORCA and the National Network of Coffee Grower Organizations (CNOC), have taken a more pragmatic stance. They carefully maintain their autonomy as nongovernmental organizations but are willing to enter into agreements with the government and its agencies.

In the 1980s there developed a coincidence of interests between the government and rising numbers of campesino farmers. This mutual interest in raising production was the foundation of what was called the "new campesino movement." Even elements in the CNC, an organization molded around the agrarian reform program, began to stress issues of production, prices, and services, and thereby increased its influence.

Before he took office in 1988 Carlos Salinas let it be known that the government's relations with the peasantry would be restructured. Salinas, who had investigated the problems of the campesino economy as a graduate student, promised to revive agricultural production and to launch a process of *concertación* (consensus negotiations) with campesino organizations that fell outside the state's corporatist structure. Although opposition candidate Cuauhtémoc Cárdenas did capture a large campesino vote in numerous states (including Michoacán, Oaxaca, Guerrero, Morelos, and in the region of La Laguna in the Northeast) candidate Salinas was able to win the support of many campesinos on the basis of his campaign promises and his support by *campesinistas* (including Gustavo Gordillo and Hugo Andrés Araujo, a founder of UNORCA) prominent in the productivist wing of the campesino movement. Salinas promised a policy of "shared responsibility" that would modernize relations between the state and campesino producers by emphasizing productivity, decentralization, and an end to government paternalism.

As president, Salinas did substantially change the structure of state/campesino relations, fulfilling his modernization promises. One of the first indicators of this change was the creation in 1989, on the anniversary of Zapata's assassination, of the Permanent Agrarian Congress (CAP) as a forum for negotiations between the state and the peasantry. No longer would the CNC be the privileged intermediary to the government, at least on a national level.[24] The productivist organizations were encouraged by this innovation, but the CNPA and other more radical groups declined to participate in CAP.

At issue was whether CAP represented a serious commitment to *concertación* or whether it was a manifestation of neocorporatism. The willingness of government agencies, particularly the National Indigenous Institute (INI) and the newly created National Solidarity Program (Pronasol), to distribute funds and hand over productive facilities to autonomous campesino organizations without insisting on their political support was unprecedented. These new relations, as well as the adoption of some of UNORCA's policy recommendations and the renegotiation of guarantee prices for corn, affirmed the wisdom of the pragmatism of UNORCA-affiliated groups. Largely because of the influence and proposals of the more productivist-oriented organizations and the *campesinistas* within government, the Salinas administration recognized the need to assuage the impact of the radical restructuring of the agricultural sector with programs like Pronasol and Procampo that targeted poor rural producers.

But *concertación* was limited and selective, not an inclusive commitment designed to formulate a new agricultural policy. With its new policy of *concertación* with autonomous campesino organizations, the Salinas administration entered into policy discussions with UNORCA and other organizations. Issues such as pricing, credit, and support for local marketing initiatives were jointly discussed, but the major issues affecting peasant welfare and production continued to be discussed behind closed doors by government planners.

The government proved willing to discuss production issues with those farmers involved in agroexport production or capable of producing a marketable surplus of basic grains. But it proved less willing to discuss the problems faced by landless and semi-subsistence peasants, especially those clearly associated with the PRD (such as those in Michoacán) or those who were at the center of challenges to local power structures (such as those in Chiapas). The limited character of *concertación* was also evident in the government's failure to consult seriously with campesino organizations about such crucial issues as the direction of its macroeconomic policies, free trade, and the changes to Article 27.[25] Both the agrarian and productivist tendencies in the nongovernmental campesino movement have been shaken by the momentous political and economic changes of the 1980s and early 1990s. Trade liberalization, privatization or elimination of government agricultural programs, declining public- sector investment in agricultural infrastructure, the end of agrarian reform, and the impact of economic stabilization and structural adjustment programs created a deep sense of insecurity in the farm community.

By the end of the Salinas sexenio, a dizzying array of political and economic changes had left the campesino movement disoriented and searching for new directions. The campesino movement, together with most Mexican farmers, was affected by six major changes: 1) the withdrawal of government-subsidized inputs, 2) high interest rates and lack of access to credit, 3) the end of land distribution and the new status of ejidal land, 4) an increased flow of cheaper food imports, 5) inadequate government measures to upgrade productivity and competitiveness, and 6) a widely criticized new subsidy program called Procampo.

Free trade and the devastating impact of the macroeconomic policies of the 1982-94 period, together with the continued decline of commodity prices, undermined previous enthusiasm for "appropriating the production process," "associative" or "social" enterprises, and other productivist-based strategies. At the same time, the more agrarian and radical tendencies of the campesino movement had been unable to mount concerted opposition to changes in Article 27, and their continued focus on land distribution and populist solutions kept them out of touch with changing times.

The recent *zapatista* rebellion did not provide the policy vision the campesino movement has been seeking, but it did confirm the judgment of those who insisted that agrarian issues could not be ignored or dealt with by targeted social welfare programs sponsored by Pronasol.

The attention given by the Chiapas rebels to the lack of democracy in Mexico pointed to the failing of both the agrarian and productivist tendencies within the campesino movement to incorporate demands for local and national democratization into their platforms for social change.[26]

A Country People Who Do Not Want to Move

Mexican campesinos have a long and heroic history of holding onto the past but at the same time leading the way to the future. When faced with the alternatives presented by capitalist modernization, Mexican campesinos have sometimes opted for tradition over what has been hailed as progress. Whether it be losing village lands to become laborers for the sugar mills of the 1890s or competing as producers in a "free" and integrated global market, campesinos have often decided that they would rather retain what they already have than face an uncertain future.

Looking to the past for salvation and tenaciously holding on to traditional agricultural practices, although understandable in the face of the destructive forces of capitalist modernization, have not necessarily improved the lot of Mexico's campesinos. It is true that the peasantry in Mexico has persisted, confounding the predictions and economic projections of liberals, Marxists, and neoliberals. Yet it is also undeniable that campesino society and economy are in ruins and do not, at least as presently structured, offer a hopeful development alternative.

To acknowledge the problems of the campesino economy and society is not to applaud capitalist modernization. The attack on communal lands by the liberals of the last century did not create a modern democratic republic of property holders but led instead to increased land concentration and social polarization. After the revolution the Mexican government, in the name of economic modernization, focused on the development potential of the large landholders of the Northwest, leading to a distorted pattern of development that left a large section of the population without a productive place in the economy and the country unable to feed itself. Neoliberal restructuring and free trade are proving equally unsuccessful in terms of their ability to provide jobs, ensure the availability of adequate food supplies, and support broad economic development.

Just as the genetic resources of tropical forests are being lost, so too are the communitarian values and social structures of campesino and indigenous communities. Economic modernization strategies promote individualism and the private sector. But unless individual initiative and private-sector endeavors occur within a moral framework of social justice and community responsibility, they can lead to social disintegration and economic polarization.

The disintegration of campesino villages and loss of communal structures—a process that will likely accelerate under the revised Article 27—have economic and social implications. Although inefficient in terms of percapita productivity, the commitment of traditional peasant agriculture to provide work and subsistence for all family and community members has helped alleviate the burden of unemployment and poverty in Mexico. The longevity of communities has helped slow migration to overcrowded cities. Rural life is undeniably harsh, but the poverty of the countryside is not as degrading and ultimately debilitating physically and mentally as the destitution of impoverished urban life, where cash income may be higher but quality of life lower.[27] In the city, the stability and continuity of the rural village environment is traded for the insecurity of living with neither land nor an extended family network.

With the destruction of campesino society, particularly the indigenous community, Mexico faces the loss of such values as communitarianism and respect for nature that are sorely missing from urban, modernized life. Unless efforts are made to preserve the campesino economy and community, Mexico will also lose its cultural pluralism as the *campo* is drained of its inhabitants. The simplicity of rural communities, the healthfulness of living close to nature, and the satisfaction of being members of integrated village communities are products of the past. But they also could be models for an economic and social modernization that looks more toward creating local and regional solutions to problems of unemployment, hunger, and lack of productivity.

A return to the countryside should not, however, be romanticized. The vision of self-contained, egalitarian, and communal rural villages was always a fiction and has become ever further removed from the reality of rural Mexico. Market forces, profit motives, individualism, and the struggle for the survival of one's own family have eroded more traditional social and economic patterns. Nonetheless, important moral, social, and productive values still exist in campesino communities and are worth preserving and propagating. But all is not ideal in the social and cultural life of rural villages. The absence of education and health services, the lack of opportunity, and the dirt-poor conditions of campesino life all explain why so many look to the lights of the city.

At the same time, however, there are numerous cases of campesino communities regrouping in the face of increasing economic misery and lack of opportunity. Often these center around strategies to control the production process, as in the case of the small-scale coffee growers. But also important are new community development efforts that focus on alternative survival strategies based on mutual-help organizations and basic-needs production projects, sometimes called "backyard" economies or "self-managed" development. Individual families are encouraged to work together in community *molinas* (corn grinding), gardens, livestock projects, sewing workshops, crafts marketing, and food provision.[28] To a large degree, the fate of the peasantry is being determined by the capacity of the rural population to act to protect its interests and to organize into local and regional organizations that let it be known that campesinos will not passively accept the fate being dealt them by economic and political elites.

Agrarian and Agricultural Issues

Along with the prominence of democratization demands, the uprising in Chiapas also revived the issue of land distribution. Two years after reforms to Article 27 had terminated the government's land distribution program, the campesinos of Chiapas insisted that inequitable land distribution was still a leading concern. The revision of Article 27 in 1992 was not the final chapter in Mexico's agrarian reform, as the Chiapas rebels and the scores of land invasions that followed the initial uprising clearly demonstrated. At the center of the neo-*zapatistas*' demands was the old *zapatista* slogan of "land to those who work it." Echoing the agrarian demands of the EZLN and elements within the newly created CEOIC coalition, campesinos in other states, particularly in the South and Southeast, also insisted that the government renew its agrarian reform program. The depth of rural sentiment against the reforms revealed the gap that had developed between campesino leaders who had given their conditioned approval to the Article 27 reforms and the large numbers of landless and semisubsistence campesinos who bitterly opposed them.

It is certainly the case that Mexico needs more equitable land distribution. However, renewed land distribution will do little to improve production or the lot of the peasantry in Mexico unless it is accompanied by a campesino-oriented agricultural policy. While agrarian injustices need to be resolved, the main focus of stuggles of the peasantry must necessarily be on the economic issues of increased productivity, better marketing, improved government services, and its role in the emerging world trading system.

Important elements for such a policy are found in the experiences of the UNORCA network and other campesino organizations that have since the mid-1970s been focusing on production and marketing issues. The lack of success of many of these groups came not for want of trying or innovation but more from the adverse impact of the government's macroeconomic policies and its failure to provide needed credit, technical assistance, and marketing support. The advances that these organizations did make on the local and regional level in "appropriating the production process" and establishing social enterprises could not be transferred to the national level for these reasons.

The wonder of the peasantry is its endurance. At each stage of capitalist modernization, campesinos have found ways to adapt. Recent neoliberal reforms and increased global economic integration make survival ever more difficult. In the late 1990s and into the next century, campesino and farm organizations will be forced to take new forms to meet the new challenges. Some of these changes are already apparent, such as the creation of product-specific organizations that bring large and small corn, coffee, and sorghum growers together to defend common interests and negotiate with the state for more responsive agricultural policies. Changes to Article 27 mean that the sharp distinction between *ejidatarios* and small private farmers is fading, presenting the possibility of more unified activism of the social and private sectors.

As both *ejidatarios* and private farmers focus on influencing government policy with regard to the products they market, the danger persists that the interests of subsistence and infrasubsistence farmers will be ignored by both the government and farm organizations representing the more-privileged strata of growers. The less-privileged sectors that exist on the margins of the market economy need their own organizations that integrate productivist issues with concerns about human rights, environmental conservation, local democracy, and the basic needs of campesinos. As Mexico's *proletaristas* and *descampesinistas* have long advocated, the formation of new farmworker organizations will also be critical to ensuring that the increasingly proletarianized peasantry gain decent wages and working conditions.[29]

At the same time that more cross-class coalitions become necessary, and as the adverse impact of the withdrawal of government intervention in the rural economy deepens, class conflict in the countryside is likely to intensify. The government has by no means totally removed itself from the *campo*. In fact, programs such as Procampo and Procede (land certification) have added new dimensions to its rural presence. But these programs are generally oriented to individual growers, not to communities, and are designed to open the countryside to the unrestricted forces of supply and demand. By committing itself to market solutions to the problems of rural production and welfare, the government has shedded much of its mediating capacity, creating the possibility of increased concentration of wealth and of increased control by intermediaries, moneylenders, and rural bosses.

Looking toward the future can be dangerous. In the same way that neoliberals have let ideology disguise the reality of the peasantry, so too can projections of certain present trends be misleading. It is certainly true that the campesino economy has become subsumed in a wider capitalist economy and that global economic integration is dramatically changing the shape of Mexico's agricultural economy. But this does not mean that campesino farmers are in the process of becoming small capitalist farmers like those in the United States or that they are becoming fully proletarianized.

For the *campesinado* to persist, it must continue to adapt and evolve. Elements of traditional peasant agriculture remain not just because of inherited cultural patterns but because they make sense as individual, family, and community survival strategies. These same elements could also become important components of national economic, social, and environmental strategies. Rather than blindly pursuing economic modernization projects based on the experiences of more industrialized nations, Mexico's leaders might do well to consider the important productive, labor-absorption, and environmentally sustainable attributes of the small-farm and cooperative agriculture of its campesinos, the people of the land.

A farmer from rural Oaxaca holds a Mexican flag and stands at attention in front of a statue of Emiliano Zapata. He is part of a march to commemorate the 75th anniversary of the assassination of Zapata. David Muang/Impact Visuals

A CALL TO ARMS

"We have nothing to lose, absolutely nothing, no decent roof over our heads, no land, no work, poor health, no food, no education, no right to choose our leaders freely and democratically, no independence from foreign interests, and no justice for ourselves and our children. We are the millions of dispossessed, and we call upon all our brethren to join our crusade."

—Zapatista National Liberation Army (EZLN),
Declaration of the Lacandón Jungle, December 1993.

For most outside observers, the Chiapas rebellion was seen as the first armed rural rebellion since the legendary exploits of Zapata and Villa. Although it is certainly true that the absence of rural conflict has contributed to Mexico's historic political stability, especially when contrasted with the experience of its Central American neighbors, this general observation has served to obscure the history of localized violence in the Mexican countryside since the revolution.

In the late 1910s and throughout the 1920s, the Carranza and Calles governments combined repression with selective land distribution to pacify campesino militias scattered throughout Mexico. During the 1920s the government's anticlerical and antiagrarian policies led to the Cristero rebellion of campesinos concentrated in *mestizo* communities in central Mexico. In the 1930s President Cárdenas encouraged armed campesinos to mobilize in support of his efforts to dismantle the economic and political power of the *hacendados*. At the same time, the populist president isolated and repressed more radical rural organizations that were more difficult to integrate into the emerging corporatist state.

Agrarian militancy did not end with Cárdenas, although the state's promise to distribute land to petitioning campesino groups did serve to direct agrarian demands through official channels. By the late 1950s land invasions became more frequent as campesinos grew frustrated with the government's agrarian bureaucracy and as ranchers and large landowners increasingly extended their control over the best lands. In many cases, land conflicts escalated into armed confrontation with the military and large landowners.[1]

Land, however, was not the only concern of Mexican campesinos. In fact, issues of democracy and the lack of control over the productive process proved central to several cases of armed campesino resistance in the 1940-75 period. This was clearly the case in Morelos, where the *zapatistas* had won back control over land and water lost during the *Porfiriato* but were losing their economic and political freedoms. In the 1940s Rubén Jaramillo, who had served as a captain under Emiliano Zapata, began organizing campesinos and farmworkers to challenge the monopoly of the ruling party and to defend themselves against landgrabbing and exploitation by ranchers and mill owners. Jaramillo's attempts to form an independent political party of workers and campesinos and to form productive associations were met with repression, which forced Jaramillo and other activists to flee their homes and to form clandestine self-defense units. In 1962 the army shot Jaramillo along with his pregnant wife and three children as part of the government's campaign to crush all efforts to organize campesinos outside of its own corporatist channels.

In most cases, rural violence took the form of state-sponsored repression of campesinos and workers who were challenging the tight control of the PRI and local economic elites. These struggles often counted on the support of students, teachers, and university professors, who not only sympathized with the plight of the poor but were also expressing their own political aspirations. Armed confrontations, campesino attacks on military barracks, and massacres of squatter groups occurred throughout Mexico in the 1960s, although the northern state of Chihuahua and the southern state of Guerrero experienced the most militant campesino organizing.

In fact, it was in Guerrero that Mexico's first modern campesino guerrilla armies emerged. Brutal repression in the 1960s and early 1970s of civic and campesino groups led to the formation of two campesino-based but teacher-led guerrilla uprisings, the first of which emerged in the Chilpancingo area and the second in the hills of the Costa Grande. In 1967 the Guerrero Civic Association, which had since the beginning of the decade challenged the PRI's authoritarian control of the state, converted into a small political-military organization led by Genaro Vásquez that harassed the army until it was eliminated in the early 1970s.

The state of siege that reigned in Guerrero and the PRI's intolerance of independent civic and campesino organizing resulted in the formation in the late 1960s of the Party of the Poor and a military arm called the Campesino Justice Brigade. Lucio Cabañas, a charismatic and highly respected school teacher and community leader, organized the guerrilla war after a military crackdown of civic organizing in Atoyac. Widespread campesino support for the guerrillas posed a real political and military threat in Guerrero, even though the guerrillas failed to create a coordinated national network of clandestine leftist groups, which limited the national implications of the localized uprising. After massive military mobilization had failed to eliminate the guerrillas, the government organized a civic action campaign, called the Guerrero Plan, which aimed to reduce popular support for the group through the provision of government services. By 1974 this combination of counterinsurgency and civic action proved fatal to the Costa Grande rebels.[2]

Twenty years later Lucio Cabañas and his men are still remembered as heroes in Guerrero. The Guerrero Plan and the populism of the Echeverría government raised popular hopes that the state would help improve the socioeconomic conditions in this desperately poor region. The villagers of the Costa Grande region claim that conditions are worse today than they were in the late 1960s. The roads constructed under the Guerrero Plan are now badly deteriorated and in some cases completely covered by vegetation. The telephone system planned for rural communities was abandoned, and the agroprocessing industries created by the government have been shut down.

Not until the Chiapas rebellion of 1994 was the Mexican government confronted with another major guerrilla challenge in the countryside. But rural Mexico has in the past two decades become ever more violent. Tensions between campesinos and cattlemen have erupted in violent confrontations throughout southern and southeastern Mexico. As rural communities have become more stratified as landlessness has increased and the market economy has deepened, conflicts involving village *caciques* have increased. Worsening economic conditions and environmental degradation combined with population pressures have sharpened tensions between neighboring ejidos and villages, where struggles over boundaries often result in bloody clashes. Rising rural violence and human rights abuses are also the product of the dramatic increase in narcotics production and trafficking. The *narcotraficantes* are becoming the new warlords in the remote mountain communities of Sinaloa, Chihuahua, Michoacán, and many other Mexican states.

Rebellion of the Damned

The rebellion by mainly indigenous campesinos living on the margins of the Lacandón Jungle brought to national and international attention the plight of Mexico's peasantry. It was a cry of a people who felt dispossessed by decades of economic modernization and by new government policies designed to increase foreign trade and investment. Excluded from the political process and repressed by the military and vigilantes hired by local ranchers, they believed they had no alternative but to take up arms to fight for a place in Mexico's economic and political future.[3] For those who see the peasantry as a disappearing social sector, the rebellion in Chiapas represented the last gasp of precapitalist forces, while others who have a more hopeful view of the peasantry concluded that the uprising constituted the first postmodern rebellion against the unsustainable New World Order.

From the beginning the neo-*zapatistas* were careful to situate their local demands for economic and political reforms in the national context. By appropriating the name of Emiliano Zapata, the Chiapas rebels directly linked themselves with the Mexican Revolution and its agrarian roots. While calling themselves revolutionaries, they themselves were not attempting to seize control of the national government. Instead, they intended that the armed rebellion would be the spark needed to renew the country's nationalist, populist, and agrarian traditions (albeit with a democratic, not statist, framework) at a time when the government was undermining these traditions with neoliberal policies. In addition, they had explicit economic objectives and implicit political ones in Chiapas.

Like most campesinos throughout Mexico, the indians who took up arms in the Lacandón Jungle felt victimized by economic policies that seemed to leave no room for their survival. The signing of NAFTA and the 1992 amendment that terminated land distribution confirmed the fears of many indian campesinos that they were being written out of the future of the country. According to the EZLN, the free trade agreement with its attack on the campesino farm economy represented the "death certificate for the indian peoples of Mexico." For the EZLN, NAFTA was more than a trade agreement—it represented the entire package of the economic reforms of the PRI technocrats. According to Subcomandante Marcos, "It's NAFTA that really directed the reforms of Article 27."[4] The EZLN, through its spokesperson/leader Marcos, offered no detailed analysis of economic integration but noted that it objected to NAFTA because it contained no protections for indian labor and pitted the technology of U.S. agribusiness against the Mexican campesino. The Chiapas rebels became the voice of all campesinos who felt abused and threatened by the government's neoliberal policies and its acceptance of the free trade imperative. Similarly, the political demands of the *zapatistas* reflected widespread frustration with the country's continuing failure to democratize.

In its second public communique, the EZLN explained its focus on democratization: "The grave conditions of poverty of our compatriots have a common cause: the lack of liberty and democracy. We think that the authentic respect for freedom and the people's democratic will are the indispensible prerequisites for the improvement of the social and economic conditions of the dispossessed of our country. For this reason, just as we call for the improvement of the living conditions of the Mexican people, we demand freedom and political democracy."

Similarities between the earlier and latter-day *zapatistas* abound. Both armies closely linked their agrarian and political demands, projected their local rebellions to the national stage, and captured the public imagination with their captivating style and leadership. Both demanded democratic control over their communities but recognized that local political change was predicated on revolutionary reforms at a national level.[5] Both armies counted on the strategic and intellectual talents of leftist activists attracted by the revolutionary potential of an organized peasantry.[6]

More than eight decades, however, separated the Plan of Ayala and the Declaration of the Lacandón Jungle, bringing with them new problems and challenges for Mexico's campesinos. The original *zapatistas* demanded the return of ancestral village land, while the EZLN troops came largely from the outer margins of the country's agricultural frontier, where they were forging new lives for themselves and their families. The *zapatistas* of Morelos wanted control over the water and rich bottomlands around their villages. In contrast, the *zapatistas* of Chiapas had migrated to the jungle because erosion, soil depletion, political tensions, and population pressures had made subsistence farming unviable in their native villages. Unlike Zapata's early supporters, the Chiapas rebels identified themselves by their common circumstances as frontier campesinos rather than by having strong village identities. Their bonds were forged not in closed corporate communities but in their common fight to survive on the agricultural frontier.

A confrontation with economic modernization was at the heart of both struggles. For the villagers of Anenecuilco, modernization meant losing their lands and becoming peons on the mechanized sugar plantations and mills that were spreading through Morelos. In Chiapas, the campesinos had experienced various cycles of economic modernization—the successive booms of the cattle, timber, and petroleum industries and the construction of hydroelectric dams—none of which improved the lot of indian communities.[7]

With the coming of free trade, they saw a series of economic and social reforms supposedly designed to modernize agriculture. Yet these reforms were making their life more difficult by depriving them of subsidized inputs and government services and crushing their hope for land distribution. They were told that they must become competitive on the international market. But what would their families eat if they did not grow corn? And how would increased international trade benefit them? A century-long history in Chiapas of producing timber, hennequen, cotton, sugar, and coffee for the international market gave little reason to hope that increased international integration would result in a brighter future. In fact, the plummeting prices of coffee, which meant less work for farmworkers and less income for small coffee growers, increased the sense of desperation among Chiapas campesinos and helped spark the rebellion.

During revolutionary times as well as during the Chiapas uprising, the *zapatista* cause was fired by more than economic issues. The Liberation Army of the South had joined Francisco Madero's political movement against the Díaz dictatorship not because they wanted national political power or even increased federal attention to their problems. Instead, they wanted to be free of a repressive national government that interfered in local affairs on behalf of the new capitalist elites that were taking control of their communities. Likewise, the new *zapatista* rebels complained of the exploitive practices of the economic power structure, particularly the ranchers, and the government's alliance with these landed elites.

In contrast with the more self-reliant posture of the first *zapatistas*, however, the Chiapas rebels demanded more state intervention, not less, in the provision of technical assistance, credit, transportation infrastructure, electrification, and health and educational services. The state, with its repressive military and corrupt politics, was their enemy, but the services that a modernizing welfare state could provide represented at least part of the solution to their socioeconomic problems. In this sense, then, the EZLN was not postmodernist but espoused modernist goals that mirrored the traditional modernizing demands of most other campesino organizations for increased services, infrastructure, and inclusion in the country's economic advancement.

As important as the national context was in fueling the Chiapas rebellion, the particular experiences of indian life in the highlands and jungle are what produced and shaped the EZLN. Nowhere else in Mexico is racism so pronounced, and nowhere else does there exist such a tight alliance (the self-designated *familia chiapaneca* or Chiapas family) among the political elite, the military, and large landowners. This combination of a caste structure and class polarization makes Chiapas one of the poorest states in Mexico, with literacy, mortality, and percapita income levels fall far below the national average. Nowhere else in Mexico is the peasantry so politicized, repressed, and organized; although as elsewhere in the country, there are deep divisions between radicals and moderates, agrarianist and productivists, and anti- and pro-government organizations.

Also important in explaining the rebellion in Chiapas is the central role of agriculture in the state. While on a national level, 22 percent of the economically active population is employed in agriculture, that figure rises to 58 percent in Chiapas and 88 percent among the indian population. Furthermore, nowhere else in Mexico were tensions between campesinos and large landowners and ranchers so high. In 1992 when the reforms to Article 27 took effect, the unresolved land claims and unimplemented presidential land-distribution resolutions constituted neary 30 percent of the *rezago agrario* (land reform backlog) in Mexico.

The occupation of San Cristóbal de las Casas and several other centers of political and commercial control on January 1, 1994 was at the same time a shout of outrage, a call for dignity, and a cry for help. Social tensions and political conflict had escalated during the previous two decades throughout rural Chiapas. Since the 1930s government coloniza-tion programs (which aimed to reduce land pressures elsewhere and promote economic development in the agricultural frontier) had ushered campesinos, ranchers, and logging companies into the remote jungles of southeastern Mexico.

Beginning in 1950 this inflow of population increased rapidly, and soon the seemingly unlimited expanses of tropical lowlands and river valleys descending from the highlands were caught up in the same kind of agrarian conflicts seen elsewhere in Mexico. Chiapas became the main source of beef for central Mexico, and the large ranchers pushed the *milpa* agriculturalists farther into the diminishing jungle. The rising population of the Lacandón region also meant that campesino communities fought among themselves over land boundaries.[8] These two sources of conflict were aggravated by the degradation of the lush jungle environment. After five years of cultivation, previously forested lands could no longer be farmed because of rapid nutrient depletion and soil erosion resulting from heavy tropical rains. Increasing the pressure on the colonists and their new frontier environment were oil exploration and hydrological energy devel-opment by Mexican government agencies.

These pressures alone do not explain why the Lacandón Jungle became the breeding ground for a campesino army. More than two decades of campesino organizing—shaped to varying degrees by leftists, the Catholic Church, and state agencies—contributed to the formation of the EZLN. The first missionaries to the Lacandón region were from the evangelical Summer Institute of Linguistics. They were invited in by the Mexican government in the 1930s as part of its efforts to acculturate the indigenous population. But despite government attempts to limit the activities of the Catholic Church, especially those associated with liberation theology, church outreach into the highlands and the jungle increased after 1960, the year that Samuel Ruiz became bishop of the diocese of San Cristóbal de las Casas.

By the 1970s the church had become the leading advocate for the indian people, and the populist Echeverría government asked it to sponsor an indian congress to commemorate the quincentenary of the death of Fray Bartolomé de las Casas. The 1974 congress proved a watershed in indian activism by sparking a wave of popular education and organizing work throughout the highlands and lowlands.

Leftist organizers, who came to the region in the 1970s as part of the post-1968 commitment to grassroots organizing, were also behind the surge of indian activism. Working with the rural communities, leftists from the Popular Politics organization (especially its Proletarian Line spinoff) provided valuable support in the efforts of jungle communities that sought government recognition for new ejidos and the formation of inter-ejidal credit unions. The 1968 generation was also found in the National Indigenous Institute and the various rural development agencies created in the 1970s.

Recruits for the insurgency came not from the highland communities, the traditional center of indian society but from the relatively new and even more deprived jungle communities. As the highland communities became more stratified and land became increasingly scarce, there was an exodus to the jungle. The landless, the young, and those who objected to the tight, self-interested control of village *caciques* made their exodus to the jungle. Although the different ethnic groups tended to congregate in new communities, the Lacandón Jungle became the stage for an unprecedented mixing of the five major ethnic groups. Also brought together in frontier settlements were *mestizo* colonizers and squatters who had left Guerrero, Michoacán, and other poor regions. They, like the Chiapas natives, were seeking economic salvation in the jungle. This distancing from traditional sources of village authority and the consciousness of their common plight as campesinos help explain the rebels' lack of ethnic nationalism and why the rebellion arose in the remote frontier region.

A combination of economic misery and a history of dashed expectations contributed to the rebellion. Those campesinos living in the jungle are the poorest of the poor. They have the highest mortality and birth rates in the state, while having little or no access to government health and educational services. Although some of the first settlers did manage to carve out enough good land to ensure subsistence, most of the jungle's campesino population lead a precarious existence. Initial hopes instilled by the government and the church (whose missionaries had likened the sparsely populated jungle to the "promised land") for land and liberty soon changed to disappointment and anger. Although now free of the strictures of traditional communities, the colonists found themselves isolated not only from government services but also from the mutual aid structures of their former villages.

Along with their counterparts elsewhere in eastern Chiapas, the frontier communities organized to defend themselves and pursue their demands. Despite the brutal repression they often faced, campesinos of the highlands and the lowlands did succeed in forming strong regional organizations. Some of these groups, such as CIOAC and the CNPA-linked Emiliano Zapata Peasant Organization (OCEZ), focused on pushing forward land claims. Also important were the less-militant but highly successful service organizations, namely the Ejido Unions and the ARIC Union of Unions. The difference in objectives and tactics of these organizations reflected the various tendencies of national campesino organizing. The OCEZ and the closely linked Emiliano Zapata Independent Campesino Alliance (ANCIEZ) assumed a highly militant and uncompromisingly anti-government position, stressing that campesinos should not organize with "two faces" —one face that opposes that state and the other that seeks favors from it.[9]

At the other political pole were the leadership of the ARIC Union of Unions, the various UEs, and local groups who were more oriented to improving socioeconomic conditions and production by working with state agencies and staying clear of political entanglements and confrontations. Between these two poles was CIOAC, which had maintained an activist stance while at the same time establishing an agreement with the government to channel farm credit to campesino organizations.

The presence of Maoist organizers and links to revolutionary organizations elsewhere in Mexico undoubtedly contributed to the insurgency, but the Chiapas rebellion was largely homegrown. Frustrated by a history of unfulfilled government promises and repression, dissatisfied with the limited accomplishments of their own organizations, and driven to desperation by the lack of opportunity, a couple thousand inhabitants of the Lacandón frontier chose armed revolt to call attention to their plight.

Although not necessarily direct supporters of the EZLN's violent tactics, campesino and indian organizations throughout Chiapas expressed their agreement with the *zapatista* demands and took advantage of the insurgency to press forward their own demands for land, increased government support, and democratic control of their municipalities. Not only was the government facing a campesino army but also a broad coalition of campesino organizations and nongovernmental organizations. Many of these were grouped within the State Council of Indian and Campesino Organizations (CEOIC) formed in January 1994, which included radical agrarian groups, productivist organizations, and unions and associations closely linked with the state and federal governments. In addition, the *zapatistas* and other campesino activists in Chiapas attracted widespread expressions of support throughout the country.

Neither in Chiapas nor in the rest of Mexico was the campesino movement as united as it might have seemed. In the wake of the Salinas reforms, particularly the changes to Article 27, many campesinos whose organizations had worked closely with the Salinas administration began to question the appropriateness of collaborating with the neoliberal government. By sticking to strictly economic demands and to a nonconfrontational posture, some organizations, notably the ARIC Union of Unions, came under increasing fire for being dupes of the government's neocorporatist strategy. This polarization came to the fore when the government published a newspaper announcement in which ARIC rejected the EZLN's position that violence was necessary and the EZLN angrily reacted by labeling the ARIC leaders as traitors. Several member organizations split to form an alternative organization after the ARIC president accepted the PRI candidacy for federal deputy from Ocosingo.

The Chiapas rebellion highlighted the deep campesino sentiment that land distribution remained a major problem in the Mexican countryside. It also pointed to the strong links between the economic and political concerns of campesinos. After all, it was not the banks or businesses that were the main targets of *zapatista* attacks and subsequent rural militancy but the municipal buildings and police stations. The narrow focus of organizations like ARIC on such issues as credit and prices, and their failure to address more structural issues such as the control of land and political power, proved inadequate, especially in the face of macroeconomic policies and constitutional reforms that threatened the very existence of the peasantry.

The EZLN did not, however, present a clear agenda for the campesino and indigenous movements in or outside of Chiapas. Certainly, the Chiapas rebellion underlined the need for a stronger position on the part of campesino organizations with respect to local and national democratization. The uprising also pointed to the need for all sectors of the campesino movement to formulate a more unified response to the government's declaration of the end of its land distribution program.

The economic platform of the *zapatistas* and their closest supporters such as OCEZ did not, however, coherently address the pressing need to formulate campesino-oriented development policies that recognized the realities of economic integration, environmental degradation, increased population pressures, and unsustainable agricultural practices. Instead, it was more a reactive platform. It did not offer positive, realistic, and sustainable solutions—something that other, admittedly more economically privileged groups of producers, such as those associated with UN-ORCA, had been doing during the Salinas administration. By taking up arms and through their remarkable public relations skills, the *zapatistas* did, however, at least temporarily succeed in pushing forward the democratization process in Mexico and focusing attention on the society's racism and economic polarization.

An infusion of government assistance and international aid combined with the military isolation of the *zapatista* leaders and selective repression of campesino leaders may successfully pacify the region. But more comprehensive and long-lasting solutions will have to be found to address the needs of a burgeoning rural underclass that has been left without land or economic opportunity. Otherwise, the decision made by the *zapatista* troops to risk their lives in a fight to protect their basic rights might be one that is repeated by other campesinos who feel dispossessed of their dignity and their future.[10]

Liberty and Democratization

Campesinos in Mexico have, since the last century, organized under the banner of "Land and Liberty." This combination of agrarianism with demands for political freedom and self-determination was expressed most clearly in Zapata's Plan of Ayala. Throughout Mexican history, struggles for control of land and water have often been closely linked with civic mobilization against undemocratic political institutions, particularly on the municipal and state levels.

Campesino movements have had a mixed relationship with political parties. It was the ruling party under President Cárdenas that shaped the first national campesino organization and gave the organized peasantry a voice in government. This corporatist relationship, however, had the long-term result of creating a dependent, passive agrarian sector. Instead of guaranteeing land and liberty, the Mexican Revolution gave the campesino movement land and the state. The government maintained a tight hold on the peasantry by channeling demands for land and services through organizations and associations that it financed and controlled and by keeping the ejido's *comisariados* incorporated within the government's structures of clientelism and political patronage.

Important nongovernmental campesino organizing was often spearheaded by national leftist parties, but this centralized control often meant that the organizing agendas of local campesino organizations were determined by the political strategies of Mexico City-based parties. There has also been a history of more independent political organizing by campesino organizations that have attempted to pursue their demands through political channels. In Morelos, Sonora, Guerrero, and Oaxaca, campesinos joined with workers and other popular sectors to create home-grown political parties to challenge PRI hegemony. In all instances, the government responded to such political challenges with repression, largely discouraging further attempts by campesinos to organize politically.

The campesino organizations that emerged following the failures of Echeverrian populism stayed clear of party politics. By the late 1980s this commitment to political independence and autonomy became an increasingly questionable strategy. Fearful of being subsumed by a Cardenista corporatism, the more radical wing of the campesino movement declined to throw their direct support behind opposition candidate Cuauhtémoc Cárdenas in 1988.[11] With an eye toward entering into agreements with the new PRI government, the pragmatic wing also distanced itself from the Cárdenas candidacy. Both tendencies focused on their agendas of advancing agrarian reform and changing agricultural policy while leaving issues of political democratization to the opposition political parties, the expanding civic movement, and localized challenges to municipal power structures.

Although campesino movements were not a major factor in national efforts to push the democratization process forward in the 1987-94 period, campesinos had become increasingly concerned with issues of internal democratization.[12] Due to the withdrawal of the state support they had formerly brokered, the power of the ejidal *comisariados* faded in the late 1970s and early 1980s. Paralleling this decline, new credit, food distribution, and other service organizations emerged, as did new campesino organizations with new leadership and more grassroots participation. The declining influence of the CNC and the creation of new local and regional organizations linked to national networks also created room for a more democratic campesino movement. Important, too, was the participation of the "generation of 1968" as technical advisors and academic consultants to the new organizations.

The increasingly democratic character of the campesino movement was also a product of the integration of traditional community organizations into producer networks. This was especially evident in the National Network of Coffee Growers Organizations (CNOC), which was firmly anchored in local and regional organizations that combined the structures of direct and representative democracy. The vibrant democracy of village assemblies and the regular regional meetings of village delegates contrasts sharply with the top-down character of Mexican political institutions and demonstrates the viability and efficiency of bottom-up social structures.

Since the 1970s campesino organizations have made great strides in creating more democratic structures. Many shortcomings remain. The clientelistic, elitist, and paternalistic behavior for which Mexican political parties and government agencies are criticized is also found within campesino organizations. The exclusion of women and women's concerns also deserves attention, although among campesino organizations there is a rising awareness of the importance of integrating women's concerns as well as environmental issues. Overdependence on one leader or honcho persists in many organizations, the most prominent case being that of the EZLN and its "spokesperson" Marcos.

The creation of autonomous regional organizations and national networks in the 1980s was just one element in the development of a more active civil society in Mexico.[13] Another model for democracy was found in the Zapotec municipality of Juchitán. Agrarian struggles by indian students evolved into a radical coalition of campesinos, workers, and students that since the early 1970s has been struggling for political power in the isthmus region of Oaxaca. In response to the mobilization of the Worker, Student, and Campesino Coalition of the Isthmus (COCEI) for democratic rights and economic justice, the government militarized the region. But the determination of the coalition and its innovative mixing of militant tactics and electoral politics eventually gave COCEI control of the municipal government.[14] The successful experience of COCEI points to the feasibility of combining economic and political struggles, and offers lessons about the interplay of class and ethnic issues.[15]

The example of COCEI also offers a hopeful alternative to armed conflict as a way to resolve class and ethnic issues in the countryside.[16] The problems that faced the incipient popular movement in Juchitán are much like those that confront campesinos and workers in such other conflictive areas as Chiapas, Hidalgo, Veracruz, Guerrero, and Michoacán where political violence is common. COCEI demonstrated that a combination of militant mobilization and electoral campaigns can reduce the power of reactionary elites and give the poor majority a voice in local government. By forging a coalition of students, workers, campesinos, and progressive professionals, COCEI was able to change the balance of power in the isthmus. Although rooted in the popular movement, COCEI recognized that successful governance required moderation and sophisticated negotiating skills. The struggle of COCEI to represent the interests of the poor and to win political power is an important model for other popular movements. At the same time, however, the mainly urban and highly localized character of COCEI limits its relevance to campesino movements that arise in more remote regions.

In the late 1980s and early 1990s, the distancing of the campesino movement from politics reduced its influence and contributed to the isolation of the campesino sector. Although political fraud and the corruption of municipal officials were rising rural concerns, the campesino movement provided little leadership and stayed removed from the battle for democratization in Mexico. This failure to join political demands with economic and agrarian ones was highlighted by the Chiapas rebellion, in which democratization was clearly a leading demand of the campesino rebels. The rash of campesino occupations of municipal buildings and the ouster of town officials that followed the January insurgency amply demonstrated the extent to which poor campesinos associated their economic plight with their lack of democratic rights.[17] Once again, the calls for liberty as well as for land reverberated through the Mexican country-side.

Campesino organizing, like many sectors of the emerging organized civil society in Mexico, has been caught in the dilemma of wanting to stay clear of politics in an effort to maintain an independent voice while acknowledging that real change will come only when the political system changes. Under the corporatist system, the ability of the ruling party to co-opt the campesino movement has been an abiding preoccupation for campesino organizations. Yet as a more pluralistic political environment develops in Mexico, the lack of integral links between an organized peasantry and political struggles has become a major obstacle to pushing campesino demands forward. Responsibility for this disjuncture between campesino organizing and the political opposition lies mainly with the two leading opposition parties, the Democratic Revolutionary Party (PRD) and the National Action Party (PAN), neither of which have opened much space for campesinos within their ranks. The PRD's intel-ligentsia-center approach distanced it from grassroots groups despite the party's *campesinista* rhetoric, while PAN's ideology is fundamen-tally anti-campesino.

The failure of campesino organizations to adopt democratization as one of their principal demands is not too surprising considering that they were being forced to respond rapidly to changing agricultural and agrarian policies. With little background in economics and trade, campesinos together with the leaders and staff of their organizations have found themselves trying to understand the new national political economy, liberalized markets, and the forces of globalization. Being fundamentally local and led by those with mainly local experiences, campesino organi-zations have had a difficult time adjusting to the political and economic policies that are being increasingly shaped by global forces. Nonetheless, campesino groups are proving themselves to be remarkably resilient and are increasingly integrating an understanding of globalization into their own strategies and injecting a strong measure of democratization into their own internal decisionmaking.

In the wake of the August 1994 presidential election won by PRI candidate Ernesto Zedillo, the limits and the advances of Mexico's democratization process became more clearly defined. In part because of the Chiapas rebellion, the election was closely monitored by both national and international observers. As a result, the election was not characterized by the widespread fraud of past elections, although voting irregularities were still common, particularly in more remote areas.

In contrast to 1988, there was little doubt which of the candidates received the plurality of the votes. The democratization process had advanced in the form of national elections whose results were not thrown into question by fraud and electoral engineering by the PRI government. In addition, the country had a new set of electoral regulations and a system of citizen vote monitoring. For all of these advances, the *zapatistas* with their demands for "liberty and democracy" deserved much credit.

Furthermore, the EZLN had set in motion a grassroots movement for democratization that was at least as important as the electoral aspects of democratization. In Chiapas, a State Assembly of the Chiapanecan People formed in July 1994 as a loose coalition of citizen groups, campesino organizations, democratic union currents, and NGOs. Responding to the call of the EZLN, a National Democratic Convention was held immediately before the August 1994 elections that brought together human rights groups, leftist academics and scholars, and popular organizations, united in their conviction that Mexico lacks true democracy.

Formal institutions such as the National Democratic Convention and the State Assembly of the Chiapanecan people were established largely as a result of the EZLN's call for organized civil society to take the lead in pushing for a from-the-bottom-up process of democratization. This grassroots movement for liberty took hold at the village level in Chiapas as communities began to challenge the pervasive hold of the *caciques* in the Altos de Chiapas and to confront municipal authorities with charges of corruption. The rising recognition in Mexico that the deep racial and caste divisions need to be addressed and a reinvigorated sense of indigenous idenity have also been important advances in the creation of a more democratic society in Mexico.

Although there has been important progress in the democratization process in Mexico, many obstacles remain. Democratization means more than fraud-free elections, and liberty means more than the building of a popular movement or organizing civil society. Elections in Mexico are becoming freer, but their fairness is still highly questionable given the PRI's manipulation of government revenues for political ends (seen most clearly in the Pronasol programs), the state's alliance with the media and large business, and the repression of dissident political forces, particularly those on the left. This lack of a level playing field is one of the major limits to Mexico's democratization process.

But the lack of true democracy is not just at the political level—it extends and to a certain extent arises from the absence of democracy at a more grassroots level. One problem is the equation on the popular level of *liberty* with *power*. This was seen in the CNPA's founding slogan: "Today we fight for land, and tomorrow for power." The increasingly politicized character of agrarian politics was reflected in the rewording of the slogan in 1982: "Today we fight for land and for power."[18] Yet power and democracy are not necessarily the same, and often are in conflict.

The absence of a democratic culture at a grassroots level is seen clearly within CEOIC in Chiapas. The government predictably attempted to manipulate this civic coalition by making political and economic deals with the *oficialista* groups like the CNC and the productivist organizations like Campesino-Teacher Solidarity (SOCAMA). At least as damaging to the integrity of CEOIC as a representative of popular interests has been the righteousness, confrontational tactics, and power-grabbing tactics of groups like the radical OCEZ that claim to be the true and only voices of the peasantry. Further complicating the process of internal democratization is that on both sides the spokespeople of the campesino organizations are often not "campesinos" themselves but administrators, technical consultants, and political ideologues. Both formal electoral democracy and the internal democracy of campesino organizations have taken a stronger hold in Mexico since the mid-1980s, but there are still major gaps that campesino organizations with their new banner of "liberty and democracy" need to address. Democracy in the Mexican countryside is also limited by economics.

It has been said that Mexican indians vote *en corto* (in short), meaning that they vote for short-term economic considerations, such as projects or financing promised by the ruling party, rather than for longer-term, unproven alternatives.[19] According to Mexican anthropologist Guillermo Bonfil, politics is "based on short-term consideration that have nothing to do with political programs that propose alternative models for the society in the future. The vote is seen more as a resource for the here and now, exercised toward the promise of finishing a road, building a school or a drinking-water system, moving forward a land-certification process, and other small benefits which help to resolve ancestral problems that shape their daily lives."

Democracy and economic justice are closely linked, as the EZLN observed. This does not necessarily translate into voting for the opposition, which is not necessarily more democratic, may be no more able to ensure economic justice, and is not even able to offer the short-term economic benefits that people need. A fundamental part of this problem is the PRI's tactics of "divide-and-rule" and co-optation, facilitated by the targeting of government revenues and favors. The continuation of voting *en corto* also can be attributed to the failure of opposing political factions—whether they are political parties, popular movements, or guerrilla armies—to persuade the Mexican people of their own democratic credentials and their capability of ushering in a new era of economic progress and stability.

The *zapatista* rebellion, the failure of the PRI to capture a clear majority of the vote, and the deepening impoverishment of rural and urban populations all indicate the urgent need for alternative policies that can credibly offer liberty and development, justice and peace both in the short and long terms. Mexico's *campesinado*—with its ability to adapt, its determination to survive, and its will to work and struggle—may prove crucial in both making and implementing viable political and economic alternatives.

A woman cuts stems off freshly harvested garlic in a field near Ixmiquilpan, Mexico. Jack Kurtz/Impact Visuals

ON THE EDGE: INDIANS, WOMEN, AND MIGRANTS

"The indian is rising up. We will no longer let ourselves be
fooled. We have seen a change thanks to our *zapatista compañeros*, who had the courage to awaken the country."

—Domingo López Angel, leader of Regional Indigenous
Council of the Altos of Chiapas (CRIACH), September 1994.

The farm crisis in Mexico is more than a crisis of production and
prices, or even of access to land, credit, or technology. The economic
upheaval resulting from the globalization of market relations is shaking
rural society at its roots. This chapter examines three social sectors in
Mexico—indians, women, and migrants—that are among those most
adversely affected by these changes.

Particularly vulnerable are Mexico's indians, who face language
barriers, caste discrimination, and cultural obstacles in adapting to the
patterns of the global market. Because of deeply rooted patriarchal behavior and structures, women and their children are hit hardest by the
fragmenting of traditional communal structures and by the expanding
economic crisis.

The tragic character of the social and economic upheaval in rural
Mexico is probably best illustrated by the increasing number of campesinos
who are choosing to leave home. Pushed to the edge of survival in the

countryside, they seek security and opportunity in Mexican cities and in the United States.

Indian communities exist throughout Mexico—from Quintana Roo to Baja California. In its museums and tourism promotion, the government glorifies the nation's indian, past and present. Yet the extensive indian population is largely out of view, missing from the image of a modern, developing Mexico.

Only if you leave the main roads and venture into the country's mountains, deserts, and jungles are you likely to encounter the centers of today's indian society. In thousands of remote campesino villages, you will find what Mexican anthropologist Guillermo Bonfil Batalla aptly termed "México profundo"—the deepest, most profound part of Mexico that represents the persistence of the native people of Mesoamerica.[1] In Mexico the indian people have been ignored and continually pushed aside in the quixotic search for the modernity promised by western civilization. Indian Mexico is a "civilization denied," despite constituting nearly 10 percent of the entire Mexican population.[2]

Unlike the United States, where indian identity is defined racially, being indian in Mexico is more of a cultural category. A person can have indian parents but not be considered indian. By speaking Spanish, moving to the city, and adopting western dress, indians can lose their indian identity and be considered *mestizos* or *ladinos* (term for nonindians used in Chiapas and Guatemala). Villages that were once considered indian have over time lost their native dress and language, although these can usually be distinguished from *mestizo* villages by different cultural practices. In the national census, language is the determining characteristic of indian identity. Using this criteria, eight million Mexicans are indian.[3] A broader definition that included all those with cultural and racial features of indians would dramatically expand the sector of the population considered to be indian.[4] As indian consciousness rises in Mexico, it is likely that the number of individuals and communities that consider themselves to be indian will increase.

Mexico is commonly described as being a *mestizo* (mixed blood) nation. But acculturation is perhaps more important than the mixing of the blood of two different races in explaining the deindianization of Mexico.[5] In many parts of rural Mexico, especially in the South, the physical characteristics of the *mestizo* population are largely indistinguishable from those of the indian community. In other words, over time campesinos stopped being "indian" without any racial mixing.

Table 10

Socioeconomic Indicators of Indian Mexico

46% illiteracy rate among those fifteen years or older.

14% of adults have completed primary school.

28% of children ages six to fourteen do not attend school.

63% of indian municipalities are losing population to migration.

83% of indian-majority municipalities are very poor or extremely poor.

Source: INI, *Indicadores socioeconómicos de los pueblos indígenas de México* (Mexico City: 1994).

Mexico's indigenous population comes from 56 linguistic groups. The major one is the Nahuatl in the central mesa region around Mexico City, followed by the Mixtec, Zapotec, and Mayan languages in southeastern Mexico.[6] In northern Mexico, where the concentration of indian communities is much smaller, the Yaqui people in Sonora and the Tarahumaras in Chihuahua are the most prominent groupings. In descending order, Oaxaca, Veracruz, Chiapas, Yucatán, Puebla, México, Hidalgo, and Guerrero are the states with the largest concentrations of indians.[7] Yucatán is the state in which the highest percentage—53 percent—of its inhabitants speak an indian language. In Oaxaca and Quintana Roo, well over one-third of the population speaks an indian language, and more than one of every four people in Chiapas is an indian.[8]

Disease and war decimated the indian population during the period of conquest, and the remaining communities were gradually pushed farther into the mountains and less fertile areas by the *criollo* (Mexican-born but of Spanish heritage) and *mestizo* society. Because of high birth rates and declining infant mortality rates, the indian population as a percentage of the total population has risen steadily since 1950.[9] More than 2,300 Mexican villages of under 5,000 inhabitants are primarily indian.[10]

Wherever they are found—in the hills of Chiapas and Oaxaca, in the squatter colonias on the edges of Mexico City, or in the migrant labor camps of Sinaloa—the indian people are the poorest of the poor (Table 10). A combination of geographical isolation, cultural tradition, institutionalized racism, and systematic land-grabbing and repression by local elites have kept Mexican indians at the bottom of the nation's socioeconomic ladder. They have benefited the least from Mexico's economic development and suffered the most from the gradual integration of the peasantry into labor and trade markets.

When Lázaro Cárdenas visited Tarahumara communities as part of his campaign to incorporate the peasantry into a national economic development strategy, he asked a village elder to explain to him what was the major problem facing his people. The Tarahumara campesino motioned for Cárdenas to sit next to him in the town plaza but then proceeded to force the president to the edge of the bench, pushing him inch by inch with his own body. According to the story, which is still recounted in the Tarahumara region, the elder then explained to the discomfited Cárdenas, "This is exactly what happens to us indians."

Being pushed to the side has been the fate of indian people throughout Mexico. The racism of a predominantly *mestizo* society uncomfortable with its indian roots may explain part of the marginalization of the indian population.[11] In San Cristóbal de las Casas, the commercial center of the Chiapas highlands, the indians of the surrounding communities were not even allowed to walk on the sidewalks until the 1950s. In many regions of Mexico, *indio* is a term of contempt, used to signify "lazy and uncivilized." In rural areas, *mestizos* sometimes call themselves *gente de razón* or "people of reason" to distinguish themselves from their indian counterparts.

Racist stereotyping is used to justify the socioeconomic position of Mexican indians, but it is a history of economic exploitation more than of discrimination that explains the destitution of native communities. The fact that the indian people live in the most remote and least productive areas is not a matter of choice but the result of having been pushed out of the agricultural valleys and into the hills. Anthropologists call these post-conquest areas of settlement "internal colonies" or "refugee regions."[12] Going back to the economic reforms of the 1850s and 1860s, the communal lands of indian communities have been either expropriated outright or exploited without adequate compensation by cattlemen and timber companies.[13] Even today indian communities complain that government agencies look the other way as communal lands are deforested and overgrazed by outsiders, usually without financial compensation.

Indigenismo

The Mexican government has tried to have it both ways with the country's indian population. In the effort to forge a nation-building ideology after the revolution, the government tapped the research of early ethnographers to shape an image of a noble indian civilization in Mexico that formed a unique blend with European culture. But while glorifying indianness in its nation-building rhetoric, the government set about to force the assimilation of the *indios* and has done little to eliminate the caste-like treatment of the native population by Spanish-speaking elites. The government, moreover, has facilitated the exploitation and despoliation of indian lands with its national economic development policies.[14]

At the same time, however, the Mexican government has undertaken numerous programs to promote improved socioeconomic conditions for indians. For the most part, these programs have had an incorporationist thrust rather than seeking to protect and sustain indian communities. While exalting the past in monuments, museums, and rhetoric, postrevolution governments have sought to forge a modern nation by trying to incorporate indians into the dominant society and economy. Underlying this incorporationist philosophy was the belief that history was moving forward toward a more enlightened and industrial future. Both the Liberals of the 1800s and the revolutionaries of the twentieth century shared this conviction that progress was inevitable and the belief that indian culture had little if anything to contribute to it.

In the 1920s the government established the first rural schools and "cultural missions" for indians. The Cárdenas presidency created the first government agency for indian affairs and sponsored the first international indian conference. In 1948 the government created the National Indigenous Institute (INI), which has since been the coordinating agency for all the government's indian programs. This outreach to indian communities by government and educational institutions has constituted what is termed *indigenismo* in Mexico.

The challenge facing *indigenismo* has been to find the best ways to ensure that indian communities participate in development and share in its economic rewards. Good intentions alone, however, have not been the sole motivations of the *indigenistas*. The government's commitment to indian programs can also be explained by its concern that "backward" indian communities slow the pace of modernization and nation-building and present a source of political instability.

Although incorporationism has dominated INI and other government programs for indians, *indigenismo* has taken various forms. During the Cárdenas and Echeverría years (1934-40 and 1970-76 respectively), government officials joined with indians to push forward popular organizing and the extension of agrarian reform. INI agents have frequently been forced out of areas by local mercantile elites, *caciques*, and large landowners who see their own interests threatened by INI's development efforts. Over the years the strong incorporationist stance of early *indigenismo* weakened as faith in modernizing solutions diminished in many sectors of Mexican society. Disenchantment with the PRI, the collapse of the oil boom, the shortcomings of industrialization, and the stagnation of the agricultural economy all undermined incorporationist sentiment. Similarly, the persistent survival of the peasantry and indigenous communities into the late twentieth century bolstered those advocating pluralism and support for community-based solutions.

By the mid-1980s cultural pluralism had made its way into the government's rhetoric. President de la Madrid described Mexico as a federation of nationalities. A revision of Article 4 in the constitution during the Salinas administration recognized Mexico as a multicultural and multiethnic society, reflecting the weakening in official commitment to an incorporationist philosophy of development.[15] Official discourse notwithstanding, the old patterns of incorporationist *indigenismo* and paternalism persist within national and state governments. On a local level, however, INI offices were often instrumental in supporting more autonomous and pluralistic approaches to economic and social problem-solving, so much so that INI officials themselves became targets of repression by area elites.

Paternalism has long characterized *indigenismo* in Mexico, as most clearly seen in the nonindian control of INI and its incorporationist goals. Even INI's research projects to study indian customs, while generally sympathetic, have not been undertaken to help preserve or promote indian structures of education, politics, or production. Instead, the government has supported such studies largely in the belief that a better understanding of indian culture is essential to the overall objective of transforming and modernizing the indian peoples.

To Be Indian

The indian rebellion in Chiapas made embarrassingly clear the failure of Mexican policies to improve the situation of the rural indian population. But while there was widespread recognition that the socio-economic and political conditions of the Chiapas indians were shameful, the causes of this underdevelopment and appropriate solutions were not clearly identified.

Was the problem that the government had failed to integrate indians into the capitalist economy or that it had failed to protect them from the dominant economic forces? Was the Chiapas uprising an indian rebellion or a campesino rebellion in which the insurgents happened to be indian? To what degree was race and caste responsible for the deprivation of Mexican indians, or was it more a matter of class? Does ethnic identity reinforce class conflict or does it prove an obstacle to the development of class consciousness? For anthropologists and analysts of rural popular movements these were not new questions but old ones that they had long debated.

At the heart of the debate is the question of what it means to be indian in Mexico. In the early days of anthropological research in Mexico, it was thought that only the communities most isolated and least integrated from the dominant society were indian and worthy of study by ethnographers. "Indian" meant being primitive as well as being the living transmitters of the belief systems of ancient civilizations. In this sense, only the several hundred Lacandón indians living in the Lacandón Jungle of Chiapas would probably have qualified.

As researchers broke out of the strict boundaries established by the early schools of anthropology (ethnographic particularlism and functionalism), they began to see rural Mexico as a continuum of acculturation, ranging from the most isolated to the most integrated.[16] Although accurate in some respects, this observation still incorrectly assumed that the only real indian culture is a vestige of some ancient past. It also implied that as indians became more closely integrated with the market economy they became better off—which has not been the case with most indian communities.

Research beginning in the 1960s, especially by anthropologists in the schools of cultural ecology and historical structuralism, had an entirely different view of the foundations of indian culture. Rather than focusing on the attributes of isolation, they highlighted the extent of contact with other cultures and of integration with regional, national, and international economies. Instead of being formed by their isolation, they concluded that the shape of indian societies and culture is largely the result of reaction to and interaction with the dominant society.

In his studies of the Zinacanteco indians in the Chiapas highlands, cultural ecologist George Collier found that these Mayan indians were much less detached from the nonindian world than previously assumed. He concluded that their indianness was largely a "dynamic, active, and adaptive response" to the relationship with the dominant economic structures and culture.[17] "Ethnic tradition is an adaptive response by which exploited groups establish and defend a protective niche, a niche whose distinctiveness peripheral elites recognize and support because it contributes to their position of dominance."

This process of adaptation in some cases leads to assimilation but in others it results in the persistence of ethnic people continuing to live in marginalized "internal colonies" or "refugee regions." Those native people who are more centrally located often lose their indian identity while those in more remote regions retain their ethnicity to protect themselves from exploitative Hispanic and *mestizo* elites.

Eric Wolf and other anthropologists reformulated the concept of closed indian communities. Instead of being the remnants of Mesoamerican civilization, the tightly knit villages in Oaxaca and elsewhere in southeastern Mexico were seen as the product of a Spanish colonization strategy that sought to isolate and divide indian peoples. Indian villagers themselves took advantage of these "closed, corporate communities" to isolate and defend themselves against the incursion of outsiders.[18]

Although some anthropological studies emphasize the reactive or negative essence of indian cultural formation, others highlight the proactive or positive nature of ethnic identity. Both sides are valid, and both serve to illustrate the different dimensions of what it means to be indian in Mexico. At one extreme there are those who conclude that there is little that is truly distinct about indian people in Mexico. An anthropologist studying this question concluded that most of what others recognize as indian culture is really of medieval Spanish, rather than prehispanic origin, and thus represents the rural component of Western culture.[19] A case in point is a rendition of an eighteenth-century minuet performed as a traditional dance by Zapotec indians at a festival in Oaxaca.[20]

In the *mestizo* society's attempt to distinguish itself from its indian past, it negatively stereotypes native people. As two anthropologists studying the Mixtec indians observed, "The most important element in the identification of *indios* is how the rest of Mexican society treats them, which is to say, how it exploits and represses them."[21] To some extent, then, being indian is the internalization of this pervasive discrimination and pejorative labeling. The stoicism, passivity, inwardness and traditionalism of indian behavior could well be a subtle form of resistance to repression and discrimination.[22]

The negative stigma attached to being indian speeds up the process of acculturation as indigenous people attempt to downplay or deny their cultural heritage.[23] A related observation by Mexican anthropologist Lourdes Arizpe is that a distinct ethnic identity survives only in particularly poor and underdeveloped rural regions like the Chiapas highlands that are dominated by indian *caciques* whose political power in turn depends on traditional *mestizo* elites.[24] The corollary is that these *caciques* strive to strengthen the corporate identity of closed communities as a way of strengthening their own economic and political power. The entire indian community is exploited for the benefit of urban, *ladino* centers (like San Cristóbal de las Casas and the city of Oaxaca) in a colonial fashion. Indians in these remote regions are treated as a lower caste by elites, making it almost impossible for the indian majority to improve its status.[25]

But this negatively constructed identity of indian people in Mexico gives only part of the picture. There are numerous characteristics, mostly positive, that distinguish indian villages from *mestizo* ones. The degree to which these represent adaptations to or reactions against Hispanic and *mestizo* societies or are vestiges of pre-Columbian times is hard to say. Nonetheless, such traits as an egalitarian ethos, loyalty to the community, conformity, and effective community institutions are more evident in indian communities than in *mestizo* villages, where individualism and a strong identification with the nation-state are more pronounced.[26] An example of the different value system of many indians is the principle of mutual help that binds the Tarahumara people: "Today for you, tomorrow for me."

The presence of a civil-religious hierarchy also distinguishes some indian villages, as does the greater respect for children and elders. A world view in which the dividing line between humanity, nature, and land is less distinct also characterizes indian society. Speaking an indigenous language is perhaps the most obvious sign of indian identity. However, some indian children are not fluent in their native language although they usually remain strongly identified with their indian communities. Kinship patterns, dress, rituals, and hair style are other indicators of indian identity. But above all indian identity is a subjective classification. Mexicans are indians because they feel themselves to be so.

There is, however, no panethnic indian identity in Mexico, nor even much of a sense of community among people from different villages who speak the same language. In fact, inter-village conflict is more common than joint organizing. Most often the sense of ethnic identity arises as part of a response to common problems, as when members of different villages realize they have the same demands for land, credit, and protection of human rights. In the case of the Mixtec people, it was only when they found themselves together outside of Oaxaca, working in the strawberry fields of Baja California or gathered in *barrios* in Tijuana, that their common identity as Mixtec people was explicitly defined. Back in Mixteca, ethnicity had not served as a prominent form of self-identification, "but in the frontier, it has become the basis for political activism and a means of defending themselves socially, economically, and politically."[27]

Class and Ethnicity

It is commonly thought that native communities are homogenous and not stratified by class. Yet wealth, political influence, and unequal access to land create rifts in indian communities as they do in nonindian villages. This has always been the case, and clear class divisions have been present at least since the mid-nineteenth century.

Community *cargos* or *tequios* incorporate village members into work projects (such as agricultural production, care of communal lands, and the maintenance of roads, municipal buildings, and schools) that benefit the entire community. But it is commonly the case that village *caciques* and those with ceremonial rank administer the land and labor of a community in ways that disproportionately benefit themselves. These *cargos* and village work projects, while often serving a communal function such as food self-provisioning, also ensure that the power and privilege of those with higher status is maintained.[28] Throughout indian

Mexico, the communal lands of villages continue to be appropriated as the private property of the wealthier members. The use of common lands for the extended farms and cattle ranches of the most powerful community members has left the families of the poor without access to land and food.

As communities have become less self-sufficient and more dependent on cash income, class divisions within indian villages have accentuated. As jobs have opened up in construction and in the petroleum industry in Chiapas and Tabasco and as transportation networks have expanded, the modernizing economy has favored the young over the old, men over women, and has created a new class of wealthy merchants, truckers, and moneylenders.[29] No longer is farm labor distributed as part of a community's self-provisioning strategy. Instead, field hands work for wages, a system that favors young men over the women and older community members.

New social stratification resulting from changing religious beliefs often combines with class divisions and population pressures to create major rifts in indian communities. Such is the case in San Juan Chamula, a large indian town on the outskirts of San Cristóbal de las Casas. The *caciques*, with the support of more traditional and Catholic members of the town, have expelled many hundreds of evangelicals and dissenting Catholic families.

The conflict among the Chamulas illustrates the way that indigenismo has been manipulated in Mexico to support entrenched elites. For years, the government and the left in Mexico have denounced the incursion of *evangélicos* in Chiapas as U.S. cultural imperialism and have defended the actions of village *caciques* on the grounds that they were defending their cultural heritage. In the course of doing so, the *caciques* have expelled some 20,000 Chamulas from their villages. In the 1980s, the exiled Chamulas, many of them living in squatter settlements on the outskirts of San Cristóbal de las Casas, formed the Regional Indigenous Council of the Altos of Chiapas (CRIACH). A human rights and community development group, CRIACH has, following the *zapatista* rebellion, led successful challenges against the traditional *caciques* and helped some exiles return home. Speaking about the changing perception of culture and class among Chiapas indians since the rebellion, anthropologist Jan Rus observed, "People are realizing their community doesn't serve their needs. They are forging new organizations and getting a sense of themselves as indians in a caste system."[30]

One of the largest concentrations of indigenous people is found in a region known as the Huastecas, located mainly in Hidalgo but reaching into the states of Puebla and Veracruz. In the late 1970s, it was among the most conflictive areas in the Mexican countryside.[31] At one point during a series of land invasions, fear that the "indians were coming" spread through the *ladino* town of Huejutla, and most of the town's 17,000 residents abandoned their homes. In the national press, the campesino militancy of the late 1970s in the Huastecas was described as an "indian rebellion."

Those who looked closer found that many of those seizing land were from mestizo villages and that in many indian villages ethnic identity was never an issue. Instead, for indian and *mestizo* campesinos alike the targets of their protests were the rich and the outsiders who were enclosing land for cattle ranches. Conflict over control of the land cut across ethnic and linguistic barriers since many of the large landowners were Nahuatl-speaking indians. Class divisions had long existed in the Huasteca communities, but the expansion of cattle production in the 1970s in response to rising meat prices upset the former social equilibrium.[32]

One cannot equate ethnicity with class, as was evident in the 1994 Chiapas rebellion. Appealing to ethnic identity can be useful in organizing and in attracting government or foreign attention to the injustices suffered by native peoples. In the Huastecas, compensinos in *mestizo* villages where Nahuatl had long since faded as a common language found it politically expedient to claim indian identity in their appeal to the government to redistribute land.[33]

In Mexico, there is no clear line dividing indians and *mestizos.* Indian and nonindian campesinos have common concerns and are joined by a common ancestry. Just as class positions can and do split *mestizo* society, so do levels of wealth and privilege divide *"México profundo."*

The problems and hopes of *México profundo* are not unlike those of the *mestizo* peasantry. Indian Mexico, like that of the entire campesino population, wants to benefit from the economic progress of the nation without being pushed off its land and without losing its sense of community. At a minimum indian campesinos insist on the right to survive, but they also want a better life for their children. The connection to land and locality, skepticism about modernization, sense of community, agricultural skills, and the very persistence of indian Mexico should be recognized, honored, and considered in the search for solutions to the crisis of the countryside and nonsustainable national development policies. Recognized or not, this deepest part of Mexico is a presence that is not likely to go away.

Indian Mexico endures, but it is struggling to overcome structural and cultural obstacles to development. Throughout Mexico, indian communities are often at the forefront of innovative attempts to adapt to global integration, and a liberalized market, and to adopt practices needed for sustainable agricultural development. In the Zapotec region of Oaxaca, women have recognized new opportunities to sell their crafts in the international market and have in this way revitalized economic life within some families and communities.[34] Indian villages from Chiapas to Guerrero have also been in the vanguard of efforts to reach U.S. and European coffee consumers through alternative marketing networks. Mountain and jungle communities throughout indian Mexico—the Tarahumaras in Chihuahua, Mayas in Quintana Roo, Mixtecs in Oaxaca, and Nahuas in Veracruz—are engaged in inspiring new projects that bring together land-use planning, new economic development strategies, and a return to a more communitarian ethos. In addition, some of the most impressive advances in campesino organizing to increase control over the agricultural production and marketing process are taking place in the indian communities of Oaxaca and Guerrero.

Women's Work

Sometimes rural Mexico seems like a world without women. When one thinks of the Mexican peasantry, images of men with their *sombreros*, machetes, and mustaches come to mind. Whether cultivating the *milpa* or haggling over politics at village assemblies, the voices and actors of the countryside are almost exclusively male.

A visit to many rural households leaves an entirely different impression of gender composition in the Mexican countryside. Men have only a shadowy presence. In many households, the men are rarely seen. Many have left for work (and for second or third families) in other regions or in the United States. Even when males remain in their villages, they sometimes seem more like hotel guests, sleeping and eating in their homes but having little to do with the daily tasks of maintaining the family and household.[35] Campesino women, invariably circled by children, form the heart and soul of home and village.

A stark sexual division of labor, rationalized by a strict patriarchal ideology, prevails in rural Mexico. To a greater degree than seen in many parts of the nonindustrialized world, a woman's role in biological reproduction has translated into a rigid definition of gender roles and the traditional separation of Mexican females from direct agricultural production. More than in many other agricultural societies throughout the world, women in Mexico and elsewhere in Latin America have historically been excluded from the central agricultural activities of the household.

Although there have been changes. Due to male migration and rising participation in the nonfarm economy, campesino women have been steadily increasing their direct role in agricultural production. Although men have commonly tended the family *milpa*, women have commonly participated in crop preparation and processing through such activities as seed collection, harvesting, sorting and storing of the harvest, as well as drying and preserving produce. Women have also directly participated in the self-provisioning of the rural household by caring for patio livestock and gardens, which provide meat, fruit, and vegetables that the family would otherwise be unable to afford.

Because women are not the ones who wield the machetes or drive the oxen that plow the fields, their contribution to the sustainability of the campesino economy has been undervalued. Economists, whether they are neoliberals or Marxists, generally consider only direct agricultural work as part of the campesino agricultural economy. Feminists and others who take a broader view of what constitutes productive work note that Mexican women are usually responsible for home-based processing, marketing, animal husbandry, and food preparation.[36] Moreover, as economic times worsen and as men migrate, women are taking over many jobs traditionally held by men, such as clearing, planting, harvesting, and caring for the family cattle.

Setting aside questions about the female contribution to campesino farming, Mexican women constitute the social foundation of the rural society. Their functions in biological reproduction, household maintenance, and social reproduction (rearing children and maintaining social support networks) make women central to the survival of the peasantry.[37] These tasks are all part of what feminist social scientists label the "invisible" and uncompensated work of campesino women.[38]

In rural Mexico, maintaining a household is more arduous than in most urban settings which do not require women to gather firewood, haul water, and make their own tortillas. In addition to these functions that are not often considered economic, women have traditionally provided for the family and generated income with such household crafts as weaving, basketry, crafting of household utensils, and sewing.

It is increasingly recognized that women are critical to sustainable development and self-provisioning strategies in rural Mexico. In caring for their backyard gardens, campesino women have historically been critical to the domestication of crops, preservation of genetic material, and food provision of campesino households. Many who advocate a rural-based development strategy believe that the expansion of this type of intensive gardening is essential to guarantee the peasantry adequate food without the use of expensive energy and chemical inputs.[39]

Impact of Modernization

As rural isolation decreases and market penetration increases, the archetypal campesino economy is disintegrating and with it structures of communal work and responsibility. Women have always had a subordinate position in campesino communities, but in tightly integrated villages, the community did shelter and protect widows, divorcees, and single mothers.[40] As communities have become less isolated and more integrated into the market, the overall status and treatment of women have deteriorated.[41] The penetration of manufactured goods means that the integral role of women in the economic survival strategies of rural communities has been undermined. As cheap polyester clothing and plastic utensils fill the village markets, home-crafted items that were usually made by women are no longer in demand. The dominance of the cash economy and the declining importance of subsistence production reduce the traditional role of women in the rural economy in which *hogar* and *trabajo* (house and work) were one and the same. This market integration has often made women more financially dependent on men.[42] However, the introduction of new technology, such as mills to grind corn, and the new oportunities created by new market relations, labor mobility, and education have also led to greater freedom and a sense of liberation for many rural women.[43]

With the increased importance of wage labor and remittances, women are less needed to cook and feed the men in the field. This disintegration of the traditional communal work structure has devalued women and reduced self-esteem. Asked what they do, women will reply *nada*—nothing—because they lack compensation for household maintenance and do not directly participate in the productive economy.[44]

The closed, corporate, and isolated history of most indian communities has slowed the penetration of the kind of *machismo* present in *mestizo* campesino communities. But male chauvinism, albeit of different dimensions, also pervades indian societies. One has only to look at the feet of indian women and men in Chiapas. The women walk barefoot behind the men, who generally have sandals and are better dressed. In indian families, as in *mestizo* campesino families, the men eat first, better, and more, which is stark evidence of the superior status of the male.

The patriarchal structure of most indian communities is readily apparent. This legacy of patriarchy translates into rights to farmland and the power to dispose of women's labor and reproduction.[45] In his studies of the Chiapas highlands, anthropologist George Collier found that communal work structures have long privileged males and that as indian communities become increasingly tied to the market economy, the position of women has deteriorated. As men leave home to work for cash incomes, women are often forced to work for corn for their families and complain that their husbands spend their wages not on provisioning the family but on nonessential consumer goods.[46]

Even in indigenous cultures that have been described as matriarchal, such as the Zapotec indians in the Juchitán area of Oaxaca, women are subject to basically the same gender inequalities observed cross-culturally. Woman-battering, sexual double standards, and restricted access to positions of political and judicial power are elements of this isthmus society as they are in most communities. The patriarchal nature of the Zapotec culture is readily evident in the Worker-Campesino-Student Coalition of the Tehuantepec Isthmus (COCEI), the left-of-center popular coalition that has gained political power in the region. COCEI's hierarchy is uniformly male, and women are strikingly absent from the vibrant artistic and intellectual environment of Juchitán.[47]

The ideology of gender guides the distribution and control of land in Mexico. It was only in 1971 that the Mexican government gave women the right to own ejido land and participate as voting members in the ejido general assemblies.[48] Today, women who have inherited rights from deceased brothers and husbands comprise a large percentage of Mexico's *ejidatarios*, with estimates of female control in some ejidos ranging from 15 percent to 38 percent.[49]

Cultural norms still keep women from being involved in the fate of the ejidos. As one Zapotec woman said, "Sure, women want to go to more meetings, but they can't. And when they do, they aren't listened to."[50] This lack of effective control becomes increasingly relevant with the constitutional reforms that legalized the rental and sale of ejidos. Not being equal owners of the ejidos and being marginalized from decision-making, women are especially vulnerable to disenfranchisement.[51] Changes to agrarian reform further limit the access of women to land by terminating the country's land distribution program. Moreover, while the new land certification program does guarantee some legal security for those women registered as *ejidatarios*, the majority of women living in ejido communities are excluded from decisions about how to use and dispose of their land. They have no common-law rights to the ejido parcels registered in their husbands' names and no formal role in the ejido political structure.[52]

Agricultural modernization, economic crisis, and the continuing disintegration of self-provisioning rural communities have shaken up the gender division in agricultural production. Women and children have long accompanied the male family members on their search for seasonal farm work harvesting agroexports such as coffee and cotton. Traditionally, the women provided the food for the men at work, but increasingly women and children have been incorporated directly into the agroexport labor force.

In states where such production is concentrated, it is common to see farm labor crews that are entirely female. Working all day picking strawberries with their children at their side, Mixtec women return in the afternoons to the squalor of the labor camps of the San Quintín Valley of Baja California. This feminization of the agricultural workforce is seen wherever fruit, flowers, and vegetables are being harvested in Mexico for export to the United States.[53] An estimated one-third of all the day laborers in the Mexican countryside are now women.

Agribusinesses select women for agroexport harvesting and processing because they are considered more docile and dexterous than men. They are commonly paid less than their male counterparts for farm labor.

This gender differentiation in wage structure is not dictated by the supply and demand of the labor market. It is the reflection of a sexist ideology valuing males more than females, which the companies adeptly manipulate to increase their profit margins.

Back home on the ejido, women are also becoming more directly involved in agricultural production. Migration by young and middle-aged males have left women and old men to care for the family's *milpa* and the cattle with the help of wage workers. In Guerrero, Oaxaca, Michoacán, and other states affected by increased migration, women are forming the backbone of the subsistence economy.[54] In hard times, women are transgressing gender roles, but this sharing of roles is asymmetrical. Only in rare cases do men pitch in to help women with family maintenance tasks that are traditionally considered women's work.

Increasingly women, particularly young women and widows, are migrating to the United States in search of jobs in the service economy, mainly caring for children and cleaning homes. Since the late 1970s campesino families have been sending their daughters off to the city to work as maids or in the informal economy as part of the household survival strategy. But this trend is not confined to young women. In a small village in the mountains that rises from the Costa Grande in Guerrero, a middle-aged campesino woman whose husband never returned from a trip north told of her dreams to go to the United States and leave her dirt home behind for a house with carpeting and a washing machine.[55]

Programs sponsored by the Mexican government and nongovernmental organizations have made some inroads in helping to give women a more active role in social and economic development in rural communities.[56] But much more needs to be done to support campesino women. As the rural crisis in Mexico deepens, women and children are the most adversely impacted. Solutions designed to address this crisis must incorporate remedies that focus on the special plight and potential of rural women in order to be effective.

Although gender roles are not yet a major concern within most campesino communities or organizations, grassroots women's organizing is widespread. Women are central figures in human rights struggles, community food councils, Christian base communities, community development efforts, and rural health promotion programs. For women to speak at village assemblies is no longer so rare, and the main campesino organizations have demonstrated increased concern about women's welfare and have increased female participation in organizatonal affairs.

Leaving the Countryside

The critical role of migration as a survival strategy in rural Mexico is perhaps the best indicator of the fundamental crisis facing rural society and economy. The peasantry, the country's most traditional sector, is ironically a population that is on the move. Every year hundreds of thousands of rural Mexicans leave their homes in search of work. No longer do migration flows come almost exclusively from Mexico's heavily populated central states. Migrants to the cities and to the United States are leaving their homes in all parts of Mexico.[57] As more communities are transformed by structural changes in local, national, and international economies, migration has increased and become more geographically diverse.

Historically, most migration has been temporary rather than a permanent displacement from rural Mexico. Whether returning meant traveling home from the agroexport plantations of northwestern Mexico or from the fields of California, the bulk of rural migrants have always intended to go home. Commonly, many returned in time to plant their *milpas* before the rains came. But even among those Mexicans most firmly connected to the land, such as the indigenous communities of the Southeast, a definitive break with the *campo* has become increasingly common.

Rural villages are being emptied as the campesino population leaves home searching for a better life in the cities or across the border in the fabled *el norte*. No longer does the migrant fit the stereotype of the transient, lone male. Leaving home to find work elsewhere in Mexico or in the United States has become part of the economic survival strategy for the entire community.[58] Increasingly, women and children are entering the migrant stream as it becomes clearer that the land no longer even provides minimal subsistence.[59]

Within Mexico, migrants either go to the cities seeking permanent employment or join the multitude of seasonal farmworkers. The latter group includes both those who migrate seasonally within their own region and those who follow the harvest season from region to region and crop to crop across the entire country.

Even before the Mexican Revolution, indians in Chiapas and Oaxaca left their highland homes in search of cash incomes from picking cotton, cutting cane, and working on coffee estates. Without this seasonal income, however meager, many rural villages throughout Mexico would have long ago disintegrated. The rise of labor-intensive agribusiness operations in the Northwest in the 1950s set off new migratory patterns, annually bringing more than 300,000 poor campesinos from central and southeastern Mexico to the strawberry and tomato agribusiness operations of Sinaloa, Sonora, and Baja California. These long-distance migrants often follow the picking seasons across the U.S.-Mexico border into California and as far north as Oregon and Washington.

The largest draw for rural migrants, however, is the city. Since 1960 Mexico has changed from being 50 percent urban to 72 percent urban today.[60] Population is exploding in the major cities, which are now ringed by squatter settlements sometimes called *colonias perdidas*. Despite the destitution and contamination spreading out from urban centers, city life offers more hope for economic betterment than the dead-end economies of rural Mexico.

Emigration is also a way out of rural stagnation, especially for those who can afford the long trip north and the costs of paying a *coyote* (smuggler) to spirit them across the border. On an average day, more than seven thousand people—mostly Mexican women, children, and men—cross illegally into the United States. Economic crisis in Mexico, increased U.S. demand for cheap labor in its service economy, and ever-expanding social networks joining U.S. and Mexican communities have pushed immigration flows ever higher. During the 1980s an estimated 190,000 settled in the United States each year.[61] At the U.S.-Mexico border, the U.S. Border Patrol apprehends nearly one million people annually.

No longer are most Mexican immigrants from the countryside. As the economic crisis of the 1980s spread, the profile of the immigrant population changed to include more working-class and middle-class urban Mexicans who have seen their standards of living deteriorate. Increased emigration of urban residents is related to rural-urban migration within Mexico. As more rural residents settle in cities, they exert a downward pressure on wages and increase unemployment, thereby increasing the pressure on city residents to leave.[62]

By the early 1990s the large influx of Mexican immigrants became the subject of hot political debate in U.S. society, which was suffering from slow job creation, declining wage levels, and shrinking public budgets. Sentiment against immigrants increased as did efforts to block their entry with stepped-up border patrols and higher fences.

NAFTA and Immigration

In the Mexican countryside, to migrate or not to migrate is the question that is being asked more than ever before. Not having been incorporated into the government's policymaking process about the future of the agricultural sector or informed about the implications of the free trade agreement, the Mexican peasantry suddenly found that it had been written out of the country's development plans. The uprising in Chiapas in early 1994 was the most dramatic example of this new-found concern. But throughout Mexico campesinos are suddenly coming to the same troubled conclusion. As an indian from the Chiapas coastal lowlands observed, "All these changes mean that we and our families no longer have a future on the land, and because we are campesinos working the land is all we know. Where will we go?"[63]

Debate over whether free trade would stem or spur Mexican rural migration swirled around the NAFTA negotiations. Both proponents and opponents agreed that trade liberalization would spark a surge in rural immigrants. They disagreed, however, over estimates of this increase and over whether increased flows of trade and capital would eventually lead to a diminished migrant stream.[64]

Free traders generally acknowledge that trade liberalization will provoke increased rural migration levels in the short term, especially by campesinos cultivating grains under dryland cropping systems. They argue that these higher levels of migration will eventually diminish as the wage differential narrows because of increased jobs and higher productivity resulting from rising trade and investment. According to free trade advocates, the only solution to rural unemployment is economic growth. To guarantee this growth, Mexico must reject old development models that rely on protective tariffs and state intervention while taking the hard but necessary step of fully integrating into the global market. The productivity and efficiency that result will attract the capital needed to create the employment to offset rural job loss.[65]

Just how many campesinos will be forced off the land by the economic reshuffling is a matter of conjecture. Estimates range from 500,000 to fifteen million by 2010. The widely varying estimates reflect the differing assumptions of the analysts about the job-generating potential of free trade and the importance of corn production to small farmers.[66] Part of the problem with making accurate estimates also stems from the difficulty of separating the impact of NAFTA from the impact of domestic agricultural restructuring, including the end to guarantee prices, land distribution, and extensive government subsidies for agricultural production and marketing.[67]

One of the lower estimates of the impact of regional free trade came from the U.S. government's National Commission for Employment Policy, which predicted that NAFTA would increase illegal immigration by 100,000 annually but calculated that only 10 percent would remain permanently in the United States. Another study estimated that the combination of complete trade liberalization and agricultural restructuring would force 12 percent (839,000 workers) of Mexico's rural labor force to migrate either to the United States or to Mexico's cities.[68] A forecasting study done for the U.S. government's International Trade Commission put the increased migrant population for the 1990s at five million family members.[69] One of the highest estimates came from Mexican economist José Luis Calva, who warned that full trade liberalization under NAFTA and other policy changes would displace fifteen million people from the farm sector, many of whom will seek economic refuge in the United States. Similarly Luis Téllez, then undersecretary of the agricultural ministry, predicted in 1992 the exit of one million people annually from Mexican agriculture over the next ten years.[70] Others contend that these numbers are vastly exaggerated and point out that only those corn growers producing for the commercial market will be adversely affected by falling prices and that the ongoing agricultural restructuring will create new opportunities for work and production that will offset displacement forces.[71]

There is much disagreement about the potential for free trade and neoliberal restructuring to stimulate the degree of economic growth required to create the quantity of jobs needed to absorb surplus rural labor. Even without the projected new migration from the countryside, roughly

1.2 million Mexicans are entering the overall labor force each year. In rural Mexico alone, about 350,000 youths are annually entering the labor movement. The nation's GDP would have to increase at the rate of more than 6 percent annually to absorb these new job seekers—a prospect that seems exceedingly unlikely.[72] A massive displacement of campesinos and reduced opportunities to emigrate to the United States would necessitate even more accelerated economic growth. Following the December 1994 financial collapse, it seemed doubtful that Mexico would enjoy any percapita economic growth. In fact, a deep recession appeared likely. Both the economic downturn and the fact that the devalued peso meant that Mexican wages sunk still lower in comparison to those in the United States will likely contribute to increased migration pressures.

In the past, foreign investment and export production has had an uneven record of job generation in Mexico. The *maquiladora* industry, located largely along the northern border, has created more than a half million jobs, although the quality of those jobs leaves much to be desired.[73] Yet as a whole Mexico's manufacturing sector has reduced rather than increased employment as a result of economic restructuring and liberalization since the mid-1980s.

Since the 1940s export-oriented agribusiness has created hundreds of thousands of farm labor jobs mainly in the irrigated lands of the northwest. Although these agribusinesses offer seasonal work for many in the rainfed areas of central and southeastern Mexico, the temporary jobs do not provide a permanent alternative for campesinos and in many cases encourage migratory patterns that extend into the United States. Relaxed trade and investment regulations under NAFTA have already resulted in new agroexport operations. But with the exception of agroindustries that process (canning and freezing) as well as produce fruits and vegetables for export, these investments do not provide the type and quantity of full-time jobs that Mexico needs.

Overall, neither the manufacturing nor the agroexport sector has the capacity to absorb the surplus labor being generated by rural Mexico. The number of men, women, and children who will be affected by liberalized corn prices is still a matter of conjecture because Mexico has not yet eliminated the support price for corn and because of the long phase-out period of corn tariffs under NAFTA. But the future of all 2.7 million corn farmers in Mexico looks extremely bleak, pointing to a massive displacement of farmers at all levels of productivity and a new surge in migratory flows.

Labor Flows with Trade and Capital

At least in the short run, economic development does not reduce the impetus for migration. Rather, development increases migration by disrupting and transforming social and economic structures in rural communities.[74] As traditional patterns of work and life disintegrate, the most forward-looking members of a community consider migration from their villages as an option for the first time. Perhaps the most vivid case of economic transformation sparking massive emigration is that of Western Europe in the late nineteenth and twentieth centuries. Industrialization and agricultural modernization forced hundreds of thousands of rural Irish, Swedish, German, Italian, and Spanish people to emigrate, many of them to the United States.[75]

When economic transformations are combined with economic, social, or political connections with countries with higher standards of living, labor tends to flow in that direction. As the transboundary flow of capital, trade, and services increases, so will the flow of labor, particularly in the direction of better conditions and higher wages. This is the conclusion of Saskia Sassen and other researchers who have studied the consequences of global economic integration. According to Sassen, "Measures commonly thought to deter emigration—foreign investment, or the promotion of export-oriented agriculture and manufacturing in poor countries—have had precisely the opposite effect. Such investment contributes to massive displacement of small-scale agricultural and manufacturing enterprises, while simultaneously deepening the economic, cultural, and ideological ties between the recipient countries and the United States."[76]

Over the years, closer integration with the United States has set off waves of immigration to the United States, ranging from such less-developed nations as the Dominican Republic, Vietnam, and the Philippines to such new economic powerhouses as Taiwan and South Korea. This is true for nonindustrialized and newly industrializing societies alike. As economic and political systems become more interconnected, workers tend to migrate to nations that are less socially stratified and have higher standards of living.[77]

Free trade advocates recognize that until there is a leveling out of wage and working conditions, the United States will continue to draw workers from Mexico. But they tend to be more optimistic that increased Mexican productivity will translate into increased wage levels. Others are more skeptical, noting that already high levels of underemployment combined with the displacement of rural producers and high population growth serve to drive wages down. In addition, the Mexican government represses labor organizing, knowing that higher benefits for Mexican workers would undermine the country's competitive standing in the global market.

Migration Boosts Economic Stability

The prevailing trends in Mexican population movement are rural-urban migration and emigration to the United States. A countervailing dynamic can also be seen in most parts of the countryside. As migration increases so does the construction of better homes in many villages. In the Mixteca highlands of Oaxaca, dollar remittances from the United States are underwriting new cinder-block homes that rise up alongside the traditional dirt dwellings. In many cases, these new structures remain uncompleted and empty for many years. They represent the conviction of many migrants that their future lies in the ancestral *tierra madre* not in the slums of some southwestern U.S. city.

Ironically, wages earned in the globalized labor market—tending gardens, washing dishes, roofing, and harvesting produce in the United States—are critical to the continued existence of the campesino sector. Not only do remittances contribute to survival on a micro level, they are also essential to Mexico's macroeconomic stability. Estimating remittance levels is about as scientific as estimating migration flows. There is little doubt that they are substantial and increasing. Estimates range from $3 billion to more than $6 billion annually.[78]

Even the lower estimates mean that remittances exceed the value of Mexico's entire agroexport production. Unfortunately, little of the remittances goes for productive investments in rural communities, suggesting that families see no future in farming.[79] Instead, families spend the remittances on household consumption, particularly for such modern conveniences as televisions, refrigerators, and washing machines.[80]

Economic planners make a strong argument that having more than one-fifth of the population employed in agricultrual activities is excessive, considering that just 7 percent of the GDP comes from the agricultural sector. It is certainly true that agricultural workers are less productive in terms of their direct contribution to national income than those in the United States or other industrialized countries. But such calculations should consider the varying levels of technology and farm support programs in those countries. Also to be considered is the fact that in Mexico, more than in the United States, many of those active in agricultural production also provide cheap labor to a large variety of rural industries, including agricultural transportation, food processing, and crafts manufacturing, that are not included in the agricultural GDP.

Where will this rural population, which the government regards as so unproductive, go if forced to leave the *campo*? The official answer is that they go to the new jobs created by rising trade and investment. Yet the unspoken but silently acknowledged answer is that they migrate, many to the United States. As it has in the past, northbound emigration functions as an escape valve for the impoverished majority, thereby reducing the domestic pressure for poverty-alleviation strategies and political change. Conveniently, migration also means more foreign exchange for a country suffering endemic trade deficits. Export people and import dollars is the bottom-line answer to the social side of the rural restructuring crisis.

Eleven

Sustaining Agriculture

"For Mexican campesinos, the problem is not sustainability but survival."

—Statement by Mexico City gathering of
the Interamerican Network of Agriculture and Democracy, July 1993.

Finding the right path to sustainable development is the main challenge of this and coming generations both in Mexico and around the world. There is widespread agreement that the deterioration of nature is limiting the development of human economy and society. Better ways need to be found for people to live and work in concert with global ecology.[1]

There is a consensus that cuts across class divisions and international borders that the relationship of society, economy, and environment needs to be sustainable. There is bitter disagreement, however, over just what that means and how to achieve it. Not just a question of semantics, this struggle to define sustainable development is an intensifying battle in which different social sectors seek to defend their own interests. It is a debate that reaches far beyond environmental conservation to affect the shape of international trade, the direction of national economic policies, and the fate of the peasantry and other subordinated social sectors.[2]

Although the term, *sustainable development*, has been circulating within environmental circles and UN conferences since the early 1970s, it was only in the early 1990s that it became part of the vernacular of policymakers and grassroots activists.[3] According to the UN's World Commission on Environment and Development, "sustainable development is that which meets the needs of the present without compromising the ability of future generations to meet their own needs." Popularized by the 1992 Earth Summit in Rio de Janeiro, the concept of sustainable development was adopted by both sides of the NAFTA debate.

Within Mexico, the call for sustainable development has been taken up by rural communities and leftist intellectuals. For them, like their counterparts in the United States and Europe, sustainable development is a wide-ranging concept that includes the importance of cultural as well as biological diversity, the right to democracy, and the satisfaction of basic human needs as well as recognition of the ecological limits of current production and consumption patterns. More than a code word for environmentalism, sustainable development represents a challenge to neoliberalism and a vision of a more equitable development policy.

In this view, *development* is not just another word for economic growth but implies that trade and investment are regulated to ensure sustainability of the environment and rural communities. The reduction of state and community control over such natural resources as land, water, and forests in the name of free markets and economic efficiency are considered threats to sustainable agriculture. Development is not sustainable when it signifies a widening gap between city and country, consumption and production, economy and environment. Sustainable agriculture, especially in labor-surplus and less-industrialized nations like Mexico, not only means ecological equilibrium but also a farm economy that provides jobs and food. In doing so, incomes are increased, birth rates decline, and the environmentally destructive consequences of the short-term survival strategies of the rural poor are avoided.

Sustainable development does not have the same iconoclastic connotations within the policy, business, and lending sectors. Instead, it signifies an adjustment in capitalist accumulation which factors in some environmental costs. For the booming environmental services and technology sector in the United States, sustainable development translates into new markets for pollution-control technology. For the multilateral banks and the bilateral economic-aid institutions like the U.S. Agency for International Development (AID), the new concern for sustainable development has meant a redirection of funding away from some of the more environmentally destructive projects, such as support for the cattle industry in Mexico, and into population control, environmental monitoring, and creation of natural resource reserves. Survival practices by the rural poor, slash-and-burn cropping, firewood gathering, and hillside farming, are regarded to be among the main causes of environmental deterioration.

Although there is a recognition that capitalist growth must be guided to take into account its impact on renewable and nonrenewable natural resources, government officials and business leaders in the United States and Mexico believe that economic growth and free trade represent the best hope for sustainable development. The logic behind this position is that the demand for environmental quality increases as incomes increase.[4] Furthermore, the wealthier a nation becomes, the more revenues it will have to devote to environmental protection. It follows, then, that economic growth and free trade—as the best guarantee that GDPs will expand—need to be promoted. Under this interpretation, sustainable development really means sustained profits. It is this logic that explains why the term sustainable development is found in the preamble of NAFTA.

Neoliberal policies that prioritize the free flow of trade and investment over human and environmental considerations run contrary to the logic of sustainable agriculture. The main components of sustainable agriculture—reduced dependence on traded inputs, decreased time and distance between production and consumption, increased local and national control of production and consumption patterns, the importance of food security and the satisfaction of basic food needs, the revival of rural communities, an expanded government role in promoting the stability of the small farm, and conserving natural resources—are all undermined by policies that encourage the international market and international capital to take command of our agricultural and food systems.

In the same way that freedom and liberty are thought to be products of the free market, sustainable development is purported to be the consequence of economic growth. The success of this appropriation of terms will be limited by the ability of the broader citizen community to educate and organize around a more comprehensive vision of environmentally sustainable development. More to the point, the potential of free trade and the free market to sustain economic development will be limited by nature itself.

Limits of Growth

One of the key concepts underlying sustainable development is that the world's resources are limited. To sustain development, nonrenewable resources can only be used sparingly while substitutes are explored. Renewable resources have to be replenished by careful long-range planning. This kind of thinking implies that there are limits to growth, which means that the levels of percapita resource consumption common in the industrialized world cannot be attained by less industrialized ones without dangerously depleting limited world resources. In other words, scarce oil resources and pollution from combustion engines will make it environmentally impossible for the U.S. percapita ownership of cars to be generalized throughout the world.

That world resources are finite and the world's absorption capacity limited were ideas explored in 1972 in a highly influential book titled *The Limits to Growth*.[5] Among the main conclusions of the authors were that:

* Limits of growth will be reached within one hundred years if current rates of economic growth and environmental destruction continue. The result will be precipitous declines in population (from wars and famine) and in global industrial capacity.

* Sustainable development, meaning ecological and economic stability, is a precondition for equal opportunity and basic-needs satisfaction.

* The sooner the world finds the political will to work for sustainable development, the greater chances of success it will have in avoiding the catastrophic consequences that will result from testing the limits of growth.

Industrial and less-industrialized countries dismissed the idea that growth should be limited and restructured. For the industrialized nations, accepting the limits of growth would imply that capitalist accumulation would have to be reconsidered as the driving force of development. It would also mean scaled-down lifestyles as consumption levels dropped. For less-industrialized nations, the limits of growth argument for revising development goals was considered an affront to national sovereignty and the rights of all the world's citizens to enjoy the same material comforts as U.S. consumers.

In the 1970s and 1980s, mainstream environmentalism became an adjunct of the capitalist system. Except for a small community of radical environmentalists, the idea that there should be a shift away from exponential growth and toward global equilibrium has been largely ignored. Instead, world leaders have advocated sustained growth resulting from increased world trade. Rather than serving as a foundation for a restructuring of the global economic system, international environmentalism was confined to pollution control, natural conservation, and population control programs.

The environmental, social, and economic consequences of the failure to reconceptualize development are all too apparent. The gap between the industrialized North and the less-industrialized South has widened as terms of trade deteriorated for exporters of traditional commodities and as capital flows from South to North increased as the debtor nations of Latin America and Africa struggled to pay off their international debts. The emergence of the new agrofood system has reduced the food security of nations whose small farm sectors find themselves unable to compete with the food-surplus nations of the North. As national economies have liberalized, the pressure to export has intensified while domestic farm and manufacturing sectors have stagnated. As world trade has expanded and economic globalization has restructured production and consumption patterns, the demand for nonrenewable energy has increased, placing new burdens on nature.

The concept of sustainable development is also subject to differing philosophical conceptions of humanity and nature. The more mainstream approach is one that considers environment and development as a means toward an end—sustaining humanity and improving the quality of life. A more radical concept, one heralded by advocates of Deep Ecology, rejects the anthropomorphic definition of sustainable development. Instead of putting people first, nature is put first. This position can lead to a kind of ecofascism that demeans the value of human life but more commonly is an expression of a deep respect for global ecology.

Free Trade and Sustainable Development

Sustainable development was listed as a general principle of NAFTA. In defining the rules and objectives of NAFTA the challenge of guiding regional trade along an environmentally sustainable path was completely ignored.

NAFTA did establish a trilateral and a U.S.-Mexico border environmental commission, achievements that won the support of major U.S. environmental organizations, with the prominent exceptions of the Sierra Club and Greenpeace. There is little in the agreement, however, that will further sustainable development. Natural resource extraction, for example, is not regulated by NAFTA. Under the regional agreement, each nation gains access to the natural resources of the other two signatory countries (with the prominent exception of Mexico's politically sensitive oil resources). Liberalized trade in natural resources opens the way for large transborder transfers of wood, minerals, fish stocks, and even water. Any resource management undertaken to conserve natural resources or maintain reserves for national use might be judged a violation of the accord. With respect to agriculture, environmental issues are limited to food safety and pesticide regulation, ignoring the demands of numerous farm and environmental groups for NAFTA to include protections for family farms and sustainable agriculture. According to Barbara Dudley of Greenpeace, NAFTA seeks to entrench agricultural trade practices "that will make the increased use of pesticides inevitable, devastate rural economies, and increase the energy and chemical intensity of agricultural production."[6] In doing so, NAFTA accelerates trends that can be traced to the post-World War II industrialization of agriculture.

In the United States, it was not until the onset of the NAFTA negotiations that most environmental organizations recognized the importance of international trade patterns to global ecology. The involvement of environmentalists in economic and development issues points to the possibility of new links being established among a broad range of citizen activists. Debates over the direction of international trade agreements and economic globalization have brought together consumer advocates, labor organizers, farm groups, environmentalists, and leftist academics and political activists, pointing to the possibility of establishing national and international alliances constructed around a mutual commitment to sustainable development.

In the case of the United States and Mexico, both sides have much to learn from the other. Environmentalists in the United States have much to offer the budding environmental and sustainable development movements in Mexico in the way of technical assistance, experience in establishing stiffer environmental protections, financing, and access to the international media. But there is a danger that U.S. environmental organizations, especially those with close links to corporate America and the U.S. policy establishment, will act in an imperious way and will allow their own priorities to override those of Mexicans.[7]

Most of the major U.S. environmental organizations lent their support to NAFTA, believing that the regional agreement would facilitate increased U.S. policy influence in environmental and conservation matters in Mexico. Little consideration was given to the impact of free trade on Mexico's rural population or to the overall implications that NAFTA would have on Latin America's development policies.

As environmentalists broaden their agenda from environmental regulations and natural resource conservation to sustainable development, they must recognize that environmentalism cannot simply be attached to the economic agendas of global investors and traders. To be effective it must be more closely linked to demands for broad-based economic and social development. The creation of nature reserves and the bolstering of the monitoring capacity of Mexico's environmental agency skirt the challenge of putting Mexico and U.S.-Mexico relations on the path toward sustainable development.

No doubt such organizations as Conservation International, World Wildlife Fund, and the Nature Conservancy have contributed to increased environmental consciousness in Mexico. Their financial and technical support has been essential in the creation or strengthening of local environmental nongovernmental organizations. However, they must recognize and be held accountable for the fact that by offering their support for NAFTA, they are facilitating the destructive forces of economic globalization. Like the U.S. government and its economic aid agency, the major environmental organizations must face the contradiction of supporting conservation measures at the same time they are backing economic policies that accelerate unsustainable patterns of growth and reduce the capacity of communities and nations to direct development in sustainable patterns.

The high-profile initiatives of major U.S. environmental oranizations to shape Mexico's environmental policy, including debt-for-nature swaps, the creation of reserves, and lobbying Washington to pressure the Mexican government to bolster its environmental protection capacities, raise the danger of "environmental imperialism."[8] This is all the more worrisome because of the wholesale acceptance of neoliberalism by these environmental organizations as the context in which their own environmental initiatives have the best chance of succeeding. In general, such NAFTA supporters as Conservation International and the Environmental Defense Fund believe that free trade will facilitate international communication about environmental matters and that the economic efficiency resulting from liberalized trade will lead to reductions in pollution and environmental degradation.[9]

The failure to link environmental concerns with an understanding of Mexico's internal social, economic, and political reality undermines the effectiveness of the support of environmental organizations for population control, conservation, and environmental protection. Political democracy, an increased role for nongovernmental and popular organizations, and a commitment to equitable development patterns and basic needs fulfillment are the foundation that will make sustainable development possible. Otherwise, environmentalism will remain the province of a small elite, and the rural poor will be regarded as a threat to nature rather than the victims of national and economic policies.

The proper role for U.S. organizations is assisting and working with environmental groups and campesino organizations as they develop a sustainable development strategy more in keeping with the socioeconomic needs and conditions of Mexico. They should not be setting the environmental priorities of the Mexican people, but to be international environmentalism has to go beyond simply pressuring for increased environmental monitoring and the protection of biological reserves of special interest to foreign NGOs. This is already happening in the partnerships that have been established by such groups as the Border Ecology Project, Forest Guardians, Texas Center for Policy Studies, Greenpeace international partnerships, and Pesticide Action Network, among others.

Population, Poverty, and the Environment

Population growth is a threat to sustainable development, and the highest birth rates in Mexico are found in rural areas. Population control is a leading focus of U.S. economic aid in Mexico and other third world nations because, as the U.S. Agency for International Development states, rapid population growth is a "key strategic threat" that "consumes all other economic gains, drives environmental damage, exacerbates poverty, and impedes democratic governance."[10]

Undoubtedly, increased education about birth control can contribute to improved family livelihoods, improved conditions for women, and sustainable development. But there are several problems with the focus of the U.S. government and many U.S. environmental organizations on Mexican population growth as a source of environmental degradation and increased poverty. The failure to identify the consumption patterns of the industrial world is perhaps the most glaring weakness. Industrial nations with 22 percent of the world's population consume 60 percent of the world's food, 70 percent of its energy, 75 percent of its minerals, and 85 percent of its marketed wood. Not only are nations like the United States doing little or nothing to rectify this imbalance, but also through their trade policies they are trying to replicate this pattern of privileged consumption within a narrow band of middle- and upper-class consumers in Mexico.

Another problem with the population control strategy is that it stresses population growth as a cause of poverty and environmental destruction. In rural areas, large families are at least partly the result of survival strategies in which more children mean more workers and income. Certainly, birth control education programs are needed for both women and men. But they will be more effective and better received if accompanied by support for economic policies that generate income and jobs for rural Mexicans—an objective that will likely be further undermined by the way free trade agreements are currently designed.

Although there are many well-targeted criticisms of the population reduction strategies promoted by industrialized nations, the downplaying or dismissal of the problem of unsustainable population growth rates by most social sectors in Mexico—from the popular movement and campesino organizations to leftist academics and the powerful Catholic Church—points also to the lack of a comprehensive understanding of sustainable development.

By not looking at how economic systems, international trading relationships, and class structures contribute to poverty in Mexico, the U.S. government and leading environmental organizations contribute to the belief that the main threat to rainforests and the conservation of other natural resources comes from the poor.[11] Obviously, the poor by cultivating eroded hillsides, occupying the agricultural frontier, and depending on firewood for fuel are the perpetrators of much environmental destruction in Mexico. For the most part, however, they have no other survival options given the failure of the agricultural economy to provide income and the inability of other economic sectors to provide jobs.

Although not to the degree often thought, the "ecocide of poverty" is a threat to sustainable development. Why then do the World Bank, the U.S. government, and the Mexican government itself promote economic policies that deepen rural poverty? For all the acknowledgment now given to the importance of sustainable development, there has been no deviation from agricultural modernization strategies that promote exports over basic foodstuffs, mechanization over job generation, chemical inputs over organic ones, and large-scale over small-scale farming. Moreover, recent economic stabilization and structural adjustment programs have cut back programs that kept the peasantry from falling into absolute poverty, while measures such as the reform of Article 27 and NAFTA hasten the disintegration of campesino communities.

On the whole, the consequences of liberalized trade resulting from NAFTA and GATT for sustainable agricultural development will be mainly negative. But there will be some important positive changes. Freer trade will make possible more trade in appropriate and energy-saving technologies. The gradual reduction of farm subsidies in the United States may result in declining production and higher prices, which over the long-term could create more room for increased domestic production by the less-productive farmers of Mexico. The increased focus on the environmental and human consequences of international trade, facilitated by the trilateral environmental commission established by NAFTA, may help ameliorate the largely adverse impact of free trade on sustainable agriculture in Mexico.[12]

Unsustainable Development

The lessons of the past hold the promise for a future of sustainable development. Today, both capitalist and small-scale agriculture are experiencing crises of sustainability in Mexico (Table 11). These dual crises have their origins in the country's agricultural structure.

Too often Mexico's environmental degradation is blamed on the campesino population rather than on a history of agricultural modernization that has marginalized rural communities. Technology, credit, and the country's land and water have been put at the disposal of capitalist agriculture and ranching, while campesinos have been given only enough government support to ensure that they did not undermine the nation's political stability and would continue as a source of cheap food and labor.

The highly subsidized capitalist sector has depended since the 1940s on massive government subsidies in the form of water through government irrigation projects, electricity to run its irrigation systems, and government-supplied fertilizer and pesticide inputs. In its efforts to modernize agricultural production, Mexico has attempted to replicate the U.S. success in mechanized farming. Farming methods that may be suitable for fertile, temperate zones like that of the U.S. Midwest are usually not appropriate for Mexico. Only 8 to 12 percent of Mexico's arable land is suitable for highly mechanized agriculture.[13]

Government programs and multilateral aid have supported the expansion of the country's agricultural frontier by financing cattle ranching and sponsoring cash-crop development projects in the forested tropics. The environmental legacy of this agricultural modernization includes massive deforestation, chemical contamination, and salinization of irrigated regions. Perhaps even more consequential has been the loss in most regions of the tradition of multicropping and of the storehouse of campesino wisdom about soil, seeds, and cultivation techniques.

With the waning of government subsidies and the deepening of the environmental problems afflicting commercial agriculture, the sustainability of the modern agricultural sector is uncertain. Plans for increased agroexport production, particularly for horticultural crops that require large amounts of water, may be jeopardized by the looming water crisis in Mexico. Already major agroexport regions like the San Quintín Valley in Baja California have had to abandon irrigated land because of salinized fields and reduced groundwater supplies. There are no firm figures about soil salinization, but it is commonly estimated that at least one of ten irrigated hectares in Mexico suffers severe salinization.[14] Reduced crop production because of salinization, according to another estimate, is equivalent to one million tons of grain annually, roughly enough grain to feed a quarter of Mexico City's population.[15]

A high dependence on and careless use of pesticides may also affect the competitiveness of Mexican agroexports as the cost of agricultural inputs increase with reduced government subsidization. In some cases reckless pesticide use has resulted in increased pest resistance to chemi-

Table 11

The Mexican Environment In Statistics

Land Use

Total land area | 196.8 million ha.

Permanent grazing lands — 79.9 million ha. (40.8%)
Tropical forests — 24.1 million ha. (12.3%)
Temperate forests — 25.5 million ha. (13.0%)
Shrubs & Thickets — 30.5 million ha. (15.6%)
Agricultural lands — 27.3 million ha. (13.9%)
72 protected areas in the form of
natural monuments, national parks
and biosphere reserves — 6,109,330 ha. (3.10%)

Land Tenure of Forest Resources

State owned — 7%
Privately owned — 23%
Owned by ejidos or indigenous peoples — 70%

Deforestation

Deforestation rate — 370,000-804,000 ha/yr
Temperate forests — 245,000 ha/yr
Tropical forests — 559,000 ha/yr
Current forested area — 49.6 million hectares

Causes of Deforestation

Temperate Conifers
forest fires (49%)
cattle grazing (28%)
agriculture (16%)
clandestine cutting (5%)

Temperate Oaks
forest fires (47%)
cattle grazing (28%)
agriculture (17%)
clandestine cutting (5%)

Tropical Evergreen
cattle grazing (58%)
agriculture (10%)
petroleum extraction (3%)
mining (2.5%)
road construction (1.5%)
forest fires (22%)
wood extraction (2%)

Tropical Deciduous
cattle grazing (57%)
agriculture (14%)
wood extraction (21%)
forest fires (7%)

Erosion

Soil with no erosion	20.8%
Soil showing light erosion	26.4%
Soil with moderate erosion	36.8%
Soil with severe erosion	12.2%
Soil plagued by total erosion	16.7%

The loss of fertile soils due to erosion occurs at a rate of 2,754 tons per year per hectare. 29% of Mexico's national territory is in the severe state of erosion known as desertification.

Water Withdrawal

Domestic	6%
Industry	8%
Agriculture	86%

SOURCES: Secretaría de Agricultura y Recursos Hidráulicos. 1992. Inventoria Forestal, México; Dirección General de Aprovechamiento Ecológico de los Recursos Naturales, Instituto Nacional de Ecologia, SEDESOL, 1992; Secretaría de Educación Pública. 1981, *Guia de planeacion y control de las actividades forestales,* Carlos Cortez Ruíz,"El sector forestal mexicano: entre la economía y la ecología?" *Comercio Exterior,* abril de 1993; World Resource Institute, *World Resources Report 1992-93.*

cals, leaving growers of cotton and other crops with no alternative but to abandon production.

The environmental crisis facing the campesino sector is even more severe. Salinization is not a problem because campesino land is usually not irrigated. Erosion and exhausted soil are among the main environmental problems facing the peasantry. Under the traditional *milpa* system, land was left fallow for a few years before being cultivated again.[16] But as the human and cattle populations have expanded and with the agrarian reform program slowing to a stop, there is no more land to permit this old pattern of shifting cultivation. As a result, land erosion and deforestation worsen as marginal lands are continuously cropped. More intensive cultivation of small plots has led to increased use of agricultural inputs, especially chemical fertilizers, which at a time of declining prices make farming more costly and risky.

Limited water supply is probably the main environmental limit to agricultural growth in Mexico. With the quadrupling of the population in Oaxaca, groundwater levels have dropped from one meter to ten meters in the central valley, making farming increasingly costly. When water supplies run short, the poor and those living in remote areas are usually the ones most affected. In contrast, wealthier growers have the political power and economic muscle to ensure that they have priority access to limited groundwater and water from reservoirs.

The relatively large amount of irrigated land, nearly 20 percent of cropland, has created a buffer against low rainfall. Falling groundwater levels and inadequate reservoirs mean that wells and reservoirs deplete rapidly in dry years, with the result that in years when rainfall is even slightly below average, crops are put at risk.[17] Drought-resistant seeds have allowed Mexican farmers to cultivate arid areas, but they have also increased farmer debt as growers have moved away from such traditional hazard-prevention strategies as mixed cropping and adapting planting to microclimates as their cost of inputs has increased. Inadequate water and the waterlogging and salinization of irrigated areas are likely to limit Mexico's agroexport potential under NAFTA more than the remaining tariff and nontariff barriers that protect U.S. growers.[18]

Aggravating this water crisis is the threat of global warming.[19] The projection of climate changes remains an inexact science, but some observers are warning that even small temperature and precipitation changes will present a serious threat to local and national food security in Mexico.[20]

Dependence on fuel is less of a threat to agriculture in Mexico than in many other countries without oil reserves. Nonetheless, as reserves diminish and government subsidized electricity and fuel are cut back, farmers are complaining that costs of production exceed the prices they receive. New concerns are arising about the appropriateness of highly mechanized farming, especially in a country where there is such an abundance of labor. In its attempts to replicate U.S. agriculture, Mexico has become a victim of the same high energy dependence afflicting the United States. Mexico's efforts to duplicate the yields of U.S. agriculture by following U.S. farming practices also fall short because its less-fertile and mostly arid farmlands have less productive potential.

In Mexico the cow is privileged. Cattle graze over half the nation's territory, about 90 million hectares. No other part of the farm economy has received so much state support in the form of cheap credit and land concessions. Part of the expansion of the cattle industry is tied to the U.S. market. In northern Mexico vast extensions of arid lands are devoted to the production of calves for export to the United States, where they are fattened in feedlots and then slaughtered, with increasing quantities of the packaged and frozen beef then returning to Mexican markets.[21] Overgrazing has resulted in habitat loss, soil eradication, and desertification throughout northern Mexico.

In southern Mexico, there has been an intensifying competition between the small farm sector and the cattle industry since the 1950s.[22] Forests have been cleared and campesinos pushed off their parcels and communal lands to make way for cattle and to ensure that Mexico City is supplied with beef. Although the cattle industry is dominated by large ranchers, many campesino families also raise cattle because it is less labor intensive, a better source of income than traditional corn and bean cropping, and a better use of infertile land. Like other primary food sectors, the cattle industry has slowed with the shrinking of the agricultural frontier and the opening of the international market.

More than the erosion of arable lands or the vast extensions of razed tropical forests, Mexico City is the most telling symbol of unsustainable development. It is here we best see the results of the development policies that have favored the city over the countryside. The government's cheap food policies, its focus on manufacturing and food processing, and its disdain for the welfare of rural Mexico are evident in the country's sprawling cities. Resources have flowed to the city, leaving the countryside economically depressed and environmentally devastated. Mexico City, with a quarter of the country's population, has 42 percent of the nation's jobs, 53 percent of its wages, 38 percent of its industrial plant value, 55 percent of its public investment, 40 percent of total food production, and 66 percent of its energy consumption.[23]

A Scourge of Chemicals

Widespread use of agrochemicals—nonorganic fertilizers, insecticides, and herbicides—have increased crop yields in Mexican agriculture. Indeed, most high-yield seeds require intensive agrochemical application. But chemical agriculture has come at a high cost—financially, environmentally, and in terms of farmworker and consumer health.

Within Mexico, the government has largely ignored the health consequences of the uncontrolled application of agrochemicals. Only recently, through the efforts of such groups as the Pesticide Action and Alternatives Network (RAPAM), Greenpeace, Mexican Association of Environmental Studies for Consumer Defense (AMEDEC), and the National Human Rights Commission (CNDH), has the public become more aware of the dangers of pesticide abuse. A 1993 report by the National Human Rights Commission concluded that Mexicans have one of the world's highest amounts of toxic substances in their bloodstreams.[24]

The Mexican government does not monitor produce for pesticide residues and does not enforce regulations to protect farmworkers against pesticide poisonings. Both tasks are left to the growers themselves, who have proved reluctant to institute effective self-regulation practices. Since the late 1980s the Mexican government has restricted or banned many of the most dangerous pesticides, although there are still ten pesticides that are banned or restricted in the United States but authorized for use in Mexico. Even these regulations are commonly evaded by clandestine pesticide manufacturers and smugglers who import banned agrochemicals from Central America and the United States. One of the ironies of the U.S. pesticide regulation system is that chemical producers are permitted to export pesticides to Mexico and other foreign nations that are not authorized for use in the United States because of their dangerous qualities.

For U.S. consumers, a prominent concern is that produce imported to the United States may be laden with toxic chemicals, many of which were produced in the United States and then exported.[25] This "circle of poison" is made possible by loose export laws in the United States, lax enforcement in Mexico, and inadequate monitoring of imported produce.[26] Three billion pounds of produce enter the United States from Mexico every year, but USDA agents check this produce only for cosmetic quality, while a smattering of agents from the Food and Drug Administration (FDA) check only an occasional shipment for pesticide residues. In fact, since the FDA offices are only open eight to five, those shipments crossing the border at night or on the weekends are never subject to pesticide checks. Only about one percent of imported produce actually gets tested.[27]

The tests the FDA uses cover fewer than half of the pesticides that are produced, and even when pesticide residues are discovered, the illegal imports have usually been put on grocery shelves by the time the test results get back. Horticultural producers in the United States complain that they are operating on an unlevel playing field since Mexican producers are not as strictly regulated. In recent years, pesticide use in Mexico has increased about 20 percent annually, with fruits and vegetables accounting for approximately 40 percent of pesticide applications. As trade liberalizes and Mexican agroexport production increases, pesticide use is expected to climb higher with better access to the U.S. market and increased pressure to raise productivity.[28]

Although the concerns of U.S. consumers and producers have received much more attention, those mainly threatened by the largely unregulated and unmonitored use of agrochemicals in Mexico are Mexican consumers and farmworkers. In the agroexport regions of the northwestern states, pesticides pervade the environment. In the Yaqui Valley of Sonora, blood tests of infants showed residues of ten pesticides, while traces of fourteen agrochemicals were found in mothers' milk. These findings have been associated with the high rate of leukemia in the state.[29]

Part of the problem for Mexican farmworkers is the high toxicity of the chemicals applied to the produce they pick. According to Greenpeace Mexico, an estimated 124,000 tons of agrochemicals that are among the "Dirty Dozen" of the most hazardous were applied in Mexico during the past two decades. Among the most popular are the 2-4-D compound, paraquat, and methyl parathion. The common use of aerial spraying, generally spreading over worker housing, directly exposes farmworkers to sometimes lethal doses of agrochemicals. Other spraying is done manually, usually by teenagers who are paid slightly more to walk down crop rows with backpack applicators. Lacking protective clothing and equipment, these are the farmworkers who pay the highest price for chemical agriculture in Mexico.[30]

Conquest and Colonization

The view that nature represents an obstacle to modernization has dominated Mexico's development philosophy. During the Díaz regime, the government centered its economic development efforts on opening up new territory through large land and railroad concessions. In the 1940s the PRI government began a policy of developing remote regions, particularly in the tropics, through colonization programs linked to cattle ranching, agribusiness, and infrastructure projects like hydroelectric dams and irrigation systems.[31]

Such development programs also had the explicit intent of reducing rural tensions and dissent by encouraging campesinos to seek out their fortunes in the jungles of Chiapas, Quintana Roo, Tabasco, Campeche, and Veracruz. "A march to the sea would alleviate the congestion in our central plateau," President Avila Camacho declared in 1941. This exhortation has been repeated time and again by Mexican presidents. Colonization has reduced pressure for land reform and offered a safety valve to land tensions in the countryside.[32]

Roads serve as the beachheads of economic development in the country's agricultural frontier. With the roads come landless campesinos looking for land and jobs, and ranchers looking for new pastures. Gertrude Blom, one of the leading voices for the preservation of the Lacandón Jungle, was concerned that the roads the government was building presaged the destruction of the forest. "See the woods on both sides," she wrote in 1974, "the roads are burning...wherever the road goes, the peasant follows; where the peasant goes, fire follows; where the fire goes, the stones appear; and where the stones appear, stalks hunger."[33]

Erosion and deforestation in Mexico present the most dramatic evidence that the present rates of agricultural production cannot be sustained. Deforestation is a problem throughout the country, but it is in the humid tropics of the Southeast where the rates of forest cutting have been the most shocking. The loss of the jungle along the Mexico-Guatemala border has been so complete that looking down from a plane you can see where Mexico ends and the forested Petén region of Guatemala begins. No one sector is responsible, but the ranching and forestry sectors are certainly the most egregious offenders.

Having no possibility of getting land in their highland communities, indian families, together with colonizers from elsewhere in Mexico, have sought a new, more promising future in heart of the Lacandón Jungle. However, the devastation wrought by the timber industry and by cattle ranchers has not been part of a survival strategy to meet basic needs. With the blessings and often financial support of the government, ranchers and timbermen slash down Mexico's tropical forests.

Jungle Conservation and Conflict

The campesino rebellion in Chiapas highlights the complexity of linking environmental and development concerns. Since the early 1960s economic development in the form of hydroelectric plants, oil drilling, cattle ranching, and campesino farming has turned the Lacandón Jungle from a sparsely inhabited tropical lowlands into a region crisscrossed by roads that has lost about 70 percent of its original forest cover. The population of the Lacandón region jumped from 6,000 in 1960 to as high as 300,000 at the time of the *zapatista* rebellion (Table 12).[34]

Large cattle ranchers, timber companies, and the government's energy bureaucracy have extracted great wealth from the jungle, which is part of the largest remaining tropical rainforest in North America. Yet most of the jungle's residents are desperately poor, and they joined the *zapatista* army in its demand for better roads, renewed land distribution, and rural electrification. Their demands were just and reasonable. They wanted land, democracy, opportunity, and modernization; but how much more development could the jungle absorb without being finally lost? When asked this question, Subcomandante Marcos replied, "We don't agree with this preoccupation with the trees over the death of our people.

Table 12

The Ecology of the Zapatista Rebellion

* Chiapas has 30% of Mexico's surface water, and its hydroelectric dams supply as much as one-half of the country's hydroelectric power. The state ranks last among Mexican states in households with electricity.

* Population growth rate in the Lacandón Jungle is more than 7% annually, about the same as the rate of deforestation.

* Chiapas (together with Veracruz and Tabasco) is one of the three leading suppliers of beef to Mexican cities; but the nutritional levels of these states are among the worst in the nation, and more than fifty percent of their populations rarely eat beef.

* By 1980, 80% of the cleared area in the Lacandón Jungle was dedicated to cattle pasture.

* An estimated 45% of Chiapas is used as pasture by some three million cattle.

* Only 30% of the Lacandón Jungle remains intact.

Sources: *La Jornada Ecológica*, April 21, 1994; *Cultural Survival Quarterly*, Spring 1994; *New York Times*, January 4, 1994.

We say, we want trees, we want mountains. But we also want a dignified life for our people."[35]

In the Lacandón Jungle, Mexico is facing a conflict between conservation and development that offers tragic testimony to the unsustainable character of the country's economic modernization strategies. As late as 1960 the jungle still had 90 percent of its forest cover, but a renewal of logging in the mid-1960s began to open the jungle up to campesino colonizers and cattlemen. New roads were bulldozed into the dense tropical forest to extract the mahogany and cedar that earlier, river-based logging teams had failed to reach.[36]

Together with the World Bank and Inter-American Development Bank, the Mexican government promoted the growth of extensive cattle industry in southeastern Mexico to meet the rising demands for meats by an increasingly urbanized nation. At the same time the government attempted to deflate the demands of the peasantry for more land and higher prices by encouraging the colonization of the agricultural frontier. The unpopulated jungles of the Southeast served as safety valves for rural political tensions elsewhere in the country.

In the early 1970s the government decreed an indigenous reserve of 641,000 hectares, declaring that the small Lacandón Maya community was the sole owner. Rather than slowing deforestation, the creation of the jungle reserve facilitated the signing of new timber agreements in which the government's own development bank Nafinsa had chief interest. More roads were blazed to access the valuable timber. Adding to this road network in the late 1970s were the drilling roads built by the state oil company, Pemex. Also part of the government-directed development boom in Chiapas were two hydroelectric dams constructed on the Grijalva River.

By the 1980s the Lacandón Jungle was rapidly disappearing as campesinos competed for land with cattle ranchers. Colonizers who previously regarded the vast jungle as a promised land found that once the forest cover was cleared the soil quickly eroded. Often lacking clear land titles, the campesino colonists were frequently pushed off their lands by the more powerful cattlemen, who were backed by the army and their own private militias. Land tensions were aggravated by a natural population growth rate of more than 3 percent and by a nearly 4 percent annual increase from new settlers—a growth rate that doubles the population every ten years.[37]

In 1978 the government took the first step to conserve at least a small part of the tropical forest from depredation by establishing the Montes Azules Biosphere Reserve. Stricter measures were gradually adopted in the 1980s to stop the spontaneous colonization of the jungle and the spread of the cattle industry. In 1990 the governor of Chiapas declared a total ban on logging and woodcutting in the Lacandón reserve, angering many campesinos who felt the prohibition further threatened their ability to survive in the jungle.

In its demand for land, the *zapatista* army never suggested that protected lands be distributed. Rather it targeted the large cattle ranches in the region. Nevertheless, the rebellion did spark a wave of land occupations throughout the jungle, that have already resulted in more deforestation.

Like the Lacandón Jungle, most of Mexico's other forests and jungles are disappearing as the poor and the rich seek ways to exploit these natural resources for wood, pastures, and agriculture. Through the creation of protected areas and biosphere reserves, the Mexican government has taken very limited steps to stop deforestation.

Too often the government has declared the creation of reserves without adequately considering how conservation can be integrated with development planning. Rather than protecting the forests, such declarations can result in the acceleration of deforestation as campesinos, ranchers, and loggers rush in to lay claim to resources before stricter land controls are implemented. For just this reason, the Sierra de Santa Maria Biosphere in Veracruz has lost more than one-fourth of its tropical forest since its creation in 1980.[38]

In the same way that the government has built hydroelectric dams without considering the fate of the poor campesinos who will be displaced, it has mapped out bioreserves with little knowledge of the affected region or of its inhabitants. In some cases, the government, in its eagerness to please the World Bank and other sources of foreign financing, has declared biospheres in regions without even notifying the inhabitants of the area. Too often this failure to consider the livelihood needs of area communities results in resentment and distrust of environmentalism.

To retain the rich biodiversity of Mexico's forests, careful land-use planning is needed to integrate community development and conservation.[39] Some of the best of this planning is being done by ejidos and agrarian communities with the technical assistance of socially committed nongovernmental organizations.[40]

Underlining the argument that sustainable rural development depends on the participation of the peasantry is the fact that 70 percent of Mexico's remaining forests and jungles are found within the boundaries of the ejidos and agrarian communities. In Mexico, the most important concentrations of biodiversity are under the stewardship of the roughly fifteen million members of the social sector.[41] "Not only do campesinos have the vision to implement a sustainable development, they have the resources," says Armando Bartra of the Maya Institute in Mexico City.[42]

Creating Sustainable Agriculture

"Sustainable agriculture," says Fernando Bejarano of Greenpeace-Mexico, "involves ecological, technical and social components which allow the production of food and fibers without putting at risk the conservation of natural resources or the biological and cultural diversity of future generations."[43]

Another helpful definition of sustainable agriculture is one which incorporates sustainability (conservation of natural resources), stability (not subject to catastrophic declines in production due to climate changes), productivity, and equity.[44] Traditional shifting *milpa* cultivation was highly equitable and sustainable (when Mexico was less densely populated) but often unstable and not highly productive. The objective is to incorporate all four components. In the interests of stability, sustainability, or equitability, however, productivity may be less than optimum.

Most campesinos are not familiar with the term *sustainable development*, but there is an increasing realization by campesino organizations that the survival of the peasantry depends more than ever on the sustainable management of its resources. The Interamerican Democracy and Agriculture Network (RIAD) brings together campesino organizations throughout Latin America and the Caribbean that are committed to promoting campesino-based and sustainable agricultural development. In Mexico, a widening array of campesino organizations and research institutes, including UNORCA, Maya Institute, the CNOC, Research Center for Change in the Mexican Countryside (CECCAM), and Environmental Study Group (GEA), are spearheading a campaign to make the struggle for sustainable development a central element in the campesino movement.[45]

This realization comes into conflict, however, with the accelerating disintegration of traditional community and even family structures. The economic crisis, the penetration of the market economy, and the increased social stratification within campesino villages have given rise to individualistic survival strategies. With more campesinos leaving their villages to join the migrant stream and to find work in the urban informal sector or on agroexport estates, communitarian ethics are fast disappearing.

In most rural villages, communal work teams have traditio~ helped maintain village irrigation ditches, roads, and communal lar individual survival strategies become dominant, community ins~

are losing their influence and the respect for communal welfare is fading, leading to increased land conflicts, the appropriation of communal lands, and deforestation.[46] This loss of traditional communal structures and a sense of collective identity has accelerated with the penetration of the capitalist market that converts traditional use values into commodities to be bought and sold. Advocates of sustainable agriculture contend that the resurrection and strengthening of community institutions are as crucial to an alternative agricultural strategy as are appropriate farming practices.

Another related concern applies equally to city and countryside, industrialized and nonindustrialized nations. As the agrofood system assumes dominance, agricultural production loses its integral connection with local food consumption, and people become farther removed from nature, their perception of nature changes. The essential understanding of how closely the fate of humankind and nature are linked is lost. Sustainable agricultural practices that seemed natural before have to be relearned along with the communitarian ethics that facilitate and shape a better interaction between economy and ecology.

Sustainable agriculture is taking hold in Mexico mostly as a survival strategy in the face of rising costs for agrochemicals, reduced state support, and the rapid deterioration of local farm economies. The increased reliance on organic inputs, better land-use planning, and integration into alternative marketing networks are among the main traits of sustainable farmers. The organic farming movement is expanding in Mexico, but the use of natural fertilizers and pesticides is hardly new. Before credit was available, organic farming and poor people's farming were one and the same. As credit became more available and farmers more dependent on crop loans, farming that relied on natural inputs became increasingly difficult because banks refused to lend to farms not blessed with agrochemicals.

The advocates of sustainable agriculture do not reject international trade. Instead, they have joined an international movement to reorder economic relations between producers, traders, and consumers. Sustainable agriculture networks have improved the livelihood of many small farmers, although they have only an insignificant market share, and have pointed the way toward international trading relationships that are at once more equitable and less destructive environmentally.

Among the most prominent participants in these new trading relations are the organic coffee growers of Chiapas, Oaxaca, and Guerrero.

Through marketing agreements with alternative trading organizations in the United States and Europe, some campesino communities sell their organic coffee under their own brand names in the premium and natural foods markets. The direct, high-price contracts with socially aware foreign trading organizations helped these organic growers survive the collapse of world coffee prices in 1989.[47]

Because no brokers are involved and because organic coffee commands premium prices, these foreign buyers can pay higher prices to Mexican coffee growers. Commonly, the foreign buyers provide technical assistance to their suppliers to ensure the coffee they market is totally organic and of high quality. By including information about the growers, these marketing networks also give foreign consumers a taste of what the political and economic conditions are like in the communities that produce the coffee they drink. Alternative marketing networks can be a source of revenues for communities that trade goods produced using sustainable techniques, such as organic fertilizers and nonchemical pesticides. But unless democratic controls exist over production and marketing, the profits may go to the same local *caciques* that have historically accumulated wealth and land in rural towns.

Promoting the shift to organic fertilizers and natural pest control is the Mexican Association of Ecological Farmers (AMAE). Farmers associated with AMAE are experienced growers who have discovered that organic methods not only cost less but usually result in yields comparable to those of chemical agriculture. AMAE, which includes some forty organizations representing more than 13,000 growers, exports organic fresh vegetables, honey, peanuts, sesame seeds, vanilla, mescal, and other products to foreign markets, with organic production doubling every year in Mexico. Organic agriculture for domestic consumption, however, is much more widespread than the small agroexport market in organic produce. Necessity, more than the enticement of foreign markets, is causing many Mexican farmers to return to natural organic inputs as part of a self-provisioning strategy in hard economic times.[48]

At least part of any sustainable development solution to the crisis in rural Mexico involves a return to such indigenous practices as mixed cropping. Some agroecologists claim that of all the agriculturally based cultures, those of Central America and Mexico were among those with the most truly ecological agriculture.[49]

A return to traditional farming methods, however, will not be enough to sustain agricultural production at levels that provide farmers with a decent livelihood. Campesino farmers have accumulated agronomic wisdom, but sometimes this traditional knowledge is based more on belief than science. To be successful, small-scale agriculture needs modern technical assistance that incorporates appropriate technologies and practices.[50] This assistance will depend on better coordination among campesino communities, state extension services, multilateral research institutions, and nongovernmental organizations.[51] Unlike the Green Revolution, which focused on large commercial farming operations, new technical assistance programs should also be oriented to small growers and should focus on more appropriate inputs. The "small is beautiful" principle must be incorporated into agricultural extension and other technical assistance programs in Mexico, where the small farm sector is so prevalent.[52] But the beauty of sustainable agriculture, sometimes called agroecology, comes more from its compatibility with the environment through the use of inputs that are natural rather than energy intensive.[53]

Productivity could increase and soil erosion slow if Mexican farmers would incorporate such sustainable practices as contour plowing, terracing, use of cover crops, integrated pest management, and better water management. In addition to providing better technical assistance, the government and nongovernmental organizations could help reduce postharvest losses if farm communities had better access to crop storage and processing facilities.

It is not coincidental that many who adopt sustainable agriculture methods live in areas which have suffered social and ecological disruption. Sustainable development represents a realization by those most directly affected by unsustainable practices that changes must be made, and that the global ecological and social crisis has arrived in the Mexican countryside. Those marginalized by the agricultural, economic, and social policies of the neoliberal government have had no choice but to develop an alternative that will allow them to sustain their livelihoods.

Throughout Mexico, from the Tarahumara communities of the Sierra Madre in the Northwest to indian communities in the Sierra Juárez in Oaxaca, rural communities have recognized the importance of better land-use planning and sustainable agricultural and forestry practices. On the Yucatán peninsula, groups such as the X'pujil Ejido Union in Campeche and the Civil Forestry Society of the Maya Zone in Quintana Roo are developing sustainable ways to use their forest resources. In Veracruz, Santa Marta Mountains Project (PSSM) combines different productive activities including cattle, coffee, and small farms with an environmental plan to protect important biological resources. Using a biosphere model of a protected core surrounded by mixed use zones, the PSSM seeks not to exclude people, but to manage the impacts of human activity to maintain ecological balance.[54] In many cases, the history of exclusion by the clientelistic structures of the ruling PRI and associated control over their villages by *caciques* has served to intensify the struggle for an inclusive, participatory approach to organizing and alliance building.

An inspiration for alternative agriculture is found in Nochixtlan, Oaxaca, an indian community that was slowly turning into a ghost community because of out-migration before World Neighbors began its alternative agricultural program. Using legumes and terracing, experienced promoters have demonstrated that agricultural yields can be dramatically improved without chemical inputs. World Neighbors encourages mixed cropping and seasonal diversification to ensure self-provisioning while at the same time securing a source of income from cash crops. Rather than buying pesticides, the villagers who have joined the World Neighbors program use such natural insecticides as chile water, tobacco, and onion soup. Instead of chemical fertilizers, which over time deplete the soil's natural nutrients, the campesinos involved in the World Neighbors project use "green manure" (nutrient-creating cover crops) and livestock droppings.

Back to the Future

Just as campesino-led strategies present an alternative to export-led growth and a possible solution to food dependency, strategies that stress the central role of rural communities may offer the best hope for sustainable development in the countryside.[55] Analysts from the *campesinista* tradition as well as an increasing sector of environmental activists say that the revitalization of campesino communities could reverse the cycle of poverty and ecological destruction.

The crisis of the *campo* can be turned into opportunity if governments and lending agencies support campesino cooperatives and village councils in their search for sustainable survival strategies.[56] Small-scale production to meet basic needs not only contributes to food self-sufficiency but also broadens the domestic market for local manufacturers by increasing the income of the peasantry. In the process of ensuring the livelihood of campesino families, village and small town life are renewed, thereby easing rural-urban polarization.

Not just a populist dream, the concept of a sustainable development strategy based on support for the small farm sector is one that some economists find credible. Analysts consulting for the OECD Development Center concluded that a development model based on stimulating campesino agriculture and consumption would be the best economic option for Mexico. Because of the important backward and forward linkages that would be created, a dynamic small farm sector could serve as motor of economic growth for the entire society.[57]

In adopting an export-oriented model as the best hope for development, Mexico and other Latin American countries hope to follow the success of the newly industrializing countries of Asia. Overlooked, however, is the fact that nations like Taiwan and South Korea based their industrialization process to a large degree on agricultural systems in which the government supported labor-intensive, small farm agriculture and agrarian reform programs.[58]

Campesino-oriented development strategies do not want to shut down the agroexport economy. Rather they advocate a better balance between food production for the local and foreign markets. David Barkin, an expert on Mexican agriculture, has proposed that the government support grain production on rainfed lands while irrigated lands would be devoted to agroexports. Under such a system, large landowners would be expected to internalize all costs of irrigation.[59] Because an agricultural strategy promoting increased grains production would likely mean higher prices, it would have to be combined with increases in urban wages and target subsidies for those in greatest need.

Individual villages or regions may successfully adopt the principles of sustainable development, especially if they are ensured of a good and stable market for their produce. However, political and economic conditions in Mexico work against local campesino-based agricultural development projects. This has been the problem with the social enterprises associated with the campesino groups CNOC and UNORCA. Without state support in the form of better access to capital, land, water, and technical assistance and within the framework of free trade that pits them against growers throughout the world, campesino-based projects are likely to fail.

In their struggle to survive, rural communities may find they can improve their circumstances by adopting more appropriate technologies and returning to traditional practices of organic agriculture and cooperative production. But to reverse the underdevelopment of the Mexican countryside will require a new restructuring of the state's agricultural and trade policies—a prospect that seems unlikely in the short and medium terms.[60]

LESSONS AND OPTIONS

"The ghost of Zapata has been seen again in the countryside. It never completely disappeared, of course, but it is now assuming a stronger presence. The new government will have to face the materialization of this phantom from the past, and the problems of governability that face Mexico's future will have much to do with how the social pacts that have been abolished [between the government and the peasantry] will be reconstructed."

—Luis Hernández of the National Network of Coffee Grower Organizations (CNOC), March 1994

There is no going back to earlier revolutions or liberal ideologies for answers to today's dilemmas. At best, we can learn some lessons from the past and draw inspiration for the challenges and struggles ahead.

Returning to Anenecuilco, the birthplace of *zapatismo*, we are reminded that poor campesinos had the conviction and the courage to challenge an exclusive political system and a modernizing economic system that offered no place for the common people. Just as important as their heroic struggles against oppressive governments was the political and social vision of the *zapatistas*. They proposed an alternative, the Plan of Ayala, that incorporated what they knew was right and just about village life in Morelos with a reform program for the future. Although limited in scope, the Plan of Ayala did identify some of the main development problems of Mexico, including the lack of democracy, political centralization, appropriation of land and water by an economic elite, and the exclusive character of agricultural modernization.

Despite the 1910-17 revolution, many of the same constraints to broad-based economic development remain. In addition, Mexico, like most poorer nations, faces a new assortment of problems arising from its changing rural/urban mix and from its new place in the global economy. The historic demands of *"tierra y libertad"* persist, but they arise in a new national and international context.

Given the mobility of capital and the country's reliance on international financing, the options for pursuing nationalistic development strategies that shape production and consumption are limited. Having embraced the dominant economic ideology of neoliberalism and thrown its doors open to the international market, Mexican workers, farmers, and businesses are finding that their worth is measured by global standards of efficiency and productivity. Mexico, closely integrated into a global trading and production system, is increasingly dependent on imports of agricultural commodities and processed foods. It desperately needs to increase its export offerings to pay for its imports and to attract foreign capital to bolster its productive capacity.

Just as there is no going back to past revolutions, there is no returning to a world where national economies could be managed in relative isolation from the rest of the world. Economic globalization is a reality that must be recognized, as Mexico has done, but this does not mean that world markets are free or that there is no longer a role for the state.

What are the best policy options for ensuring that a country meets the needs of an urbanizing society while at the same time helping the farm sector survive in a market that is increasingly globalized? Policy choices range from the wholesale adoption of the free market to the return to more state involvement in economic development and regulation.[1] Measures such as liberalizing prices and opening the domestic market to inexpensive imports may seem appropriate from a narrow view of the economics of comparative advantage but may be neither economically nor politically sound from the point of view of the broader development needs of Mexico. Policies that benefit the urban consumer may undermine rural production, or conversely policies that improve the lot of farmers, such as higher prices and the channeling of government services to the countryside, may adversely affect most urban consumers.

This concluding chapter summarizes some of the lessons of the past and current agricultural, agrarian, and food policies in Mexico. It also reviews some of the benefits and problems of different broad policy options that Mexico could pursue.

Agrarianism, Agricultural Modernization, and State Legitimation

Largely because of Zapata's Liberation Army of the South, agrarianism has long held a central place in the postrevolutionary Mexican state's efforts to maintain its legitimacy as a government of the people. During the Cárdenas *sexenio*, a strong campesino-government alliance accelerated agrarian reform and gave the ejido a central place in agricultural development. Once having solidified campesino support for the ruling party through corporatist channels, subsequent governments rejected an agrarian-based development strategy in favor of one that promoted capitalist agriculture on large private estates and ranches. Ejidos and indigenous communities were no longer regarded as potential sources of economic dynamism and domestic market expansion but merely as a source of cheap food and labor.

The bimodal system of agricultural production showed signs of breaking down by the late 1960s as percapita food production turned negative and food imports increased. Rather than moving toward a unimodal system, such as that of Taiwan, Korea, or China, which would have required a greater degree of redistributive and structural reforms throughout the countryside, governments in the 1970s and early 1980s expanded the state's presence in the small farm sector through integrated rural development programs. New state institutions provided credit and marketing assistance to small growers, and thereby diminished the control of local private intermediaries. But this new government intervention on behalf of the social sector occured within the context of a corporatist state in which political patronage and self-serving bureaucracies ruled and in which large agribusiness and the cattle industry were given priority treatment. Not only did the bimodal structure persist but the sector of infrasubsistence campesino farmers expanded substantially, leading to what David Myhre of the Center for U.S.-Mexican Studies has called a *trimodal* structure.

By the mid-1980s the fetish of the free market came to replace state capitalism and statist populism as the source of legitimation for the ruling government. To the business sector, the government offered parastatal companies at bargain prices and a liberalized economic system. Consumers were rewarded with a flood of imported food and merchandise. To the peasantry, the government promised less state control over the ejidos and their organizations. Paternalism would be replaced by a more equal relationship between the government and a self-directed, mature social sector. This new relationship between state and market and between the government and the farm sector is fraught with problems that have implications not only for the viability of the agricultural economy but also for the legitimation needs of the Mexican state.

Macroeconomic policies of economic stabilization and structural adjustment that address problems of inflation, costly public-sector programs, currency valuation, and debt servicing have dominated government economic planning, with the result that no coherent farm sector policy has been formulated. A fixation on macroeconomic management has blinded policymakers to the need for state planning to address structural constraints to increased production, expanded domestic consumption, and broad-based economic development. The government has cut back on services to the farm sector at the very time a concerted program is most needed to boost its efficiency, productivity, and competitiveness in the new context of liberalized trade.

Although the government is abandoning its traditional corporatist instruments for managing agrarian problems and the agricultural economy, it has not moved to create a coherent and stable farm policy that responds to farmer needs and national development priorities. A welter of new programs and agencies has been created to push forward liberalization and to ease the adjustment to the new political economy, but these programs are uncoordinated and show little sign of coalescing into an effective farm policy. The dissolution of old agencies and creation of disparate new ones have led to widespread consternation and a sense of confusion among small farmers. Adding to this sense of uncertainty is the knowledge that government programs change from president to president with little or no input from campesino communities and farmer associations.

The end of agrarianism has had a mixed reception. While many *ejidatarios* look favorably on the end of state control of their land and the dissolution of the old agrarian patronage networks, there is also an undercurrent of fear, particularly in poorer regions, that the reforms to Article 27 presage a period of land grabbing and a return to the prerevolutionary structures of peonage. Especially in light of the Chiapas rebellion, there is reason to believe that it will be increasingly difficult for the Mexican state to maintain its legitimacy in the countryside. Given the deep historical connections that link rural Mexico and the state's identity and legitimacy, political dissidence and agrarian violence in the countryside will have implications for overall political stability in Mexico.

Future of the Peasantry

The government's commitment to neoliberal macroeconomic policies and free trade has badly shaken the peasantry. Many have rightly concluded that with the Article 27 reforms and NAFTA they are being deleted from the script for Mexico's future.

If it is true that campesinos have no productive role to play, will they find one in other sectors of the economy, such as manufacturing and agroexport production? Even in the absence of a large displacement of campesinos, Mexico's economy has not demonstrated the capacity to absorb the million or so youths who enter the labor force annually. Many campesinos have found a tenuous livelihood in the informal sectors of the major cities. But the influx of rural unemployed floods the informal sector with street vendors, depresses wages for all workers, and creates new social and environmental problems in the crowded margins of Mexico's metropolitan areas. As the barriers to immigration tighten in the United States, this traditional escape valve for rural underdevelopment and political tensions may become a less viable option.

It is difficult to project the degree to which campesinos will completely abandon the *campo*. Although increasing migration is readily evident, it is also true that many campesino families are reducing their expectations for rising beyond the subsistence level and are trying to survive through basic self-provisioning outside the market economy. If the levels of Pronasol and multilateral funding for rural areas decline, as they are likely to do, it is likely that malnutrition and hunger in the countryside will become more pervasive.

Campesino organizations have not been passive observers of this restructuring of the agricultural economy and the end of agrarian reform. Although there is a widely shared belief that more lands that are now uncultivated or part of large ranches should be redistributed, there is also an increasing recognition that improved agricultural productivity, more well-informed participation in the market, and diversification are the keys to progress.

However, those campesino organizations that have attempted to take firmer control over the production process in line with the market-oriented policies of the government have found that the withdrawal of state services and adverse market conditions make turning a profit all but impossible. Not only have these production-oriented campesino organizations found themselves alone in the market without adequate credit, infrastructure, and technology assistance, but they have also found themselves responsible for caring for the basic needs of their members as the government has cut back its own social services.

Although broader economic and political conditions are chiefly responsible for the tragic circumstances facing most campesino families, there are also problems on the individual and community levels that need to be addressed. These problems include the marginalization of women and children, lack of family planning, dependent behavior, and the discarding of communitarian traditions. Similarly, it must be recognized that creation of new *minifundios* is not the solution of the rural crisis of landlessness. Inefficient smallholdings should be consolidated, preferably under the management of community enterprises that can take advantage of the economies of scale while avoiding the pitfalls of uneven community development. A hopeful sign is that campesino groups have become increasingly aware of the need to promote sustainable agriculture practices, while the use of natural fertilizers, better soil conservation, and increased land-use planning has given new life to some campesino communities.

The challenge facing the organized peasantry and government policy makers is to tap the traditional strengths of campesino society and economy without turning away from the need to increase efficiency and productivity. Simply because campesino producers may not be competitive with highly capitalized growers does not mean that they cannot be more competitive with appropriate government support or that they have no place in Mexico's development strategy. Moral values, communal organization, ethic of hard work, democratic structures, farming skills, and experience with production and marketing cooperatives are not to be ignored in the search for modernization and progress.

Liberalizing Markets

There is a saying that markets are good servants but poor masters. In the Mexican countryside, the market has become the new master—not just the local, regional, or national market, but primarily the international one. There are many tangible benefits of liberalized trade, such as cheaper manufactured goods and food products, although few of those reach the isolated *campo*. Opening up markets allows prices to respond better to supply and demand while encouraging producers to make cropping decisions based on competitiveness and comparative advantage. Rather than protecting the inefficient production of staple goods, it is argued that Mexico will do better by increasing agroexports and opening its economy to trade and investment. With the increased foreign exchange that results, Mexico can buy cheap foodstuffs. If international supplies shrink and prices rise above the costs of domestic production, Mexican farmers can always switch back to producing more basic foods.

The liberalization of domestic and international trade make good economic sense, according to the neoliberal logic. By importing cheaper food, Mexico directly benefits from the subsidies offered by foreign governments and the higher productivity of foreign farmers. National savings result because the imported food is less expensive. The government also saves because it no longer is required to subsidize the difference between high production costs (relative to the international market) and low consumer prices. International competition forces farmers to become more productive, to switch to more profitable crops, or to drop out of the market. Furthermore, market deregulation will attract new capital to a sector that suffers from the lack of productive investment.

Neoliberal technocrats in the Mexican government have pushed reliance on the free market as the country's best development alternative. Yet it is also important to recognize that there is a strong measure of sympathy even among the peasantry for policies that reduce the involvement of corrupt and inefficient state institutions in the nation's economic life. Markets and international trade that are less protected clearly can have a constructive role in solving Mexico's production and consumption problems, although the limits to market solutions must also be recognized.

Applying market solutions across the board does not necessarily lead to free markets. It is certainly true that the forces of globalization are opening up markets around the world. But as NAFTA made abundantly clear, trade remains regulated, managed, and shaped by corporations and national governments. Neoliberalism falls short in explaining how real markets work, as did the classical liberalism on which it is based. Although it is universally the case that markets are imperfect, it is particularly evident in rural areas, which are more controlled than freely responding to supply and demand. The withdrawal of state regulation and institutions from rural markets will not result in free markets but ones in which a small circle of oligopolists, *caciques*, moneylenders, and *coyotes* hold sway. Although the state is not perfect or impartial itself, its capacity to moderate market distortions that leave people without food and growers subject to exploitative practices should not be so easily dismissed. In the Mexican countryside, the free market that neoliberalism envisions is more ideology than reality.

Not only are markets becoming the masters of economic development, but the ideology of the market has become dominant. It is an ideology that pushes aside such other considerations as the importance of maintaining cultural pluralism, the responsibility of the government to ensure that basic needs are met, and the need to find a place for those who increasingly find no productive place in the international market.

Internationalization of Agriculture

The farm crisis in Mexico and questions about the state's relationship to the peasantry take place within the broader context of the globalization of agricultural trade. Mexico can benefit from agricultural internationalization in the form of increased investment in agroexport production and agroindustry. But food-deficit nations like Mexico can become dangerously dependent on surplus grains from the United States and other food-surplus nations, undermining the nation's capacity to meet the nation's food needs, particularly in times of drought, high international prices, or scarce international supplies.

With their control of markets, technology, and capital, transnational corporations skew trade, making it especially difficult for small producers to find a profitable niche in the global market. Close integration with the international market largely precludes a role for the government to pursue development strategies aimed at expanding the domestic market, ensuring jobs for those workers or producers whose productivity falls below global standards, and guaranteeing that most food needs are met by national production.

The comparative advantages offered by natural resources, climate, and wage levels do open some new export possibilities in a liberalized international market. But these are often undermined by the declining terms of trade for agricultural commodities, the global competition to meet the limited and shrinking demand in the industrial world for tropical commodities, the threat of product substitution, and the lack of competitiveness resulting from technological backwardness and reduced government support.

A rising concern is that advances in biotechnology developed for temperate climates will undermine the comparative advantages enjoyed by Mexico and make agricultural production even more dependent on imported seeds and agricultural technology. Another danger is that food production for the global supermarket targets consumers with large disposable incomes and stimulates desires for products like snack foods that lead to higher incidence of malnutrition, especially among the poor.

The internationalization of agriculture is not a trend that can be reversed by government policy. Instead, the challenge facing Mexico and other less-industrialized nations is to chart out food policies that recognize the irreversibility of economic integration but at the same time guarantee a certain level of autonomy for the government. Autonomy is needed to protect and to support sectors of the farm economy and elements of its food policy deemed critical to national economic and social welfare.

State Intervention

Corruption, inefficiency, and self-serving bureaucracies have created a popular base in Mexico for proposals to reduce state involvement in economic life and give more freedom to nongovernment actors in the economy. The great irony is that it has been the PRI government itself that has pushed forward the neoliberal agenda of privatization, liberalization, and deregulation.

But more than just an ideological turn toward the right and away from the historic populism and nationalism of the Mexican government, the current emphasis on the primacy of market forces is a reflection of the forces of global economic integration. To guarantee access to international capital and markets, especially those of the United States, the Mexican government has been forced to back away from state-managed capitalism and its traditional role as arbiter of class relations.

This change has been particularly evident in the farm economy, which has been sent into a state of shock by all the abrupt changes resulting from decreased government intervention. The end of guarantee prices, land distribution, subsidized credit and inputs, and marketing assistance has set the farm sectors—both large and small—reeling.

Mexico's involvement in the farm sector had its origins in the revolution's agrarian and populist traditions. But in the 1940-70 period the state's agrarian programs were largely overshadowed by the government's efforts to boost the large farm sector through input subsidies and infrastructure creation, most notably the extensive irrigation projects in the Northwest. In the 1970s and early 1980s another layer of state involvement was added with the establishment of state intermediary institutions designed to make the production and consumption of basic foods less vulnerable to the profiteering and speculation of private intermediaries.

Food security and rural development programs, which require a high degree of state planning and intervention, run contrary to the logic of the marketplace. The National Food Program was the first to fall. The economic withdrawal of the government also resulted in cutbacks or elimination of state marketing agencies, credit and insurance agencies, and commodity distribution services. The result has been the disintegration of one of the most advanced food production and distribution systems in the less-industrialized world.

But small growers and low-income consumers have not been the only ones impacted by reduced state intervention in the agricultural economy. In fact, medium- and large-scale growers had disproportionately benefited from guarantee prices, cheap credit, and input subsidies. Perhaps more than any other sector, a country's food production and distribution sector can only function well with some degree of government involvement. Only state regulation can overcome production and distribution shortfalls and inequities that stem from: 1) the highly imperfect nature of the agricultural economy resulting from lack of equal market access, 2) risks of weather (floods, drought, plagues, etc.), 3) seasonal character of production, and 4) inadequate purchasing power.

There is widespread agreement that too extensive state involvement spawns inefficiency and dependency. But poor and rich countries alike have found the need for a strong government presence in the agricultural and food economy. Few nations have been willing to sacrifice totally their capacity to produce basic foodstuffs in the interests of further global economic integration and economic efficiency. At the very least, most governments have found the need for agencies that provide the following services: establishing food reserves to protect against seasonal variations in supplies and prices, providing credit, guaranteeing that poorer citizens have access to basic foodstuffs, preventing commodity speculation, and ensure that natural disasters do not completely ruin the farm sector. Some government role in regulating the cross-border flow of agricultural commodities may also be needed to ensure that sudden increases in inexpensive imports do not ruin part of the national farm economy.

The outright rejection of state involvement in the agricultural economy is not practical in Mexico. Even advocates of free trade and the free market recognize the need for the state to soften the impact of market adjustments. But more than handouts to ease the transition and delay its full impact, there is a need for state training, extension, market information, and technological assistance programs that boost the productivity and competitiveness of all sectors of Mexico's weak farm economy.

To ensure that these programs are effective, they need to be closely coordinated with farm communities and organizations, especially those of the less-privileged classes. Farmer groups, including the National Union of Autonomous Regional Campesino Organizations (UNORCA) and the National Network of Coffee Growers Organization (CNOC), have already demonstrated their eagerness and their capability for such a task.

Social Liberalism

Even the most ardent free market advocates usually acknowledge that nonmarket strategies are needed, at least in the short term. Government intervention is needed to ease the transition to a free market, free trade economy. Because the benefits of neoliberal reform do not come immediately, the government needs to address the likely social consequences of restructuring. By satisfying some of the basic needs of the population hit hardest by economic stabilization and structural adjustment, these programs aim to forestall political unrest and maintain support for the government.

In Mexico, this adjunct to neoliberalism is known as social liberalism. The National Solidarity Program (Pronasol), launched by President Salinas, serves as the flagship agency for the government's social liberalism. This more human side of neoliberalism has also manifested itself in the government's nutrition programs and its subsidy program for grain farmers (Procampo).[2]

At a time when the government was lifting its protections and eliminating input subsidies and soft credit for farmers, it opened up new channels of support for the peasantry, offering credit through Pronasol and direct income support through Procampo. Neither program was designed to boost productivity or to address seriously the rural development crisis. Rather, they served only to take the edge off the crisis while at the same time giving the peasantry reason to maintain its support of the PRI.

Not only did the Mexican government succeed in better targeting its social funding in ways that reached the poorest of the poor, but it also managed to minimize political opposition to its neoliberal restructuring in most parts of the country while also minimizing opposition within the ruling party to the Salinas-led modernization.[3] The social liberalism of the PRI technocrats was paralleled and financed in part by multilateral funding from the World Bank. Along with stabilization and structural adjustment programs, the World Bank has promoted basic needs programs throughout Latin America that target those likely to be most gravely impacted by changing economic policy. In Mexico, the World Bank has supported Pronasol, which it regards as one of the world's most successful "social investment funds," backed targeted feeding programs, and sponsored poverty-alleviation efforts in southeastern Mexico.

Just as the World Bank played a central role in the restructuring of the agricultural sector, it also was a major figure in overhauling Mexico's nutrition policy. In 1990 the recommendations of a World Bank study calling for a more targeted food program were adopted by the Salinas government.[4] Over the years the Mexican government has attempted to target the poorest of the poor with food handouts and food coupons, replacing more generalized food subsidies that benefited all sectors.[5] Neither the government's social liberalism nor the World Bank's social funding for rural Mexico is driven by a development objective. Long-term solutions to the problems of food production, job creation for displaced campesinos, and rural stagnation are left to the international market.

For all the shortcomings, misplaced objectives, and political manipulation associated with the Pronasol program, there have been a number of positive contributions of Mexico's social liberalism that point to positive new directions for the state's food and farm policy. Although the government should give a higher priority to supporting production-oriented alternatives that form part of a more comprehensive rural development strategy, there is a need for government social intervention that provides a buffer against the destructive impacts of changing patterns of production and marketing.

Although support for the campesino economy is not a main focus, Pronasol has provided important resources to innovative campesino production, processing, and marketing initiatives, such as those of the coffee growers. Some funding for *empresas sociales* (social enterprises) has pointed to the potential of a more positive, less paternalistic relationship between the government and autonomous campesino organizations, although also creating the danger of neopaternalistic structures. Efforts to decentralize government social funding, to target resources more efficiently, and to establish pluralized relations with popular organizations have also proved largely positive.

Exports and Food Production

No contradiction necessarily exists between agroexport and domestic market production. Mexico needs both, but establishing a good balance between the two is a difficult challenge. It means evaluating the best use of natural resources and state revenues and assessing the different economic and welfare benefits of the two sectors. Ideally, a country could maximize its agroexport potential without seriously cutting into its domestic food production. Export cropping and food cropping can be, and should be, complementary.[6]

Agroexports bring in foreign exchange, while the production of basic foodstuffs requires higher prices or subsidies from the government and consumers. However, Mexico's ability to increase agroexports both as a strategy to foster rural development and to pay for food imports depends largely on maintaining substandard wages for farmworkers. The technology gap and the escalating environmental crisis impede the development of an alternative strategy to improve competitiveness based on increased productivity and better access to land and water.

Although agroexports are generally more profitable and are a source of dollars, the impact on the domestic economy of the generated revenues is reduced by the high cost of imported agricultural inputs, the flow of profits out of the country, the high level of mechanization, the low wages paid seasonal farmworkers, the barriers to small-farmer participation, and the limited linkages with the domestic economy. In contrast, basic grain production, particularly corn production by the small-farm sector in Mexico, is highly labor intensive, reduces the need for food imports, has greater linkages with the domestic economy, maintains the integrity of rural communities, benefits from a less elastic market (less subject, at least nationally, to fluctuations in demand), and enables its producers to self-provision.

The main issue that policymakers and farm groups need to consider is to what degree the Mexican economy should be driven by the import-demand of industrial countries, whose growth is slowing while competition to supply these markets is increasing. There may be substantial benefits for a narrow stratum of society that can participate in the modernized farm sectors and benefit from the opportunities offered by the emerging global trading system. But the vast majority of campesinos and even those medium-scale farmers dependent on production of grains for the domestic market are finding they have no viable place in the internationalized agricultural system. Alternatively, even within the new context of internationalized agriculture, Mexico could shape an overall agricultural development policy that was driven more by local market demands. Such a policy would aim to increase effective domestic demand by raising productivity through appropriate technology and by supporting the diversification of the rural economy, including support for cash-crop production and for decentralized processing and manufacturing operations. Such a strategy could not only produce high rates of growth but it would also ensure broader participation.

Self-Sufficiency vs Free Trade

Closely associated with an evaluation of the benefits of basic grain production is the proposition that less-industrialized countries without strong export sectors should strive for a high degree of self-sufficiency in basic foodstuffs. Arguments for greater self-sufficiency run directly contrary to the persuasive logic of free trade since it requires a high degree of state intervention and market protection.

The objective of achieving a high level of self-sufficiency is fourfold: to promote rural development by providing a guaranteed market for basic grains; to protect the nation against sudden market fluctuations that decrease food availability and increase prices; to create effective demand in rural areas; and to bolster national sovereignty by making the nation less vulnerable to political pressure from exporting countries. Even given the validity of these objectives, few would embrace autarchy or complete self-reliance as a credible development strategy. There are simply too many political, economic, technological, and social advantages of economic integration, especially for smaller nations.

The special place of food in the hierarchy of human needs has given rise to policies of self-sufficiency. Most countries, including the wealthiest ones such as the United States, Japan, and members of European Community, have agricultural policies that promote a degree of self-sufficiency in food. Having achieved superior productivity in grain production, the United States is now pushing for more liberalized agricultural trade, but other nations like France and Japan still insist on protecting their farm sectors.

Mexico, backing away from earlier food security programs, has tied the fate of its farm economy and its food distribution to the wisdom of the international market. At a time when grains on the world market are plentiful and inexpensive (a situation that will likely persist in the short and medium terms), Mexico has decided that it does not make good economic sense to support the production of food that is available at lower prices from other countries. Free trade, economic restructuring, and a wave of neoliberal thinking have pushed food security off the policy agenda in Mexico. Yet there is a strong current of resistance from many agricultural specialists who feel that boosting the national production of basic grains, particularly corn, is essential for cultural, political, social, and economic reasons.[7]

The reasons to support full or selective self-sufficiency stem primarily from social, political, and security considerations. But a number of analysts have offered economic rationales that make the costs of food self-sufficiency in food grains seem less formidable. The challenge facing economic policymakers the world over is to maximize the efficient use of available resources. Free market proponents argue that private-sector decisions will perform this task best.

Yet in an economy marked by high levels of unemployment and underemployment, there is obviously a large waste of human potential. In such an economy, the free market conclusion that displaced workers (such as farmers and hired hands) will find more productive work elsewhere is highly questionable. The real choice in Mexico for the foreseeable future is not between farming and other productive activities, but between farming and even more marginal activities.

One possibility is a policy of selected self-sufficiency based on social, cultural, environmental, and economic considerations. Such a policy would designate certain foods as deserving special protections. One consideration is the elasticity in demand for a commodity. There is a constant demand for corn, which cannot be easily substituted for, but meat has a higher elasticity in the Mexican diet. Another important factor is whether farmers can quickly convert to crops whose prices and availability may shift suddenly. Mexico could, for example, easily increase wheat production but would have a more difficult time increasing milk production because of the lead time needed to increase herds and production facilities.[8]

But the conversion factor may not be the only relevant consideration in a country like Mexico in which so large a portion of the population depends on corn production for basic nutrition. Mexico could determine that the production of corn on rainfed lands deserves special consideration because maize production is so important to the peasantry's survival and to the social and cultural pluralism of the country. Under such a policy, the importation of most grains would be liberalized given that they are readily available for better prices on foreign markets. But corn production would receive continued protection either until Mexico could become competitive (unlikely given the low productivity of campesino cultivation) or until sufficient job opportunities could be created elsewhere in the economy.

In the context of NAFTA, the long-term possibilities of self-sufficiency in food grains are slight. Mexico could decide to move toward agricultural prices more in line with the international market but support local production with direct income subsidies to farmers. Nominally, it has done just this with its Procampo program. But the income payments fall far short of what would be needed to cover the differential between production costs and international prices for most basic grains. Alternatively, Mexico could maintain high guarantee prices to cover domestic production costs for part of the phase-out period of NAFTA's tariff rate quotas. Both policies would be expensive for the government to maintain. Only in the event that international prices increased or supplies dropped dramatically might such polices be economically feasible.

Under free trade, self-sufficiency policies of grain-deficit countries like Mexico are effectively excluded from the range of development options. Free trade locks in policies that facilitate the internationalization of agriculture: the main winners of free trade are corporate agribusiness, and the main losers are small farmers.

Campesino-Oriented Development

To satisfy its basic food needs, Mexico could (1) rely on imports to cover shortfalls, (2) increase production by commercial-level farmers, or (3) increase production by the peasantry. Historically, the agrarian reform and colonization programs have maintained a large campesino base that has provided about 70 percent of the nation's corn and beans.

There is little doubt that Mexico enjoys the capacity to become self-sufficient in basic grains. Higher corn prices offered during the SAM program in the early 1980s and the decision by the government in the early 1990s to maintain corn guarantee prices while eliminating guarantees for other grains led to a boom in corn production, especially by commercial growers. As a result, corn imports plummeted.

With sufficient protections, price levels, and subsidies, Mexico's medium- and large-scale growers could likely satisfy the country's demand for other basic grains as well, especially if more land were incorporated into irrigation projects and productivity levels increased. Corn yields could easily double or triple on rainfed lands and increase 75 percent on irrigated lands with the proper technical assistance. More government assistance to improve production, warehousing, and processing technology could increase the competitiveness of Mexican agribusiness in the international market. But the cost to the government of subsidies and guarantee prices combined with the opportunity cost of having commercial-scale producers cultivate basic grains rather than agroexports would be extremely high. Such a strategy to improve self-sufficiency would improve the country's agricultural trade balance, but the concentrated and capital-intensive character of production would mean that problems of rural unemployment and economic desperation would remain unsolved.

Another possibility would be what some have called a "peasant-oriented" or "agrarian wage" solution to the problems of food security and economic development in Mexico.[9] Rather than focusing state attention on improving the capabilities of commercial growers by extending irrigation systems and technical assistance, the government would concentrate on improving the productivity and welfare of the small farm sector.[10]

Through a targeted system of direct subsidies, technical outreach, credit, and guarantee prices, the government would encourage increased corn and bean production on rainfed lands by campesinos. Although expensive, such a development program would have a number of advantages over expanded commercial production of basic grains. It would provide more employment because of the labor-intensive production practices of the peasantry, slow rural-to-urban migration flows, and give greater stimulus to the domestic economy because increased campesino income would translate immediately into greater consumer spending.

According to some proponents of such a strategy for Mexico, corn imports could be easily substituted by production on uncultivated drylands, giving jobs to as many as 750,000 campesinos. At the same time, corn production on irrigated land would be discouraged and agroexport production encouraged.[11]

But a campesino-oriented strategy would require extraordinary political will by the government. The Cardenista state/campesino alliance of the 1930s would have to be renewed to counter increasing resistance from large agribusiness. Moreover, a campesino-oriented development strategy would mean a break with free trade, thereby threatening Mexico's place in the integrated regional and global economy.

Unless combined with a plan to increase urban wages and keep food prices low, such a strategy would also increase rural-urban tensions. If not carefully coordinated, an effort to increase production by the peasantry could increase environmental degradation as uncultivated land was brought into production. Another danger of any rural development strategy that increased state intervention in campesino agriculture is that it would further corporate control by the ruling political party while deepening a dependency mentality among the peasantry. Mexico's campesinos would remain "the chosen children of the regime," rather than becoming mature participants in an evolving economy. Similarly, a strategy whose central element was campesino production of corn and beans would risk propagating the *"hombre de maíz"* (man of corn) prototype of the Mexican campesino. Although there are many good reasons why campesinos cling to traditional cultivation patterns, their survival as independent producers will increasingly depend on diversifying production into more profitable cash crops and on adopting more appropriate farming practices and technology.

To be successful, a campesino-oriented development strategy will need to update and revise the *hombre de maíz* image. Campesino organizations in Mexico have already taken important steps in this direction by demanding that they have a role in formulating and implementing agricultural policy.[12] Campesinos do not want to be dependents of state agencies. They want to be productive farmers who meet the nation's food needs and also export into the world market, but they recognize that they will need access to the same kind of government agricultural services that are offered to farmers in the industrial world. If given access to credit, technical assistance, and a profitable market, representatives of Mexico's new campesino movements contend that small farmers will act in profit-maximizing ways and become increasingly productive.

Adapting to the international market and adopting new appropriate technologies are among the tasks facing the evolving Mexican peasantry. Yet the new *hombre de maíz* will also have to incorporate traditional strengths that have been worn down by the penetration of capitalist relations in the countryside. Foremost among these is the recognition of the importance of working together as communities and organizations. Only in the rare case will the individual campesino or family be able to succeed in the market without the support of a cooperative production or marketing organization. Communitarian practices, a sense of reciprocity, a respect for communal lands, and the democratic character of village assemblies are all traditional traits that will enhance a renovated system of campesino production.[13]

Rethinking Development

Broadly conceived, Mexico's food production and distribution problems are symptoms of the country's development crisis. In concert with foreign donors, government policymakers have chosen neoliberal remedies to solve the stagnation of Mexican agriculture and the plight of the peasantry. But if these policies fail to attract investment to the agricultural sector, boost agroexports, and provide jobs to displaced campesinos, then these policies may have to be revised.

Such issues go to the heart of the development debate that is taking place not only in Mexico but throughout the nonindustrialized world. Increasingly this debate is also stirring within development institutions like the U.S. Agency for International Development and even to a certain extent within the World Bank. Although trade liberalization and deregulation can lead to greater efficiency of production on a global scale, they do not necessarily lead to broad development.

In the end, whether the choice is free trade or more inward-looking economic policies or some amalgam, countries like Mexico with a large campesino population will have to find ways to productively employ the large number of these currently noncompetitive producers. These jobs can either be in industry, agroexport production by agribusiness, or diversified production by a vibrant small farm sector. Otherwise, unemployment and migration from the countryside will increase. If such an increase occurs, the country will be faced with the challenge of providing for the basic food needs of and pacifying an expanding rural and urban underclass of Mexicans who have no productive place in the formal economy.

In the process of rethinking the economics and politics of development, it is now widely accepted that development has to be sustainable, meaning that immediate development practices should not preclude future development by depleting natural resources. There is, however, sharp disagreement about whether sustainable development implies a radical redefinition of what we mean by economic development and economic progress or if it merely means increased attention to environmental protection and conservation. In either case, a commitment to sustainable development points to some of the failings of free trade and the neoliberal overhaul of agriculture.

A more liberalized climate for global investment and trade without an accompanying set of standards to ensure food security, biodiversity, ecological security, and democracy may be the best path for sustaining the profit levels of the transnational food corporations and the food-surplus nations. But such a policy is unlikely to result in anything that can remotely be characterized as environmentally sustainable development. Among the characteristics of a more sustainable system of agricultural development would include:

* More concern with meeting the agricultural and livelihood needs of smallholders, who comprise the vast majority of Mexico's farmers.

* Attention to local land-use planning and economic development that recognizes the heterogeneous character of the farming community.

* Recognition of the harm that cheap food policies (either because of low guarantee prices or the availability of imported surplus grains) cause the rural economy.

* A better balance between agricultural and industrial development strategies that does not make the mistake of trying to imitate the capital-intensive, energy-intensive, and environmentally destructive patterns of development of more industrialized nations.

* Planning that reduces the unsustainable rural/urban split by promoting increased agricultural production, food processing, and small-scale manufacturing in rural communities.

* Recognition of the essential role of campesino communities in preserving biodiversity and natural resources.

* A more equitable sharing of the benefits of economic progress among those who currently exist on the margins of economic growth, such as women, children, and farmworkers.

* A better appreciation of the sustainable character of small-scale production and the promotion of appropriate farm technology.

* Active participation of farm groups in policymaking and economic planning as one of the best ways to ensure the integrity of rural communities and the preservation of local environments.

For agricultural development to be sustainable, it has to be people-centered, respectful of the environment, and responsive to local needs—objectives that will be undermined by blind obedience to the forces of supply and demand. With the term *sustainable development* having been increasingly appropriated by those who see free trade as the best way to ensure economic growth and by companies eager to sell the latest in pollution-control technology, it is important to stress the contradictions between traditional concepts of development and what is environmentally sustainable. At the same time, however, the need for social and productive investment to improve the socioeconomic circumstances of the poor and to reverse North-South inequities cannot be ignored.

There is a danger of being overly romantic about traditional agricultural communities. There is no glorifying cultivation by the hoe and planting sticks. And there is no denying the fact that a U.S. farmer can produce about fifteen times as much corn in a day as the average Mexican farmer, or that the indians working the eroded lands of the Altos of Chiapas are ten times less productive than the average Mexican corn grower. Self-exploitation or the exploitation of family labor can not be regarded as a solid foundation for sustainable development.[14]

Increased productivity based on new research and technology does not necessarily contradict the principles of sustainable development. With adequate support and with the freedom to organize, campesinos have demonstrated a remarkable ability not only to sustain themselves but to diversify production, adapt new technologies, and explore new forms of productive organization.

Elements of a New Equilibrium

Since the early 1980s, not just in Mexico but throughout the "developing" world, the politics of economic stabilization and restructuring have prevailed over those of sectoral economic development, poverty-alleviation, and extension of social services. Projects that promoted integrated rural development and promoted food production gave way to macroeconomic policy reform shaped by neoliberal convictions. Market-oriented price incentives, deregulation, privatization, and state minimalism shaped the new political economy.[15] This restructuring conveniently paved the way for the free trade agenda of trade and investment liberalization pursued by transnational economic actors and the leading industrial governments.

These reforms, while moderately successful in stabilizing economies and eliminating inefficiencies resulting from excessive state economic interventions, have been narrowly focused on fiscal, monetary, and exchange policies. The result has been the crisis of the 1990s, brought on by reduced state attention to economic and social infrastructure, basic needs, and industrial and agricultural production. In addition to the problems of deteriorating infrastructure, socioeconomic conditions, and domestic productive capacity, Mexico faces severe employment and environmental crises. While regional economic integration may provide some relief in the form of new export opportunities, cheaper food, and increased foreign investment, it holds little promise of reversing the country's development crisis.

Dependence on multilateral funding and foreign investment flows and Mexico's adherence to the liberalized trading rules of GATT and NAFTA limit its policy options for addressing the development crisis of the 1990s. But it is becoming increasingly clear that a new equilibrium needs to be established between state and markets and that organized civil society should play a critical role in creating this new balance. In Mexico, grassroots groups of consumers and producers have shown a remarkable capacity to fill in where both the state and the market have fallen short. As the state deregulated, new coalitions of campesino producers have moved in to "appropriate the production process," create alternative credit institutions, and forge innovating marketing strategies.

Outside the formal market, Mexicans have created thousands of microenterprises and have come together as communities in mutual assistance organizations. The community food councils that emerged to distribute food to remote rural villages demonstrated the remarkable capacity of many campesino communities to find solutions to common food supply and distribution problems. A proliferation of grassroots organizations are addressing such diverse problems as the lack of adequate land-use planning, human rights abuses, the absence of democratic local governments, housing shortages, and the need for new community-based economic development projects.

Mexico's *mestizo* peasantry and indigenous population are rejecting the paternalism, corruption, and clientelism of state tutelage. At the same time, there is a recognition of the need for a state that can provide poor consumers and growers with a buffer against food and farm markets that leave them hungry and desperate. Neoliberal reforms have dramatically reduced the state's protective capacity and have left the farm sector without the infrastructure, credit, technical assistance, and inputs it needs to produce for the market. In the wake of the single-minded deregulation and privatization of the De la Madrid and especially Salinas administrations, the need for a developmental state remains in Mexico.

More public-sector investment in rural Mexico is necessary to provide employment and to create the infrastructure that can make the farm sector more competitive. Similarly, improved state services are essential, especially in education, to ensure that basic needs are met and to improve the productive capacity of Mexico's farmers and workers. Unlike in the past, the developmental state, to be most effective, has to listen to market signals and the voice of organized civil society. Without the participation and monitoring of nongovernmental actors, state programs will be ineffective and state officials unaccountable. The active involvement of organized producers and consumers will be the best insurance that a new complementarity of state, market, and civil society serves the interests of democracy and development.[16]

The formulation of new food and farm policies would be an appropriate starting point to pursue a new strategy of sustainable development.[17] Just as targeted food subsidies and programs to address differing rural and urban needs help make a national food policy more effective, an effective agricultural policy should recognize the heterogeneity of the farm sector.

The polarized structure of the farm community creates the need for differentiated responses. Equal policies for unequal sectors would be a recipe for failure. Targeted support to increase the productivity of those sectors that are potentially the most competitive in the new world trading order should not mean that other sectors are ignored. Not only do different classes of producers have varying needs, so do different regions, especially in terms of the environmental sustainability of different methods of production.

Although the objective of a renovated farm policy would be to increase the productivity of all classes of growers, it would be misdirected to assume that, even with the proper government assistance and support for self-organization, the subsistence and infrasubsistence peasantry will eventually find a niche in the world trading system. Campesino-based food production systems are probably structurally incapable of being competitive in the world market or providing the same standards of living enjoyed by those created by modern (unsustainable) agribusiness.

Nonetheless, until the economy can provide other productive employment, the peasantry merits government support in its attempts to diversify production and increase self-provisioning. Without such a targeted farm policy that benefits the peasantry, Mexico faces accelerating urbanization, disintegration of rural society, and loss of cultural diversity.

The cost of a developmentalist farm policy can be covered at least in part by the revenues saved by better targeted food programs and reduced state subsidies resulting from liberalized trade. The institution of more progressive tax policies among other redistributive economic policies can also help support government measures aimed to rejuvenate Mexican agriculture.

Zapata's Bequest

Emiliano Zapata was at the heart of the violent political unrest of Mexico's revolutionary period, but it was largely because of the struggle of the *zapatistas* that Mexico recognized the need to establish social pacts with its peasantry. The country's agrarian reform program and a history of alliances between government reformists and rural organizers contributed substantially to Mexico's political stability and economic growth.

With the old social pacts having been exhausted and the limits of agrarian politics widely recognized, Mexico now needs to forge new popular alliances that will ensure future political stability and economic development. Clearly, the paternalism, dependency, corruption, inefficiency, strident nationalism, manipulative populism, and environmental carelessness of the past should be left behind. At the same time, however, there remains the need, perhaps more than ever, for policies that establish national development priorities, protect the economically weak, and direct special attention to the needs of peasantry. But such policies cannot be dictated; they need to be shaped democratically with a *campesinado* that over time has demonstrated its perseverance, flexibility, and determination.

Mexico cannot escape its rural origins and impoverished conditions by turning its back on the people of the land. Nor can the spirit of Zapata be exorcised with an incantation of free trade and neoliberalism. Instead, that legacy of agrarian justice, democratic community, and heroic struggle should help guide an economic and political future for Mexico that is just and sustainable.

NOTES

Introduction

1. Phrasing from Marilyn Gates, *In Default: Peasants, the Debt Crisis, and the Agricultural Challenge* (Boulder, CO: Westview Press, 1993), 107.

One

1. James O'Connor, *The Fiscal Crisis of the State* (New York: St. Martin's Press, 1973), 6. Although focusing on the United States, O'Connor's description of the "two basic and often mutually contradictory functions [of government]—accumulation and legitimation" are seen clearly in Mexico.

2. *Encuesta nacional agropecuaria ejidal, 1988* (Aguascalientes, INEGI, 1990)

3. Steven Sanderson, *Agrarian Populism and the Mexican State* (Berkeley: University of California Press, 1981), 211.

4. Ibid., Chapter 3.

5. At least 38 million hectares were distributed to *hacendados* and survey companies during the *Porfiriato*. Ibid., 38-39.

6. Ibid. Baja California was the major exception to the generalized condition of landlessness in Mexico in the prerevolutionary period.

7. Charles Cumberland, *Mexico: The Struggle for Modernity* (New York: Oxford University Press, 1968), 204.

8. Gerardo Otero, "Agrarian Reform in Mexico: Capitalism and the State," in William C. Thiesenhusen, ed., *Searching for Agrarian Reform in Latin America* (Boston: Unwin Hyman, 1989), 278.

9. Adolfo Gilly, *La revolución interrumpida* (Mexico City: Editorial el Caballito, 1974), 21.

10. Sanderson, *Agrarian Populism*, 41.

11. A good source on the history and influence of the Liberal movement is Jesús Reyes Heroles, *El liberalismo mexicano* (Mexico City: Fondo de Cultura Económica, 1961).

12. Sanderson, *Agrarian Populism*, 62; and Frank Tannenbaum, *The Mexican Agrarian Revolution* (Washington: Brookings Institution, 1929). There have been various

interpretations of the 1915 decree, some concluding (like Tannenbaum) that it set the foundation for Article 27 and the agrarian reform program that followed while others (like Sanderson) emphasizing the commitment of Carranza and the other Constitutionalists to private property.

13. There are various interpretations of Article 27. Some analysts assert that the land reform clause represented a clear victory for the progressives while others regard it as a compromise measure that satisfied neither the socialists nor the *zapatistas*. It is generally agreed that Article 27 and Article 123 (which guaranteed labor rights) were regarded as paper reforms to win the support of the progressives but with which the postrevolutionary elite never intended fully to comply.

14. The categories of farm land were clearly defined in the founding principles of the National Revolutionary Party (the predecessor of the PRI) in 1929. Jesús Silva Herzog, *El agrarismo mexicano y la reforma agraria* (Mexico City: Fondo de Cultura Económica, 1967), 46.

15. Adolfo Gilly, *The Interrupted Revolution* (London: Verso, 1980), 33.

16. Although he supported another candidate, Calles did not oppose the party convention's nomination of Cárdenas. But soon after beginning his campaign Cárdenas distanced himself from the Jefe Máximo and became convinced that his power as president would come more from popular support of peasants and workers than from the narrow political and economic elites.

17. Corporatism refers to a network of state-structured social organizations that contribute to the political stability of the ruling party.

18. Cynthia Hewitt de Alcántara, *Modernizing Mexican Agriculture: Socioeconomic Implications of Technological Change, 1940-1970* (Geneva: UNRISD, 1976), 4.

19. Jonathan Fox, *The Politics of Food in Mexico: State Power and State Mobilization* (Ithaca, NY: Cornell University Press, 1993).

20. The ruling party's name changed again in 1946 to the Partido Revolucionario Institucional (PRI).

21 An excellent study of the Cárdenas era and its "progressive alliance" is found in Nora Hamilton, *The Limits of State Autonomy: Post-Revolutionary Mexico* (Princeton: Princeton University Press, 1982).

22. Along with his agrarian populism, the other major element of the reformist legacy of Cárdenas was his nationalism, as demonstrated by his expropriation of the British and U.S. oil industry in 1938.

23. This conservative trend was evident even before Cárdenas left the presidency. Economic stagnation and accumulating rightist and foreign pressure obligated Cárdenas to reign in the popular sectors, whose militancy had previously been supported by the government, in the interests of consolidating the economy. See Sanderson, *Agrarian Populism* and Hamilton, *Limits of State Autonomy*.

24. The gap between ideology and practice in Mexico is examined in John J. Bailey, *Governing Mexico: The Statecraft of Crisis Management* (New York: St. Martin's Press, 1988).

25. Industrialization in Mexico meant import-substituting manufacturing in which Mexican industries (or foreign corporations investing in Mexico) produced consumer and intermediate goods for the domestic market. Its main weaknesses as a development strategy were the heavy dependence on imported capital goods, the limited domestic market, and the inefficiency resulting from high tariff barriers to competitive imports.

26. One indicator of this capital transfer was apparent in the banking system, which received 19 percent of its financial resources from the agricultural sector from 1942 to 1962 but returned only 12 percent to the sector during this period. Centro de Investigaciones Agrarias (CIDA), Empleo, *Estructura agraria y desarrollo agricola en México* (Mexico City: Fondo de Cultura Económica, 1974), 181.

27. The authoritative source on agricultural development in the 1940-70 period is Hewitt de Alcántara, *Modernizing Mexican Agriculture*. Other good sources include CEPAL, *Economia Campesina y Agricultura Empresarial* (Mexico City: Siglo Veintiuno Editores, 1982) and Merilee S. Grindle, *State and Countryside* (Baltimore: Johns Hopkins University Press, 1986).

28. This cheap food/cheap labor analysis comes from Alain de Janvry, The *Agrarian Question and Reformism in Latin America* (Baltimore: Johns Hopkins University Press, 1981).

29. The term *Green Revolution* was coined by William S. Gaud, a director of the U.S. Agency for International Development (AID).

30. One of the earliest criticisms of the negative impact and narrow focus of the Green Revolution was a hardhitting article by Nicholas Wade, "Green Revolution (I): A Just Technology, Often Unjust in Use," *Science* (786), September 20, 1974.

31. Hewitt de Alcántara, *La modernización de la agricultura mexicana* (Mexico City: Siglo Veintiuno Editores, 1978), 23.

32. Ibid., 26.

33. Hewitt de Alcántara, *Modernizing Mexican Agriculture*, 309.

34. David Barkin and Billie DeWalt, "Sorghum and the Mexican Food Crisis," *Latin American Research Review* 13(3), 1988; David Barkin, Rosemary L. Batt, and Billie R. DeWalt, *Food Crops vs. Feed Crops: The Global Substitution of Grains in Production* (Boulder: Lynne Reiner Publications, 1990).

35. Grindle, *State and Countryside*, 93.

36. Ibid.

37. John Womack, Jr., *Zapata and the Mexican Revolution* (New York: Random House, 1968), ix.

Two

1. Observations about the "pendulum effect" in Mexican politics are found in Dale Story, "Policy Cycles in Mexican Politics," *Latin American Research Review* 3, 1985; Steven Sanderson, "Presidential Succession and Political Rationality in Mexico," *World Politics* 35, April 1983; Susan Kaufman Purcell and John Purcell, "State and Society in Mexico: Must a Stable Polity Be Institutionalized?" *World Politics* 32(2), 1980; and Wayne Cornelius and Ann Craig, *Politics in Mexico: An Introduction and Overview* (San Diego: Center for U.S.-Mexican Studies, 1988). Cornelius and Craig categorize Calles, Alemán, Díaz Ordaz, and De la Madrid as conservatives; Cárdenas, López. Mateos, and Echeverría as progressives or reformists; and Avila Camacho, Ruiz Cortines, and López Portillo as transition figures or consolidators of the status quo.

2. Proyecto de Inversiones Públicas para el Desarrollo Rural (PIDER), established in 1973, coordinated rural development projects. It was the largest World Bank-funded rural deveopment program in the world. Marilyn Gates, "Codifying Marginality: The Evolution of Mexican Agricultural Policy and its Impact on the Peasantry," *Journal of Latin American Studies* 20(2), November 1988.

3. Luis Hernández and Jonathan Fox, *La Union de Ejidos Lázaro Cárdenas* (Mexico City: Cuadernos Desarrollo de Base 1, 1990).

4. Jonathan Fox and Gustavo Gordillo, "Between State and Market: The Campesinos' Quest for Autonomy," in Wayne A. Cornelius, Judith Gentleman, and Peter Smith, eds., *Mexico's Alternative Political Futures* (San Diego: Center for U.S.-Mexican Studies, 1989).

5. Roger Bartra, "Capitalism and the Peasantry in Mexico," *Latin American Perspectives* 9(1), Winter 1982, 36.

6. Magda Fritshcer, *Estado y sector rural en México: 1976-1982* (Mexico City: Universidad Autónoma Metropolitana, 1985).

7. Armando Bartra, *Los heredederos de Zapata: Movimientos campesinos postrevolucionarios en México* (Mexico City: Ediciones Era, 1985), 140.

8. Ibid.

9. For a discussion of the successes and failures of SAM, see Fox, *Politics of Food*, which is especially valuable for its placing of food policy within a wider political and historical context. According to Fox, "The politics of food reflect and refract the most basic tensions in Mexican state and society." Another essential source is James E. Austin and Gustavo Esteva, eds., *Food Policy in Mexico: The Search for Self Sufficiency* (Ithaca, NY: Cornell University Press, 1987).

10. A discussion of the critical role of populist reformists within government in encouraging the formation of autonomous community organizations to facilitate rural food distribution is found in Fox, *Politics of Food*.

11. The 1980 law laid the legal foundation for later ejido reforms by Presidents De la Madrid and Salinas but because of restrictive implementing guidelines it did not have much impact at the time.

12. Rolando Cordera and Carlos Tello, *La disputa por la nación* (Mexico City: Siglo Veintiuno Editores, 1982).

13. Lindajoy Fenley, "Promoting the Pacific Rim," *Business Mexico*, June 1991.

14. Mexico ranked first in the world in nonpoverty lending by the World Bank during the first three years of the Salinas administration. By 1992 it had become the institution's largest overall recipient, with more than $12 billion in outstanding loans.

15. Lynn Salinger and Jean-Jacques Dethier, "Policy-Based Lending in Agriculture: Agricultural Sector Adjustment in Mexico," Paper presented at the World Bank Seminar on Policy-Based Lending in Agriculture, Baltimore, May 17-19, 1989, cited in Philip McMichael and David Myhre, "Global Regulation vs. the Nation-State," *Capital & Class* 43, Spring 1991, 97, 98.

16. Rosario Robles and Julio Moguel, "Agricultura y proyecto neoliberal," *El Cotidiano* 34, March/Apri 1990. The authors demonstrate that shortly after receiving the first agricultural sectoral adjustment loan in 1988 the Mexican government announced a series of privatization and restructuring measures that closely paralleled the World Bank's loan recommendations.

17. Julio Moguel, "Banco Mundial y Pronasol: Un romance difícil," *Cunadernos del CECCAM 1*, July 1993.

18. Cited in David Barkin, "The New Shape of the Countryside: Agrarian Counter-reform in Mexico," Carried on PeaceNet, November 22, 1992.

Three

1. Phrasing from Dan Morgan, *Merchants of Grain* (New York: Viking Press, 1979), 231.

2. James Petras and Howard Brill, "Latin America's Transnational Capitalists and the Debt: A Class-Analysis Perspective," *Development and Change* 19(2), 1988.

3. Edward J. McCaughan, "Mexico's Long Crisis: Toward Regimes of Accumulation and Domination," *Latin American Perspectives* 20(3), Summer 1993.

4. David Barkin, *Distorted Development* (Boulder, CO: Westview Press, 1992).

5. Harriet Friedman, "The Political Economy of Food: A Global Crisis," *New Left Review* (197), 1993.

6. This section on the dimensions of the agrofood system is drawn largely from Laura T. Raynolds, David Myhre, Philip McMichael, Viviana Carro-Figueroa, and Frederick H. Buttel, "The 'New' Internationalization of Agriculture: A Reformulation," *World Development* 21(7). Also see William H. Frieland, Lawrence Busch, Fredrick H. Buttel, and

Alan P. Rudy, eds., *Towards a New Political Economy of Agriculture* (Boulder, CO: Westview Press, 1991).

7. Office of Technology Assessment, *U.S.-Mexico Trade: Pulling Together or Pulling Apart?* (Washington: U.S. Government Printing Office, October 1992), 213. Seasonal agricultural workers in the United States are paid less than workers in any other industry, earning median hourly wages of $4.85 in 1990, with fewer than half covered by unemployment insurance and fewer than a quarter having health insurance.

8. Phrasing from Friedman, "Political Economy of Food."

9. Philip McMichael, "World Food System Restructuring under a GATT Regime," *Political Geography* 12(3), May 1993. At the conclusion of the Uruguay Round, GATT members agreed to establish the World Trade Organization as the new institutional framework to conduct trade negotiations and manage trade disputes.

10. Philip McMichael and David Myhre, "Global Regulation vs. the Nation-State: Agro-Food Systems and the New Politics of Capital," *Capital and Class* 43, Spring 1991.

11. See Harriet Friedmann, "Changes in the International Division of Labor: Agri-food Complexes and Export Agriculture," in Friedland et al., *Towards a New Political Economy of Agriculture*.

12. Jaime Hernández, "Preocupa a investigadores que la nueva ley de patente beneficie sobre todo multinacionales," *El Financiero*, January 7, 1991.

13. Frederick H. Buttel, Martin Kenney, and Jack Kloppenburg, Jr., "From Green Revolution to Biorevolution: Some Observations on the Changing Technological Bases of Economic Transformation in the Third World," *Economic Development and Cultural Change* 34(1), October 1985.

14. See, for example, Miguel Teubal, "Internationalization of Capital and Agroindustrial Complexes: Their Impact on Latin American Agriculture," *Latin American Perspectives* 14(3), Summer 1987; and R. Echeverría Zuno, ed., *Transnacionales, agricultura y alimentación* (Mexico City: Nueva Imágen, 1982).

15. By the late 1970s transnational corporations were present in 27 of the 40 agricultural subsectors and were responsible for more than half of national production in eleven agricultural subsectors. Rosa Elena Montes de Oca, "Las empresas transnacionales en la industria alimentaria mexicana," in Rodolfo Echeverría Zuno, ed., *Transnacionales, agricultura y alimentación* (Mexico City: Colegio Nacional de Economistas and Editorial Nueva Imagen, 1982).

16. Miguel Teubal, "Internationalization of Capital and Agroindustrial Complexes: Their Impact on Latin American Agriculture," *Latin American Perspectives* 14 (3), Summer 1987.

17. Lloyd E. Slater, "U.S. Food Perspective," in Sidney Weintraub, Luis Rubio, and Alan D. Jones, eds., *U.S.-Mexican Industrial Integration: The Road to Free Trade* (Boulder, CO: Westview Press, 1991).

18. Both Néstle and Unilever have broadened operations in Mexico with recent purchases of U.S. firms. Unilever bought out Anderson Clayton's Mexican operations and purchased

CONASUPO's oilseed processing facilities, while Néstle bought out Carnation, which has extensive Mexican operations. S. Kenneth Schwedel and Kevin Haley, "Foreign Investment in the Mexican Food System," *Business Mexico*, Special Edition 1992. Pillsbury, another U.S. agroindustrial company which operates Gigante Verde, a vegetable procssing company in Mexico, is a subsidiary of Grand Metropolitan of Great Britain.

19. Rogelio Varela and Claudia Villegas, "Joint Ventures Flourish," *El Financerio International*, July 5, 1993.

Four

1. It is worth recalling that the protocol agreement to adhere to GATT, which was signed in 1985 and became operational in 1986, contained this provision: "The contracting parties recognize the priority that Mexico gives to its agricultural sector through its political and social policies. With the objective of improving its agricultural production, maintaining its structure of land tenure, and protecting the income and employment opportunities of its farm sector, Mexico will continue implementing a program of gradual substitution of import permits with tariff protections." In fact, Mexico proceeded unilaterly to liberalize trade not only by reducing or eliminating import permits and licences but also by dramatically dropping tariff barriers.

2. NAFTA's agricultural section is really two separate binational agreements rather than an across-the-board trinational agreement. Incorporated within NAFTA are bilateral agreements affecting agricultural trade between Mexico and the United States and between Mexico and Canada. The U.S.-Canada agreement, which took effect in 1989, regulates U.S.-Canada agricultural trade. The Mexico-Canada agreement does not provide for barrier-free trade for such products as poultry, eggs, milk, and other dairy products.

3. The most recent GATT agreement resulted in an average agriculutural tariff reduction of 36 percent for industrialized nations and 24 percent for less industrialized ones with a minimum market access commitment of 5 percent of domestic consumption of agricultural goods. In terms of trade liberalization, the new GATT will have little impact on Mexico, which since 1986 has become one of the most open economies in the developing world. New regulations that require countries to cut agricultural subsidies eventually could mean higher prices for many foodstuffs Mexico now imports in large quantity, including beef, corn, dairy products, and wheat, although the new GATT deal should encourage further agroexport growth, especially in Europe.

4. The U.S. Agricultural Marketing Agreement Act of 1937 permits the horticultural industry to enforce standards for grade, size, and other characteristics through marketing orders. Disputes between the three countries on unfair agricultural trade practices will be examined by a trinational working group on nontariff barriers, which will report to NAFTA's Committee on Agriculture.

5. Robert G. Chambers and Daniel H. Pick, "Marketing Orders as Nontariff Trade Barriers," *American Journal of Agricultural Economics* 76, February 1994.

6. Affected products for the United States are chili peppers, eggplant, onions, squash, two seasons of tomato production, watermelon, cotton, dairy products, sugar products, and peanuts. For Mexico they are slaughter pork, apples, frozen potatoes, barley, poultry, eggs, animal fats, nonfat dry milk, corn, dry edible beans, cotton, peanuts, and orange juice.

7. According to Ch. 7, Subchapter B: "Each Party may...apply any sanitary or phytosanitary measure necessary for the protection of human, animal, or plant life or health in its territory, including a measure more stringent than an international standard." However, each nation must ensure that such measures are based on scientific principles, based on a risk assessment, and are not discriminatory. Although better than many consumer advocates had anticipated, opponents still contended that the necessity of basing standards on scientific principles and risk assessments violated the assumed right of communities to establish measures that do not respond to clear scientific evidence but are simply precautionary.

8. Two exceptions relevant to agribusiness investors are the continued prohibition of direct foreign ownership of land near borders or coasts and the continued 49 percent cap on foreign equity in land-holding corporations. Loopholes in each restriction allow effective foreign control of land anywhere in Mexico, however.

9. NAFTA will, however, probably have a major effect on investment flows in banking, financial services, and other services.

10. General investment protections addressed by NAFTA, such as the right to full profit repatriation and full compensation for expropriation, apply equally to industrial and agricultural sectors.

11. For varying assessments of investment potential, see USITC, *Potential Impact on the U.S. Economy and Selected Industries of the North American Free Trade Agreement* (Washington: USITC, 1993), 22-2, 24-5.

12. The Uruguay Round of GATT, however, requires a reduction of export subsidies by 21 percent in volume and 36 percent in value over a six-year period, which means that U.S. export subsidies will be reduced but can still be utilized.

13. SARH, *Encuesta para estimar precios, coeficientes técnicos y rendimientos de la producción agrícola 1987, 1988, 1989*, cited in José Luis Calva, *Probables efectos de un Tratado de Libre Comercio en el campo mexicano* (Mexico City: Fontamara, 1991), 35.

14. Frederick Nelson and Chris Boling, "Policy Changes and Subsidies in the Western Hemisphere," *Western Hempishere*, June 1994.

Five

1. Office of Economics, USDA, *Preliminary Analysis of the Economic Implications of the Dunkel Text for American Agriculture*, March 1992; Interview with Susan Keith, National Corn Growers Association, October 3, 1994.

2. Phrasing from *U.S.-Mexico Trade: Pulling Together, Pulling Apart?* 199.

3. McMichael and Myhre, "Global Regulation vs. the Nation State."

4. See Mares for a discussion of the extent to which Mexican producers and distributors in the 1970s gained increased control in the horticultural sector.

5. Steven E. Sanderson, *The Transformation of Mexican Agriculture: International Structure and the Politics of Rural Change* (Princeton: Princeton University Press, 1986), 35.

6. David R. Mares, *Penetrating the International Market: Theoretical Considerations and a Mexican Case Study* (New York: Columbia University Press, 1987).

7. Figures from various issues of *Comercio Exterior* (Mexico City). According to one optimistic projection, the downward trend will be reversed and agroexports will account for more than 20 percent of Mexico's export value by the year 2002. World Bank and OECD study cited in *El Financiero International*, October 4, 1993.

8. Authorized direct investment in production of crops, fish, and cattle is extremely small, representing just 0.3 percent of total foreign investment in Mexico. U.S. Embassy, *Foreign Investment Climate: Mexico* (Mexico City, August 1991).

9. Among sources on contract production are Jeane Etine Dasso and Tomás Bustamante Alvarez, "Capital extranjero e industrialización de la agricultura mexicana: el caso de las multinacionales meloneras en el valle del Río Balsas," *Cuadernos Agrarios* 2, 1991; Martha Stamatis, "Hortalizas para U.S.A.," *Ciudades* 5, January/March 1990; Steven Sanderson, *The Transformation of Mexican Agriculture* (Princeton: Princeton University Press, 1986); and Mares, *Penetrating the International Market*.

10. Mares, *Penetrating the International Market*, 32; Banamex, "Agrochemicals," *Review of the Economic Situation of Mexico*, September 1992.

11. In 1988 the UNPH became the National Confederation of Fruit and Vegetable Producers (CNPH).

12. Michael W. Foley, "Structural Adjustment and Political Adaptation: The Politics of Neoliberal Reform in Mexican Agriculture," *Governance: An International Journal of Policy and Administration* 4(4), October 1991.

13. For a class analysis of contract farming that likens the contract between the farmer and processor to that of the age-old contract between the laborer and employer, see John Wilson., "The Political Economy of Contract Farming," *Review of Radical Political Economics* 18(4), 1986.

14. Lower transportation costs as well as a long history of exporting to the United States account for Mexico's dominance. But lower labor costs, extended growing seasons, and

increasing experiencing in nontraditional exports of such countries as Chile, Peru, Dominican Republic, Costa Rica, and Guatemala will make it difficult for Mexico to increase its U.S. market share.

15. Barney H. McClure, "Growing Importance for Mexican Imports," *Supermarket Business*, March 1991.

16. Steven M. Jaffee, Exporting High-Value Food Commodities: Success Stories from Developing Countries (Washington, DC: World Bank, 1993), 74

17. Robin R. Marsh and David Rusten, "From Gardens to Exports: The Potential for Smallholder Fruit and Vegetable Production in Mexico, Prepared for the XVlll International Congress of Latin American Studies Association, March 10-12, 1994, Atlanta, Georgia.)

18. Although horticultural exports do represent about half of Mexico's agricultural and food exports, more than 80 percent of total fruit and vegetable production is sold to the domestic market. Eighty-five percent of vegetable shipments to the United States are fresh, 10 percent are frozen, and 5 percent are canned.

19. See Sanderson, *The Transformation of Mexican Agriculture*, for a thorough and eminently readable discussion of the use of cheap labor in agroexport agriculture.

20. Although U.S. contract production is common, there is also an important sector of Mexican investors who have established their own distribution networks in the United States. See Mares, *Penetrating the International Market*.

21. McClure, "Growing Importance for Mexican Imports,"

22. Enrique Astorga Lira, *Mercado de trabajo rural en México: La mercancía humana* (Mexico City: Ediciones ERA, 1985).

23. Martine Vanackere, "Conditions of Agricultural Day Laborers in Mexico," *International Labor Review* 127(1), 1988, 101-102.

24. For the most recent overview of farmworker organizing, see Adriana López Monjardín, "Organization and Struggle among Agricultural Workers in Mexico," in Kevin J. Middlebrook, ed., *Unions, Workers, and the State in Mexico* (San Diego: Center for U.S.-Mexican Studies, 1991). Good Mexican sources on the plight of farmworkers are Hubert de Grammont, *Asalariados agrícolas y sindicalismo en el campo mexicano* (Mexico City: Editorial Juan Pablo, 1986), and Luisa Pare, *El proletariado agrícola en México* (Mexico City: Siglo Veintiunio, 1985).

25. Gary D. Thompson and Philip L. Martin, *The Potential Effects of Labor-Intensive Agriculture in Mexico on U.S.-Mexico Migration* (Washington: Commission for the Study of International Migration and Cooperative Economic Development, December 1989).

26. Linda Wilcox Young, "Labor Demand and Agroindustrial Development: The Evidence from Mexico," *The Journal of Development Studies* 30(1), October 1993.

27. Ibid. In her study of agricultural employment in El Bajío, Wilcox Young concludes, "The impact of widespread crop substitution and wholesale transfer of technology promoted by

transnational processing plants have both reduced the total labor employed and increased the instability of employment through heightened seasonality of labor demand."

28. Linda Wilcox Young, "Economic Development and Employment: Agroindustrialization in Mexico's El Bajío," *Journal of Economic Issues* XXII(2), June 1988.

29. Lois Stanford, "Mexico's Fresh Fruit and Vegetable Export System: Recent Developments and Their Impact on Local Economies," Presented at the Workshop on the Globalization of the Fresh Fruit and Vegetable Industry, University of California, Santa Cruz, December 6, 1991. As Stanford notes, the end of the export permit system was only one factor in the restructuring of the valley's agricultural economy. Corruption within the regional ejidatario union, increased competition from other regions, and inefficient use of agricultural inputs also led to the breakdown of contracts with U.S. purchasers.

30 . OTA, *U.S.-Mexico Trade*, 211; For more complete analysis see Santiago Levy and Sweder van Vijnberen, "Transition Problems in Economic Reform: Agriculture in the Mexico-U.S. Free Trade Agreement," *Economy-Wide Modeling of the Economic Implications of a FTA with Mexico and a NAFTA with Canada and Mexico* (Washington: U.S. International Trade Commission, May 1992).

31. Ibid.

32. David Runsten and Sandra O. Archibald, "Technology and Labor-Intensive Agriculture: Competition between Mexico and the United States," in Jorge A. Bustamante, Clark W. Reynolds, and Raúl Hinajosa, eds., *U.S.-Mexico Relations: Labor Market Interdependence* (Stanford, CA: Stanford University Press, 1992); OTA, U.S.-Mexico Trade 212-13.

33. Stephen Lande and Nellis Crigler, "Food for Thought," *Business Mexico*, May 1994.

34. Foreign Agricultural Service, *Mexico: The Market for U.S. Agricultural Products-Agxport Guide* (Washington: February 1993), 5.

35. Ibid., 1-2.

36. Lande and Crigler, "Food for Thought."

37. Interview with Kevin Moffin, Oregon-Washington-California Pear Bureau, May 10, 1994.

38. A Food and Agricultural Organization of the United Nations (FAO) study found that as agriculture export volume increases, agroexport value drops. FAO, *El estado mundial de la agricultura y la alimentación* (Rome: 1986).

39. Irma Adelman, "Beyond Export-Led Growth," *World Development* 12(9), 1984.

40. A valuable overview of the policy issues of cash cropping is Simon Maxwell and Adrian Fernando, "Cash Crops in Developing Countries: The Issues, the Facts, the Policies," *World Development* 17(11), 1989.

Six

1. Postrevolutionary Mexico has never been completely self-sufficient in basic grains, but the quantities of imported food were modest before the mid-1960s. Favorable weather and high guarantee prices have occasionally resulted in large production increases, thereby reducing the need for imports. The overall trend, however, has been toward increased imports since the late 1960s.

2. FAO, "Global Imports and Exports of Agricultural Products by Country," 1992.

3. USDA Foreign Agricultural Service, U.S. Trade Data Collection: 1980-93.

4. USDA/Foreign Agricultural Service, *Annual Grain and Feed Report 1994: Mexico* (Mexico City: U.S. Embassy, 1994)

5. These are the characteristics of food security defined by the FAO and UNRISD. See *Potentials for Agricultural and Rural Development in Latin America and the Caribbean* (Rome: FAO, 1988).

6. Lester R. Brown, "Facing Food Insecurity," in Brown, ed., *State of the World 1994: A Worldwatch Institute Report on Progress Towards a Sustainable Society* (New York: W.W. Norton, 1994).

7. For an excellent description of the strengths and weaknesses of Mexico's food distribution system and the politics that shaped it, see Jonathan Fox, *The Politics of Food in Mexico: State Power and Social Mobilization* (Ithaca, NY: Cornell University Press, 1993).

8. SAM's higher production gains came at a high cost, however. During the three years of the program (1980-82), the government's food budget grew at an annual rate of 50 percent. Armando Andrade and Nicole Blanc, "SAM's Cost and Impact on Production," in James E. Austin and Gustavo Esteva, eds., *Food Policy in Mexico: The Search for Self-Sufficiency* (Cornell: Cornell University Press, 1987).

9. Through the Export Enhancement Program (EEP) of the U.S. Commodity Credit Corporation (CCC), the U.S. government offers direct subsidies to exporters to enable them to lower prices and capture foreign markets. Increasing U.S. wheat exports to Mexico have been underwritten by the EEP, along with dairy, sunflower seed oil, and cottonseed oil products. EEP subsidies have helped U.S. exporters, particularly the large grain conglomerates including Cargill, Continental Grain, and ADM to beat out their foreign competitors for a larger share of the Mexican market. Providing even a bigger boost to U.S. grain exports to Mexico has been the GSM credit guarantees of the USDA. In the 1980s, Mexico became the world's largest beneficiary of these credit guarantees by which the U.S. government agrees to pay exporters in the event that Mexican importers default. Mexico's use of GSM programs jumped from $38 million in 1982 {TB?} billion in 1994 and an allocated $1.35 billion for 1995. Beth Sims, *On Foreign Soil: Government Programs in U.S.-Mexico Relations* (Albuquerque: Resource Center Press, 1994); Communication with Agricultural Attaché, U.S. Embassy, Mexico, May 16, 1994, January 20, 1995.

10. For more on U.S. food aid to Mexico see, Tom Barry, ed., *Mexico: A Country Guide* (Albuquerque: Resource Center Press, 1992) and Sims, *On Foreign Soil.* U.S. food aid, which was mainly channeled through Section 416 of the Commodity Credit Corporation, began in 1983 and continued through 1991. Mexico was one of the world's largest recipients of U.S. food aid in the 1980s, second only to India in 1989. From 1983 to 1991 Mexico received more than $300 million in Section 416 aid, which included powdered milk, cheese, rice, corn, and wheat flour.

11. Billie R. DeWalt, "Mexico's Second Green Revolution: Food for Feed," *Mexican Studies/Estudios Mexicanos* 1(1), 1985.

12. The shift in cropping patterns was dramatic. Whereas sorghum production area had been insignificant before the 1960s, the area devoted to this feedgrain equaled more than one-fifth the area in corn, four-fifths the area in beans, and twice the area in wheat by 1981.

13. David Barkin, Rosemary L. Batt, and Billie R. DeWalt, *Food Crops vs Feed Crops: Global Substitution of Grains in Production* (Boulder, CO: Lynne Rienner, 1990).

14. In the 1940-70 period, Mexico only achieved a surplus in basic grains from the early to late 1960s, although previous import levels were quite low, generally about 1 percent to 3 percent of production.

15. In very few places in Mexico is traditional *milpa* cropping still practiced. For a description of why this is the case and of current *milpa* farming in Veracruz see Chapter Five, a collection of essays edited by Luisa Paré, in Hewitt de Alcántara, *Reestructuración económica y subsistencia rural.*

16. Kirsten Appendini, *De la milpa a los tortibonos: La restructuración de la política alimentaria en México* (Mexico City: El Colegio de México, 1992) 22,23. Focusing on corn production and consumption, this is a valuable examination of Mexico's food and farm policies.

17. Kirsten Appendini, "Transforming Food Policy over a Decade, " in *Economic Restructuring and Rural Subsistence in Mexico: Corn and the Crisis of the 1980s* (San Diego: Center for U.S.-Mexican Studies, 1994), 145.

18. The corn surplus was exacerbated by the NAFTA agreement under which Mexico agreed to import 2.5 million tons of corn duty-free in 1994. Despite the bountiful corn harvest, corn produced in Mexico was available at lower prices, inducing the government to begin channeling corn into the feedgrain industry, substituting it for sorghum.

19. Appendini, *De la milpa a los tortibonos.*

20. The success of Chihuahuan corn growers to raise the guarantee price for the region can be attributed in part to the political challenge by the PAN in that northern state.

21. Jaime de la Mora Gómez, "La banca de desarrollo en la modernización del campo," *Comercio Exterior*, 40, No. 10, October 1990.

22. A key work for understanding the role of caciques and acaparadores in the village farm economy is Gustavo Esteva, *La Batalla en el México Rural* (Mexico City: Siglo Veintiuno, 1980).

23. Procampo covers corn, dry beans, wheat, sorghum, rice, barley, safflower, soybean, and cotton production, encompassing about 90 percent of cultivated land. Only those growers registered in 1993 as being producers of these crops are eligible..

24. Beginning in 2004 and continuing through 2008, the final year of the program, the subsidies will be reduced by 20 percent each year.

25. Centro de Estudios para el Cambio en el Campo Mexicano (CECCAM), Instituto Maya, and Red Nacional de Productores de Granos, *La apertura comercial y la nueva política de subsidios hacia los productores de granos básicos en México: 1993* (Mexico City: Friedric Ebert Stiftung, 1993).

26. Alfredo Corchado, "Mexico Farm Program Faces Growing Criticism," *Dallas Morning News*, August 15, 1994.

27. Kirsten Appendini and Diana Liverman, "Agricultural Policy, Climate Change, and Food Security in Mexico," *Food Policy*, Spring 1994.

28. Ibid.

29. Cassio Luiselli, "The Way to Food Self-Sufficiency in Mexico and its Implications for Agricultural Relations with the United States," in Bruce Johnston, et al, *U.S.-Mexico Relations: Agriculture and Rural Development* (Stanford, CA: Stanford University Press, 1987). 340.

30. Cynthia Hewitt de Alcántara, *Economic Restructuring and Rural Subsistence in Mexico* (Geneva: United Nations Research Institute for Social Development, January 1992).

31. According to the World Health Organization (WHO), 2400 calories and 65 grams of protein are needed each day to maintain good health. In Mexico, daily calories percapita have risen from 2490 in 1961-63 to 3062 in 1988-90. *FAO Production Yearbook*, 1992.

32. CEPAL, *Anuario estadídico de América Latina y el Caribe*, 1992. Percapita averages of daily grams of protein consumed during the 1969-71 and 1988-90 periods.

33. International Institute for Applied Systems Analysis, *Hunger Amidst Abundance* (Austria: 1986)

34. INEGI, *Encuesta nacional ingreso-gasto de los hogares 1992* (Mexico City: 1993).

35. Cited in Claudia Fernández, "Mexican Billionaires Booming," *El Financiero International*, July 11, 1994.

36. From 1989 to 1993 the GDP percapita fell by 13 percent, from $2,633 to $2,289.

37. One study found that the percentage of families living in extreme poverty dropped from 14.1% in 1989 to 11.8% in 1992, roughly the same percentage as 1984. CEPAL and INEGI, *Informe sobre la magnitud y evolución de la pobreza en México 1984-92* (Mexico City: 1994).

38. Kathryn G. Dewey, "Nutritional Consequences of the Transformation From Subsistence to Commercial Agriculture in Tabasco, Mexico," *Human Ecology* 9 (2), 1981; and Roberta D. Baer, "Nutritional Effects of Commercial Agriculture," *Urban Anthropology* 16 (1), 1987.

39. National Nutrition Institute, *The Food and Nutrition Situation in Mexico*, 1992; SourceMex, "Nearly Half of Rural Population Malnourished," September 27, 1990.

40. The various indicators illustrate different aspects of nutritional history. Low weight or height for age tends to indicate past malnutrition, while low weight for height is strongly influenced by current conditions (e.g., diarrhea can severely affect weight/height ratios in a matter of days). Waterlow classifications are another way of measuring nutritional levels. For example, the Waterlow category of low weight for height/low height for age indicates chronic or acute chronic malnutrition. While a simple indicator such as weight for age gives a good general indication of nutritional conditions, Waterlow classifications allow more fine-grained analysis of the situation. All these measurements require examinations by trained health personnel, making them expensive to administer.

41. *Hunger 1994: Transforming the Politics of Hunger* (Silver Spring, MD: Bread for the World Institute, 1993).

42. CEPAL and INEGI, *Informe sobre la magnitud y evolución de la pobreza en México 1984-92.*

43. SourceMex, "Notes on Malnutrition," November 7, 1990.

44. Jaime Sepulveda-Amor, et al., "Estado nutricional de preescolares y mujeres en Mexico: Resultados de una encuesta probabistica nacional," *Gaceta Médica de México* 126 (3), May/June 1990.

45. Adolfo Chávez et al., *La nutrición en México y la transición epidemiológica*, (Mexico City: Instituto Nacional de la Nutrición Salvador Zubiran, October 1993).

46. Manuel Robles, "Burocratismo, desorganización, y programas con miras político-electorales agravan la desnutrición," *Proceso*, October 29, 1990.

47. See essays on corn policy by Hewitt de Alcánara and Appendini in *Economic Restructuring and Rural Subsistence in Mexico*.

Seven

1. President Salinas announced his intentions to amend Article 27 on November 7, 1991. In the following two months, the proposed changes to the constitution were approved by both houses of the Congress and by the legislatures of all 31 states, becoming part of the constitution in January 1992. The enabling legislation, La Ley Agraria, became law in February 1992. The Article 27 amendments were paralleled by changes to the country's Ley Forestal and Ley de Aguas that gave market forces an increased role in directing the use of the country's natural resources.

2. For the best summary of the amendment of Article 27 and the implementation of the Agrarian Law see Wayne Cornelius, "The Politics and Economics of Reforming the Ejido Sector in Mexico: An Overview and Research Agenda," *LASA Forum* 23(3), 1992.

3. Mexico's new agrarian bureaucracy included three institutions: Procuraduría Agraria (Agrarian General Counsel), which is obligated to defend *ejidatarios* and *comuneros* in terms of the *Ley Agraria*; *Tribunales Agrarios* (Agrarian Tribunals), which are decentralized courts that hear disputes arising from the application of Article 27; and *Programa de Certificación de Derechos Ejidales y Titulación de Solares Urbanas* (Procede), which is charged first with defining ejido boundaries and certifying ejido rights and titling urban losts. Upon privatization, Procede titles ejidal plots .

4. The eliminated clause referred to the state's unlimited obligation of "dotar con tierras y aguas suficientes...conforme a las necesidades de su población sin que en ningún caso deje de concedérseles la extensión que necesiten."

5. See various issues of *La Jornada del Campo* (published monthly by *La Jornada*), especially the April 27, 1993 supplement, which includes essays from various critics including Carlota Botey, Julio Moguel, Armando Bartra, and Luis Hernández.

6. An excellent overview of ejidos and *comunidades agrarias* and the research on Mexico's social sector is found in Billie R. DeWalt and Martha W. Rees, "The End of the Agrarian Reform in Mexico," *Transformation of Rural Mexico* 3 (San Diego: Center for U.S.-Mexican Studies, 1994).

7. There are two main categories of ejidos: individual and collective. In theory, collective ejidos are worked jointly by their members but in practice many of the estimated thousand or more collective ejidos are divided into individual plots. Two other subcategories of ejidos are urban and coastal ejidos.

8. *Ejidatarios* can transfer their individual parcels to other members of the ejido without prior approval of the *asamblea ejidal*. The sale to outsiders, however, requires authorization through a vote by the assembly witnessed by a *Procuraduría Agraria* representative. To privatize, a quorum of two-thirds of ejido members is required. Once a quorum is achieved, a simple majority is needed to sell parcels to outsiders or to dissolve the ejido. In other words, no more than 33 percent plus one member need vote for privatization to make it effective for the whole ejido.

9. Helga Baitenmann, "La regularización del sector ejidal: Veracruz al día," paper presented at a workshop of the Ejido Reform Research Project/Center for U.S.-Mexican Studies, Tepotlzán, Morelos, November 5-6, 1993.

10. For early reactions of the campesino organizations to the new Article 27, see Julio Moguel, "Reformas legislativas y luchas agrarias," *El Cotidiano* 50, September-October 1992.

11. The maximum property size for irrigated land is 100 hectares or the equivalent in rainfed lands and pasture. Equivalencies are one hectare of irrigated land for two of rainfed, for four of good-quality pasture land, for eight of forest or arid pasture land. The maximum for property with livestock is that not exceeding the surface area needed to keep 500 head of cattle or the equivalent in small livestock. Critics point out that permissible landholdings for an individual may range from 500 hectares in the humid tropics to 12,500 hectares in the arid lands of the north. A new limit established by the revised Article 27 is that corporations

cannot hold more than 2,500 hectares in irrigated land or their equivalent, which, according to critics, creates the possibility for the legal formation of vast corporate estates with 5,000 hectares of rain-fed lands and 10,000 of good-quality pasture land.

12. Common lands, except for forested lands, can be redistributed by the ejidal assembly to ejidatarios, family members, and the landless and eventually privatized. Control over common lands but not ownership (*dominio pleno*) including forested lands can be transfered to production associations over which outside investors hold control, thereby effectively privatizing the common lands.

13. Gustavo Gordillo served as Undersecretary of Policy at thre Agricultural Ministry (SARH), and later as undersecretary of agrarian reform, while Arturo Warman was the director of INI during the Salinas presidency, later becoming the director of the *Procuraduría Agraria*.

14. Lynn Stephen, "Viva Zapata!: Generation, Gender, and Historical Consciousness in the Reception of Ejido Reform in Oaxaca," *Transformation of Rural Mexico* 6 (San Diego: Center for U.S.-Mexican Studies., 1994).

15. Estimates of the amount of land that could be distributed vary widely as do estimates of the number of land claims. Estimates of the amount of land that could be distributed range as high as five million hectares (according to the PRD's Cuauhtémoc Cárdenas).

16. The government has given landowners two years to sell lands over the hectare limit.

17. A study of the Laguna region in north-central Mexico concluded that there was widespread consensus in favor of the new agrarian law and in the certification of land titles within the ejidos. Raúl Salinas de Gortari and José Luis Solís González, "Rural Reform in Mexico: The View from the Comarca Lagunera in 1993," *Transformation of Rural Mexico* 4 (San Diego: Center for U.S-Mexican Studies, 1994).

18. But even in Chiapas an increasing number of ejidos are turning to Procede to help clarify ejido boundaries and the rights of individual *ejidatarios*.

19. With respect to the use of ejido land as collateral: Certificates of rights allow the "use of rights" but not the ownership of land to be used as collateral. Since use rights might extend for a period of five to seven years, the land is effectively "alienated" from defaulting borrowers. Once privatized, the land is fully alienable.

20. For a good discussion of the *indústria de siniestros* see Marilyn Gates, *In Default: Peasants, the Debt Crisis, and the Agricultural Challenge* (Boulder, CO: Westview Press, 1993), Chapter 5.

21. For a criticism of Procede and its methods see Helga Baitenmann, "Las irregularidades en el programa de certificación ejidal," *La Jornada del Campo*, September 6, 1994. A rebuttal by an official of the Procuraduría Agraria appeared in the October 4, 1994 edition of *La Jornada del Campo*.

22. INEGI, *Programa de titulación de tierras ejidales: Documento de presentación* (Aguascalientes: 1992).

23. Foreign investors in production associations with *ejidatarios* can own no more than 49 percent of the project's land but other aspects of the ventures can be 100 percent foreign owned.

Eight

1. Arturo Warman, *Los campesinos: hijos predilectos del régimen* (Mexico City: Nuestro Tiempo, 1972).

2. The phrasing "logic of modern historical development," comes from Rose Spalding, "Peasants, Politics, and Rural Change in Rural Mexico," *Latin American Research Review* 23 (1), 1988, 208.

3. See the writings of Roger Bartra, especially *Estructura agraria y clases sociales en México* (Mexico City: Editorial Era, 1974).

4. Roger Bartra, ed., *Caciquismo y poder político en el México rural* (Mexico City: Siglo Veintiuno Editores, 1975).

5. One of Mexico's leading *campesinistas* is Gustavo Esteva. See, for example, "La economía campesina actual como opción de desarrollo," *Investigación Económica* 38 (147), 1979.

6. The fundamental differences between the peasant economy and capitalist organization was described by A. V. Chayanov, *The Theory of Peasant Economy* (Homewood, Ill.; Richard D. Irwin, 1966). Instead of seeking to maximize production, the campesino family seeks to achieve subsistence while providing work for all members of the household. Rather than being driven by profits and growth, the traditional campesino community aims for stability and permanence.

7. See James Scott, *Weapons of the Weak: Everyday Forms of Peasant Resistance* (New Haven: Yale University, 1986).

8. Michael Redclift, "Agrarian Populism in Mexico: the 'Via Campesina'" *Journal of Peasant Studies*, July 1980.

9. The evolution of these paradigms or "mental maps" are clearly outlined in Cynthia Hewitt de Alcántara, *Anthropological Perspectives on Rural Mexico* (London: Routledge & Kegan Paul, 1984).

10. Those anthropologists inclined to emphasize mental obstacles have come from the *indigenista*, ethnographic particularlist, and functionalist schools, while the historical structuralists (strongly influenced by Marxism), cultural ecologists, and *dependistas* stress economic barriers.

11. For a history of rural rebellion in Mexico dating back to the colonial era, see Friedrich Katz, ed., *Riot, Rebellion, and Revolution* (Princeton: Princeton University Press, 1988). Especially valuable are the overview and comparative essays by Katz and John Coatsworth.

According to Coatsworth, 57, "The Mexican countryside probably witnessed more rebellions, large and small, in these two centuries [1700-1900] than any other area in the Western hemisphere."

12. The colonial government's efforts to limit the power of the Creole elite and the church by organizing indian communities into villages with protected common lands was another important factor in the lack of unified political action by the peasantry in colonial times. See essays by John Tutino and John Coatsworth in Katz, Ibid.

13. Estimates of indian depopulation come from Katz, "Introduction to Rural Revolts in Mexico," Ibid., 6.

14. Coatsworth, "Patterns of Rural Rebellion," in Katz, 58.

15. For a view, now largely discredited, that the Mexican Revolution was a generalized rural rebellion see Frank Tannenbaum, *The Mexican Agrarian Revolution* (Washington: Brookings Institution, 1929).

16. Arturo Warman, "The Political Project of Zapatismo," in Katz, *Riot, Rebellion, and Revolution*. This contrasts with the militarism of other campesino leaders, such as Villa in Chihuahua and the Cedillo brothers in San Luis Potosí.

17. Enrique Semo, "Las revoluciones en la historia de México," *Historia y Sociedad* 8, 1975, 49-61.

18. Armando Bartra, *Los herederos de Zapata* (Mexico City: Ediciones Era, 1985), Chapter 3. Bartra's book provides an instructive history of the development of the postrevolutionary, pre-1980 campesino movement.

19. For an overview of the CNC see Clarisa Hardy, *El estado y los campesinos: La Confederación Nacional Campesina* (CNC) (Mexico City: Editorial Nueva Imagen, 1984).

20. The two leading independent campesino organizations were the General Union of Workers and Peasants of Mexico (UGOCM), which was founded in 1948, and the Independent Campesino Central (CCI), which was founded in 1964. In both cases, the government succeeded in fomenting schisms that resulted in the founding of progovernment organizations of the same name, thereby diffusing the threat of an independent campesino movement.

21. Blanca Rubio, *Resistencia campesina y explotación rural en México* (Mexico City: Ediciones Era, 1987).

22. The Independent Campesino Central (CCI) was renamed CIOAC in 1975, and its key figure has been the highly respected Ramón Danzos Palomino, who represented the wing of the CCI associated with the Mexican Communist Party, and later the United Mexican Socialist Party (PSUM).

23. A valuable summary of the recent history of the campesino movement is Neil Harvey, *The New Agrarian Movement in Mexico 1979-1990* (London: University of London Institute of Latin American Studies Research Papers, 1990). Two important books examining the emergence of autonomous campesino organizations that demanded more control over the production process and agricultural policy are Julio Moguel, Carlota Botey, and Luis

Hernández, eds., *Autonomía y nuevos sujetos en el desarrollo rural* (Mexico City: Siglo Veintiuno Editores, 1992), and Armando Bartra et. al., *Los nuevos sujetos del desarrollo rural*, Cuadernos de Desarrollo de Base 2 (Mexico City: ADN Editores, 1991).

24. The CNC lost power nationally because of the fading of agrarian reform, the new emphasis on promoting production, and the emergence of Pronasol as a new intermediary in the countryside. But in some states, notably Chiapas and Guerrero, state governments continued to privilege the CNC while marginalizing and repressing nongovernmental organizations.

25. The government did consult with CAP about the Article 27 reforms but only in a cursory way and did manage to secure an expression of campesino support. But criticism from the ranks and among the *campesinista* factions outside government led many organizations to join in criticism of the reform. The rapidity with which the constitutional amendments were implemented showed the government's concern that an open debate would generate widespread peasant dissent. Similarly, the government never opened up the issue of the proposed NAFTA for discussion with and within campesino organizations.

26. There was a vibrant discussion of these issues among activist scholars such as Julio Moguel, Luis Hernández, and Armando Bartra but democratization was never taken up as a leading banner of the campesino movement. See, for example, essays in *Los nuevos sujetos del desarrollo rural*, Cuadernos desarrollo de base 2 (Mexico City: June 1991).

27. Grindle, *State and Countryside*, 115. Also see Hewitt de Alcántara, *Anthropological Perspectives*, 190-91.

28. An inspiring and eloquent account of this new concept of *trabajo social* is found in Rosario Robles, "La unión de comunidades del Valle del Mezquital: La autogestión en las tierras de la extrema pobreza," in Moguel, Botey, and Hernández, eds, *Autonomía y nuevos sujetos en el desarrollo rural*.

29. Some of the best analysis of the current state of organizing by small growers in Mexico is found in the writings of Luis Hernández, including "Las telarañas de la nueva organicidad del movimiento campesino," *El Cotidiano* 50, September-October 1992, and "Las convulsiones rurales," in Moguel, Botey, and Hernández, eds., *Autonomía y nuevos sujetos sociales en el desarrollo rural*. Also see *Cuadernos Agrarias* (Nueva Epoca), 1-7.

Nine

1. Central to many of these land invasions was the independent General Union of Mexican Workers and Campesinos (UGOCM).

2. There is limited documentation of the guerrilla struggles in Guerrero. However, for an insightful and reputedly accurate novelistic portrayal of the Party of the Poor of Lucio Cabañas, see Carlos Montemayor, *Guerra en el paraíso* (Mexico City: Editorial Diana, 1991). The civic action or pacification program included an extensive integrated rural

development program, a fortified Banrural, and direct state intervention in marketing and distribution of the main products of the region—coconut, timber, and coffee—in the form of La Impulsadora Guerrense de Cocotero, La Forestal Vicente Guerrero, and Inmecafe.

3. Among the best sources on Chiapas are the writings of Neil Harvey and Luis Hernández (peasant movements) and Thomas Benjamin and Jan Rus (history). For regular reporting and analysis see *Ojarasca* and *La Jornada*.

4. Interview in *La Jornada*, February 5-7, 1994.

5. For an overview of the innovative aspects of the Plan of Ayala and the platform of the Emiliano Zapata see Arturo Warman, "The Political Project of Zapatismo," in Katz, *Riot, Rebellion, and Revolution*.

6. Emiliano Zapata often called on an informal team of anarchist and socialist activists and intellectuals known as his "secretaries" in formulating his national political strategy and in editing communiques. The presence of Subcomandante Marcos pointed to the influence of leftist intellectuals and organizers in the EZLN.

7. The timber industry has been active in Chiapas since the late 1800s. In the 1950s the economy and society of the state began changing rapidly, with the most dramatic change being the expansion of the cattle industry. One result was the escalation of land disputes, and one study cited by Benjamin found that 87 of 115 disputes examined involved conflicts caused by the invasion of communal land by cattle herds. Social discontent was also fueled by the Grijalva-Usumacinta hydroelectric project in the central valley in the 1970s, which flooded more than 200,000 hectares of productive land. Thomas Benjamin, *A Rich Land, A Poor People: Politics and Society in Modern Chiapas* (Albuquerque: University of New Mexico Press, 1989).

8. The population of the largest municipality of the region more than doubled between 1950 and 1970, doubled again in the 1970s, and increased by more than 50 percent in the 1980s. Gabriel Ascencio Franco and Xochil Leyva Solano, "Los municipios de la Selva Chiapaneca: Colonización y dinámica agropecuararia," *Anuario de Cultura e Investigación* (Tuxtla Gutiérrez, Chiapas: Instituto Chiapaneco de Cultura, 1992), cited in Neil Harvey, *Rebellion in Chiapas: Rural Reforms, Campesino Radicalism, and the Limits to Salinismo* (San Diego: Center for U.S.-Mexican Studies, 1994), 28.

9. See Harvey, *Rebellion in Chiapas*, for analysis of origins and dynamics of Chiapas campesino organizations.

10. In mid-1994 there was some evidence of guerrilla forces active in the Huastecas region (Hidalgo and western Veracruz) and in Guerrero, as well as an increase of militancy throughout much of rural Mexico.

11. These concerns were validated after the 1988 election when Cárdenas attempted to form a new national campesino organization called the Central Campesina Cardenista, which received some support in Cardenista strongholds of Michoacán and La Laguna but never got off the ground.

12. For a discussion of the progress and problems of internal democratization see Jonathan Fox, ed., *The Challenge of Rural Democratization: Perspectives from Latin America and the Philippines* (London: Frank Cass and Company, 1990); and Jonathan Fox, "Democratic Rural Development: Leadership Accountability in Regional Peasant Organizations," *Development and Change* 23(2), 1992.

13. Gerardo Otero, "The New Agrarian Movement: Self-Managed, Democratic Production," *Latin American Perspectives* 16(4), Fall 1989; Jonathan Fox and Gustavo Gordilo, "Between State and Market: The Campesinos' Quest for Autonomy," in Wayne A. Cornelius, Judith Gettleman, and Peter H. Smith, eds., *Mexico's Alternative Political Futures* (San Diego: Center for U.S.-Mexican Studies, 1989).

14. For a history and analysis of COCEI see works of Jeffrey W. Rubin, including "COCEI in Juchitán: Grassroots Radicalism and Regional History," *Journal of Latin American Studies* 26 (1), February 1994. Also see Howard Campbell, Leigh Binford, Miguel Bartolomé, and Alicia Barabas, eds., *Zapotec Struggles* (Washington: Smithsonian Institution Press, 1993).

15. COCEI creatively used ethnic pride to push forward its class-based politics in a region in which Zapotecs not only make up the popular sectors but are also important in the PRI and in the economic power structure. According to Binford and Campbell, "COCEI transcends many of the dichotomies often used to categorize social movements: ethnic vs. class-oriented, Marxist vs. *indigenista*, rural indigenous vs. urban Westernized, parochial vs. international." Leigh Binford and Howard Campbell, "Introduction," in *Zapotec Struggles*, 17.

16. For a thoughtful analysis of the COCEI experience and its relevance to the Chiapas rebellion, see Jeffrey W. Rubin, "Indigenous Autonomy and Power in Chiapas: Lessons from Mobilization in Juchitán," *Transformation of Rural Mexico*, series 5 (San Diego: Center for U.S.-Mexican Studies, 1994). According to Rubin, "The EZLN, like COCEI, may gain negotiating power by remaining at the border between violence and nonviolence....Given the strength of old-style political and economic elites in Chiapas, and the multiplicity of ethnic groups there, it is the EZLN's *armed* uprising that has provided a threat equivalent to that of COCEI."

17. An excellent overview of the relationship of economics conditions to rural democracy is found in Jonathan Fox and Luis Hernández, "Mexico's Difficult Democracy: Grassroots Movements, NGOs, and Local Government," *Alternatives* 17(2), April 1992.

18. Luisa Paré, "The Challenges of Rural Democratization in Mexico," *Journal of Development Studies* 26(4), July 1990, 86.

19. Guillermo Bonfil, *México profundo: Una civilización negada* (Mexico City: Grijalbo, 1990), iii, as cited by Jonathan Fox, "Problems of Governance in Rural Mexico," Presented at "The Agrarian Problem in Present Day Mexico," Mexican Studies Program, University of Chicago, May 6-7, 1994.

Ten

1. Guillermo Bonfil Batalla, *México profundo: Una civilización negada* (Mexico City: Editorial Grijalbo, 1987).

2. Instituto Nacional Indigenista, *Programa Nacional de Desarrollo de los Pueblos Indios 1991-94*, 11.

3. This figure from the National Indigenous Institute is an underestimation of those speaking indian languages because it includes only those over the age of five.

4. But such broader estimations should be used with caution because it would include many Mexican peasants who themselves would deny being indian.

5. *México Profundo*, 41-2.

6. The figure of 56 languages does not include the various dialects of many languages. In some cases, such as that of the Mayan people of the Yucatán, the dialects do not represent a communication barrier. However, in the case of the Zapotec people, residents of Zapotec villages have widely varying customs and often cannot easily communicate.

7. INI, *Indicadores socioeconómicos de los pueblos indígenas de México* (Mexico City: 1994).

8. James B. Pick, Edgar W. Butler, and Elizabeth L. Lanzer, *Atlas of Mexico* (Boulder: Westview Press, 1989), 157, citing 1980 census data.

9. Ibid, 156.

10. Although primarily rural, there are more than one million Nahuatl-speaking people living in Mexico City.

11. For an analysis of racism in postrevolutionary Mexico see Alan Knight, "Racism, Revolution, and Indigenismo: Mexico, 1910-1940," in Richard Graham, ed., *The Idea of Race in Latin America, 1870-1940* (Austin: University of Texas Press, 1990).

12. Gonzalo Aguirre Beltrán, *Regiones de refugio* (Mexico City: INI, 1967); Rodolfo Stavenhagen, *Social Classes in Agrarian Societies* (New York: Anchor Doubleday, 1975).

13. The economic reforms of the mid-1800s were instituted by the Liberals, who came to power by ousting the Conservatives and the French. Promoting individual rights and fewer constraints on the spread of capitalism, the Liberals adopted reforms that made church and indigenous communal lands vulnerable to expropriation. Ironically, Benito Juárez, a Oaxacan indian, became the first Liberal president in 1860.

14. A good critique of *indigenismo* is found in Knight, "Racism, Revolution, and Indigenismo: Mexico 1910-1940," in *The Idea of Race in Latin America*.

15. A key struggle for indigenous rights and autonomy will be in the formulation of the implementation guidelines for the revised Article 4.

16. This paradigm of an acculturation continuum is examined in Viking Fund, *Heritage of Conquest* (New York: Cooper Square Publishers, 1968).

17. George Collier, *Fields of the Tzotzil* (Austin: University of Texas Press, 1975), 211-12.

18. Eric Wolf, "Closed Peasant Communities in Mesoamerica and Central Java," *Southwest Journal of Anthropology* 13, 1957.

19. Judith Friedlander, *Being Indian in Hueyapan* (New York: St. Martin's Press, 1975), as cited in Franz J. Schryer, "Ethnicity and Politics in Rural Mexico: Land Invasions in Huejutla," *Mexican Studies/Estudios Mexicanos* 3(1), Winter 1987.

20. Carole Nagengast and Michael Kearney, "Mixtec Ethnicity: Social Identity, Political Consciousness, and Political Activisim," *Latin American Research Review* 25(2), 1990.

21. Ibid., 73.

22. Ibid.

23. Schryer, "Ethnicity and Politics," 104.

24. Lourdes Arizpe, *Migración, etnicismo, y cambio económico* (Mexico City: Colegio de México, 1978), 238, cited in ibid.

25. Cynthia Hewitt de Alcántara, *Anthropological Perspectives on Rural Mexico* (London: Routledge & Kegan Paul, 1984), 42-69.

26. Schryer, "Ethnicity and Politics," 111.

27. Nagengast and Kearney, "Mixtec Ethnicity," 62.

28. George A. Collier, *Seeking Food and Seeking Money: Changing Productive Relations in a Highland Mexican Community* (Geneva: UNRISD, May 1990), 4.

29. Ibid.

30. Tracy Wilkinson, "The Defiant Return to Chiapas," *Los Angeles Times*, September 15, 1994.

31. For a fascinating, instructive study in the issues of ethnicity and class see Frans J. Schryer, *Ethnicity and Class Conflict in Rural Mexico* (Princeton: Princeton University Press, 1990). Besides helping to expose the myth of classless indian villages, Schryer's research found that indians sharing a common language had different forms of land tenure and social structures depending on where they lived in the diverse Huasteca region.

32. John Tutino, *From Insurrection to Revolution in Mexico: Social Bases of Agrarian Violence, 1750-1940* (Princeton: Princeton University Press, 1985), Chapter One.

33. Schryer, *Ethnicity and Class Conflict in Rural Mexico.*

34. See Stephen, *Zapotec Women.*

35. Direct and wide-ranging female involvement in peasant agriculture is seen to a much higher degree in southern and west Africa and in southeast and east Asia. See study by Ruth Dixon, "Women in Agriculture: Counting the Labor Force in Developing Countries," *Population and Development Review* 8(3), 1982, 539-566.

36. Important sources for a description and analysis of Mexican peasant women are found in Carmen Diana Deere, ed., *Rural Women and State Policy* (Boulder: Westview, 1987); Heather Fowler-Salamini and Kay Vaughn, eds., *Women of the Mexican Countryside, 1850-1990: Creating Spaces, Shaping Transitions* (Tucson: University of Arizona Press, 1994); Josefina Aranda, ed., *Las mujeres en el campo* (Oaxaca: Instituto de Investigaciones Sociológicas de la Universidad Autónoma Benito Juárez, 1988); Lourdes Beneria, ed, *Women and Development: The Sexual Division of Labor in Rural Societies* (New York: Praeger, 1982); Janet Townsend and Janet Momsen, eds., *Geography of Gender in the Third World* (New York: State University of New York Press, 1987). For a helpful overview of gender issues in agriculture in the third world see Laura Raynolds, "Women and Agriculture in the Third World," in William Friedland et. al., eds., *Towards a New Political Economy of Agriculture* (Boulder: Westview, 1991).

37. Maureen MacKintosh, "The Sexual Division of Labor and the Subordination of Women," in Karen Young et. al., eds., *Of Marriage and the Market* (London: Routledge and Kegan Paul, 1984).

38. See, for example, Townsend and Momsen, *Geography of Gender.*

39. Jennifer H. Bain, "Mexican Rural Women's Knowledge of the Environment," *Mexican Studies/Estudios Mexicanos* 9(2), Summer 1993, 267.

40. Lourdes Arizpe and Carlota Botey, "Mexican Agricultural Development and Its Impact on Rural Women," in Carmen Diana Deere, ed., *Rural Women and State Policy* (Boulder: Westview Press, 1987), 81.

41. Lourdes Arizpe, "La participación de la mujer en el empleo y el desarrollo rural," in Aranda, *Las mujeres en el campo*, 38; Cynthia Hewitt de Alcántara, *La modernización y las oportunidades de vida de mujeres de familias rurales* (Santiago: CEPAL, 1979).

42. Arizpe and Botey, "Mexican Agricultural Development," 67-83.

43. Michael W. Foley, "Organizing, Ideology., and Moral Suasion: Political Discourse and Action in a Mexican Town," *Comparative Studies in Society and History* 32(3), July 1990.

44. Frances Abrahamer Rothstein, "Women's Work, Women's Worth: Women, Economics, and Development," *Cultural Survival Quarterly*, Winter 1992.

45. Collier, *Seeking Food and Seeking Money.*

46. Ibid.

47. Howard Campbell, "Class Struggle, Ethnopolitics, and Cultural Revivalism in Juchitán" in Howard Campbell, Leigh Binford, Miguel Bartolomé, and Alicia Barabas, eds., *Zapotec Struggles* (Washington: Smithsonian Institution Press, 1993), 227. For a study of gender roles in one Zapotec community see Lynn Stephen, *Zapotec Women* (Austin: University of Texas Press, 1991).

48. Arizpe and Botey, "Mexican Agricultural Development," 68-70.

49. The 15 percent figure is from Arizpe and Botey in "Mexican Agricultural Development." The 38 percent figure is from Gail Mummert, "The Transformation of the Forms of Social Organization in a Mexican Ejido (1924-81)," *International Social Science Journal* 39(4),

1987. In ejidos studied in Michoacán and Morelos by Billie DeWalt and David Barkin, the percentage of land controlled by women was 23 percent and 17 percent respectively, cited in Billie DeWalt and Martha W. Rees, *The End of the Agrarian Reform in Mexico, Transformation of Rural Mexico*, No. 3 (San Diego: Center for U.S.-Mexican Studies, 1994), 19.

50. Stephen, *Zapotec Women*, 208.

51. For a valuable discussion of women and ejidos see Lynn Stephen, "Generation, Gender, and Historical Consciousness in the Reception of Ejido Reform in Oaxaca," *Transformation of Rural Mexico, 6* (San Diego: Center for U.S.-Mexican Studies, 1994).

52. Ibid.

53. Deere and León conclude that even when women are integrated into the agricultural labor force, there is "no necessary relationship between women's agricultural labor contribution and their control over the production process or the disposition of the production." Carmen Diana Deere and Magdalena León, *Women in Andean Agriculture: Women, Work and Development, Paper 4* (Geneva: International Labor Office, 1982).

54. Lourdes Arizpe, Fanny Salinas, and Margarita Velásquez, "Effects of the Economic Crisis on the Living Conditions of Peasant Women in Mexico," in *The Silent Adjustment: Poor Women and the Economic Crisis* (New York: Santiago: UNICEF, 1989). The authors conclude that because of the economic crisis of the 1980s, women constitute as much as a third of the work force in some rural areas.

55. Interview with women cooperative members in Paraíso, March 15, 1993.

56. A description of government development programs for women is found in Arizpe and Botey in "Mexican Agricultural Development" and Rosario Robles, Josefina Aranda, and Carlota Botey, "La mujer campesina en la época de la modernidad," *El Cotidiano* 52, March/April 1993. The Federal Agarian Reform Law of 1971 called for the creation of Agro-Industrial Units for Women (UAIMs), which allowed women collectively to hold use rights to ejido parcels. In 1993, only 15 percent of Mexico's ejidos had registered UAIMs, and even a smaller number were actually functioning.

57. The traditional sending states in heavily populated central Mexico are Zacatecas, Jalisco, Michoacán, Durango, San Luis Potosí, and Guanajuato.

58. An insightful and valuable overview of Mexican emigration patterns is Douglas S. Massey, Rafael Alarcón, Jorge Durand, and Humberto González, *Return to Aztlán: The Social Process of International Migration from Western Mexico* (Berkeley: University of California Press, 1987). Also see Merilee S. Grindle, *Searching for Rural Development: Labor Migration and Employment in Mexico* (Ithaca, NY: Cornell University Press, 1988) and Douglas Massey, Luis Golding, and Jorge Durand, "Continuation in Traditional Migration," *American Journal of Sociology*, 99 (6), May 1994.

59. Georges Vernez and David Ronfeldt, "The Current Situation in Mexican Immigration," *Science*, March 8, 1991. According to the authors, approximately half of current Mexican

immigrants are female. As with most immigration matters, the rise in female immigrants is the result of both push and pull factors. In this case the pull factors for women have been the increase of service jobs in the U.S. economy and the Immigration Reform and Control Act of 1986, which, by legalizing the presence of many male family heads, increased the flow of women seeking to be reunited.

60. The high rates of urbanization probably exaggerate the rural-urban split in Mexico since many of those who live in urban areas (defined as towns of 15,000 or more inhabitants) are connected to the rural economy. Even in the major cities, large sectors of the population, especially recent arrivals, regularly contribute to the economic well-being of family members left behind in rural homes and consider their real homes to be in the rural villages where they were born.

61. See Manuel García y Griego, "The Mexican Labor Supply, 1990-2010," in Jorge Bustamante and Wayne Cornelius, *Mexican Migration to the United States: Origins, Consequences, and Policy Options* (San Diego: Center for U.S.-Mexican Studies, 1989).

62. Santiago Levy and Sweder Van Wijnbergan, "Transition Problems in Economic Reform: Agriculture in the Mexico-U.S. Free Trade Agreement," Paper No. 7 in *Economy-Wide Modeling of the Economic Implications of a FTA with Mexico and a NAFTA with Canada and Mexico* (Washington: U.S. International Trade Commission, May 1992), 304-05.

63. Interview during gathering of the State Council of Indian and Campesino Organizations (CEOIC) gathering, February 15, 1994, San Cristóbal de las Casas, Chiapas.

64. The best overview of the impact of NAFTA on Mexican migrations is Wayne A. Cornelius and Philip A. Martin, *The Uncertain Connection: Free Trade and Mexico-U.S. Migration* (San Diego: Center for U.S.-Mexican Studies, 1993). The authors contend that only trade-linked development for Mexico will stem future emigration from Mexico.

65. This type of argument is present in most free trade advocacy including, for example, Gary Clyde Hufbaurer and Jeffrey J. Schott, *NAFTA: An Assessment* (Washington: Institute for International Economics, 1993).

66. Although it is important not to overemphasize the displacement effect of corn liberalization, it should be remembered that trade liberalization in basic grains is just one of the many adverse impacts facing the small farmer as a result of the restructuring of the agricultural sector. An uncertain factor in the evaluation of the displacement of campesinos by trade liberalization is the impact of Procampo, the new government direct subsidy program, which will likely have an ameliorative effort on displacement pressures, although this may be partially offset by the scheduled elimination of guarantee prices for corn and beans in 1995.

67. For a survey of the economic analysis of NAFTA's impact on agriculture and the peasantry see Tim Josling, "NAFTA and Agriculture: A Review of the Econmic Impacts," in Nora Lustig, Barry P. Bosworth, and Robert Z. Lawrence, eds., *North American Free Trade: Assessing the Impact* (Washington: The Brookings Institution, 1992).

68. Sherman Robinson, Mary Burfisher, Raul Hinojosa-Ojeda,and Karen Thierfelder, "Agricultural Policies and Migration in a U.S.-Mexico Free Trade Area," Working Paper 617 (Berkeley: Department of Agricultural and Resource Economics, December 1991). The researchers concluded that of the 839,000 migrants a total of 610,000 would migrate to the United States, including 66,000 directly from rural villages and 544,000 unskilled migrants from the cities. They describe this as a domino effect whereby the rural displaced would move primarily to the cities, which would have the effect of lowering wage levels and making jobs more scarce, thus sparking migration to the United States.

69. Levy and Van Wijnbergen, "Transition Problems in Economic Reform," 326. The authors conclude that liberalized trade in corn would force the migration of 700,000 to 1.2 million workers, meaning that at least five million would migrate if accompanying families are included in the estimate.

70. Cited in Alain de Janvry, Elizabeth Sadoulet, and Gustavo Gordillo, "NAFTA and Mexico's Corn Producers," paper presented at the XVIII LASA International Congress, March 10-12, 1994, Atlanta, Georgia.

71. Ibid.

72. The 6 percent figure used by some analysts assumes constant labor productivity. A more realistic model would assume increasing productivity, which would mean that the GDP would need to grow at a 8-9 percent annual rate to absorb the 3 percent or more growth in those looking for employment.

73. The absorptive capacity of the *maquila* industry is also limited by the low wages it offers and therefore the kind of employees it attracts, mainly young women and men who are not heads of families and have never before been included in the labor force. It is commonly claimed that the *maquilas* actually foster U.S. immigration by attracting migrants to the northern border and thereby breaking their ties to their home towns, but surveys of *maquila* workers do not show a high proportion planning to migrate to the United States.

74. Douglas S. Massey, "Economic Development and International Migration in Comparative Perspective," *Population and Development Review* 14(3), September 1988.

75. For a broad overview of the links between economic change and immigration, see Commission for the Study of International Migration and Cooperative Economic Development, *Unauthorized Migration: An Economic Development Response* (Washington, DC: July 1990).

76. Saskia Sassen, "Why Migration?" *Report on the Americas* 26(1), July 1992, 15.

77. Saskia Sassen, *The Mobility of Labor and Capital: A Study in International Investment and Labor Flow* (Cambridge, MA: Cambridge University Press, 1988).

78. Fernando Lozano Ascencio, *Bringing It Back Home: Remittances to Mexico from Migrant Workers in the United States* (San Diego: Center for U.S.-Mexican Studies, 1993). Mexico's central bank estimated that Mexican nationals sent back $3.5 billion in 1993, a sum equivalent to 1.5 percent of the GNP. The $6 billion estimate came from TELECOMM-SEPOMEX (Telecomunicaciones de México-Servicio Postal Mexicano),

Transferencias personales de Estados Unidos a México (Mexico City: TELECOMM-SEPOMEX, 1990), including higher estimates for "pocket transfers" or remittances through informal channels and direct cash transfers (excluding checks and money orders).

79. Cornelius and Martin noted that "the younger generation of workers in high-emigration communities is not disposed to taking home-town agricultural jobs, even at higher than prevailing local wages and even if such jobs could be made year-round (e.g., by irrigation projects that permit double cropping). *The Uncertain Connection*, 25.

80. Massey et al., *Return to Aztlán*, 250.

Eleven

1. See David C. Korten, *Getting to the 21st Century: Voluntary Action and the Global Agenda* (West Hartford, CT: Kumarian Press, 1990).

2. An excellent overview of the debate around sustainable development is found in Michael Redclift, *Sustainable Development: Examining the Contraditions* (London: Metheun & Co., 1987). Also see the more current review and analysis of David Barkin, "World Poverty and Sustainable Development," Unpublished manuscript, 1994.

3. The term sustainable development was used at the UN conference in Stockholm in 1972 but it was the Brundtland Commission or the World Commission on Environment and Development (WCED) in 1987 that gave the term wide acceptance in government and environmental circles.

4. For an exposition of this analysis, see Gene M. Grossman and Alan B. Kreuger, "Environmental Impacts of a North American Free Trade Agreement," in Peter Garber, ed., *The Mexico-U.S. Free Trade Agreement* (Cambridge, MA: MIT Press, 1993).

5. Donella H. Meadows, *The Limits to Growth: A Report for the Club of Rome's Project on the Predicament of Mankind* (New York: Universe Books, 1972).

6. Testimony of Barbara Dudley, Greenpeace before the Committee on Merchant Marine and Fisheries, U.S. House of Representatives, November 10, 1993.

7. For a provocative examination of these issues in Mexico, see David Barkin and Stephen Mumme, "Environmentalists Abroad: Ethical and Policy Implications of Environmental Nongovernmental Organizations," Unpublished manuscript, 1994.

8. Ibid.

9. Interviews with Peter Emerson of the Environmental Defense Fund and Ian Bowles of Conservation International, August 1994.

10. AID, *Strategy Paper: Mexico*.

11. For a good discussion of the poor and the environment, but one which avoids a critique of global capitalist accumulation and free trade policies, see H. Jeffrey Leonard et. al.,

Environment and the Poor: Development Strategies for a Common Agenda (New Brunswick: Transaction Books, 1989).

12. For a good overview on trade and the environment, see Hilary F. French, *Costly Tradeoffs: Reconciling Trade and the Environment* (Washington: Worldwatch Institute, March 1993).

13. Victor M. Toledo, *Naturaleza, producción, cultura: ensayos de ecología política* (Veracruz: Universidad Veracruzana, 1989).

14. Norman Myers, "Environment and Security," *Foreign Policy* 74, Spring 1989.

15. Sandra Postel, "Saving Water for Agriculture," in Lester Brown, ed., *State of the World 1990* (New York: Norton, 1990).

16. In rainfed areas, farmers can cultivate corn only two to three years in the same area without experiencing large reductions in productivity. See special issue on erosion of *La Jornada Ecológica*, June 20, 1994.

17. Kirsten Appendini and Diana Liverman, "Agricultural Policy, Climate Change, and Food Security in Mexico," *Food Policy*, Spring 1994.

18. USDA, *Agriculture in a North American Free Trade Agreement*, ERS Foreign Agricultural Economic Report 246, 1992.

19. Diana Liverman and Karen O'Brien, "Global Warming and Climate Change in Mexico," *Global Environmental Management* 1(4), December 1991.

20. Appendini and Liverman, "Agricultural Policy, Climate Change, and Food Security."

21. See the chapter on the World Steer in Sanderson, *The Transformation of Mexican Agriculture*.

22. "Su majestad la res," *La Jornada Ecológica*, January 16, 1992.

23. Richard Nuccio, Angelina Ornelas, and Iván Restrepo, "Mexico's Environment and the United States," in Janet Welsh Brown, ed., *In the U.S. Interest: Resources, Growth, and Security in the Developing World* (Boulder: Westview Press, 1990), 39.

24. Comisión Nacional de Derechos Humanos, *Los plaguicidas en México* (Mexico City: February 1993).

25. These include chlordane, aldicarb, lindane, paraquat, and pentacholorophenol.

26. General Accounting Office, *Pesticide Monitoring: FDA's Automated Import Information System is Incomplete* (Washington: Government Printing Office, 1991); GAO, *Pesticides: U.S. and Mexican Fruit and Vegetable Pesticide Programs Differ* (Washington: Government Printing Office, February 1993); GAO, *Pesticides: Better Sampling and Enforcement Needed on Imported Food* (Washington: Government Printing Office, September 26, 1986); and GAO, *Pesticides: Adulterated Foods Are Reaching U.S. Grocery Shelves* (Washington: Government Printing Office, September 24, 1992).

27. Tom Barry, *The Challenge of Cross-Border Environmentalism: The U.S.- Mexico Case.* (Albuquerque: Resource Center Press. 1993), 47-58

28. Banamex, "Agrochemicals," *Review of the Economic Situation of Mexico*, September 1992. The term "circle of poison" was popularized with the publication of David Weir and Mark Shapiro, *The Circle of Poison*, (San Francisco: Institute for Food and Development Policy, 1981).

29. Jan Trebilcock and Talli Nauman, "Killing Fields," *El Financiero International*, June 13, 1994.

30. For more on pesticide abuse in Mexico see: Angus Wright, *The Death of Ramón González: The Modern Agricultural Dilemma* (Austin: University of Texas Press, 1990); Iván Restrepo, *Los plaguicidas en México* (Mexico City: Comisión Nacional de Derechos Humanos, 1992); and Tom Barry, *The Challenge of Cross-Border Environmentalism* (Albuquerque: Resource Center Press, 1994). The best continuing sources of information are the newsletters of the Pesticide Action Network (San Francisco) and the Red de Acción sobre Plaguicidas y Alternativas en México (Mexico City).

31. The 1946 Colonization law permits private colonization on national land, allowing cultivation of up to 300 hectares of tropical plantation crops and between 500 and 2500 hectares for cattle ranches. But ejidos are limited to 20 hectares.

32. Jean Revel-Mouroz, "Mexican colonization experience in the humid tropics," in David A. Preston, ed., *Environment, Society, and Rural Change in Latin America* (New York: John Wiley and Sons, 1980). Other sources on Mexico's River Basin Project and colonization projects include Thomas T. Poleman, *The Papaloapan Project: Agricultural Development in the Mexican Tropics* (Stanford University Press, 1964); David Barkin and Timothy King, *Regional Economic Development: The River Basin Approach in Mexico* (Cambridge: Cambridge University Press, 1970); Fernando Tudela, et al., *La modernización forzada del trópico: el caso de Tabasco* (Mexico City: El Colegio de México/UNRISD, 1989), and Miguel Székeley and Iván Restrepo, *Frontera agrícola y colonización* (Mexico City: Centro de Ecodesarrollo, 1988). Also see *La Jornada Ecológica*, January 16, 1992, which was a special issue on the development of southeastern Mexico.

33. Gertrude Duby Blom, "Chiapas: testimonio y documentos," *El Dia*, March 28, 1974. Also see Alex Harris and Margerte Sartor, eds., *Gertrude Blom Bearing Witness* (Chapel Hill: University of North Carolina Press, 1984), especially the essay by James D. Nations, "The Lacandones, Gertrude Blom, and the Selva Lacandona."

34. James D. Nations, "The Ecology of the Zapatista Revolt," *Cultural Survival Quarterly*, Spring 1994, citing World Bank officials. There are no hard figures for the population of the Lacandon Jungle although Mexican sources estimate the population to be closer to 200,000.

35. Interview by Bill Weinberg, "From an Anti-Authoritarian Perspective: Interview with Insurgent Subcommander Marcos," Posted on Chiapas-L (Internet), May 2, 1994.

36. Nations, "The Ecology of the Zapatista Revolt."

37. Ibid.

38. *La Jornada Ecológica*, December 31, 1994.

39. R. Goodland, *Wildland Management in Economic Development* (Washington: World Bank, 1985), 3. For alternative agricultural development possibilities, see Victor M. Toledo, "La vía ecológico-campesina de desarrollo: Una alternativa para la selva de Chiapas," *La Jornada del Campo*, January 25, 1993.

40. See Theodore E. Downing, Susanna B. Hecht, Henry A. Pearson, and Carmen García-Downing, eds., *Development or Destruction: The Conversion of Tropical Forest to Pasture in Latin America* (Boulder, CO: Westview Press, 1992); Jason Clay, "Indigenous Peoples and Tropical Forests," *Cultural Survival Report* 27; David B. Bray, "The Forests of Mexico: Moving from Concessions to Communities," *Grassroots Development* 15(3), 1991; *Memoria: Segundo Taller de Análisis de Experiencias Forestales* (Mexico City: November 1990); and *Cultural Survival Quarterly*, Spring 1993, a special issue devoted to "Indigenous Peoples, Ancestral Rights, and the Forests of the Americas."

41. Janis B. Alcorn and Margaret Oldfield, *Biodiversity: Culture, Conservation, and Ecodevelopment* (Boulder, CO: Westview Press, 1991).

42. Cited in Salvador Anta Fonesca, "Economía campesina y sustentabilidad," *Cuadernos Agrarios* 7, 1993.

43. Cited in Jasmine Aguilar, "Políticas hacia una agricultura sustentable," *Pasos*, 5 (nd).

44. G. Conway, "Agro-ecosystem analysis," *Agricultural Administration* 20, 1985.

45. The best summary of sustainable agricultural development and the role of the peasantry is found in Red Interamericana Agriculturas y Democrácia, *Políticas hacia una agricultura campesina sustentable: Memoria del Taller* (Mexico City: July 1-2, 1993). Also see various issues of the magazine *Pasos* (Mexico City).

46. Raul García-Barrios and Luis García-Barrios, "Environmental and Technological Degradation in Peasant Agriculture: A Consequence of Development in Mexico," *World Development* 18(11), 1990.

47. Among the U.S. organizations and companies that market organic coffee from southern Mexico are Frontier Coffee, Allegro Coffee, Aztec Harvests Coffee, Grassroots International, Oxfam America, Earth Trade, and Cultural Survival.

48. For a valuable examination of organic agriculture in the context of new peasant organizing strategies, see the writings of Ronald Nigh of Asociación de Dana, Mexico City, including especially his "Associative Corporations, Organic Agriculture, and Peasant Strategies in Post-Modern Mexico," Unpublished manuscript, July 1992.

49. Judith Soule and Jon Piper, *Farming in Nature's Image: An Ecological Approach to Agriculture* (Washington: Island Press, 1992).

50. A persuasive exposition of this position is found in David Kaimowitz, "The Role of Nongovernmental Organizations in Agricultural Research and Technology Transfer in Latin America," *World Development* 21(7).

51. Kaimowitz, ibid, makes this point convincingly. Also see Jeffrey Bentley, "What farmers don't know can't help them: The strengths and weaknesses of indigenous technical knowledge in Honduras," *Agriculture and Human Values* 6(1), 1989. According to

Kaimowitz, "The idea of knowledge accumulated over generations is more myth than reality, considering the rapid changes which have occurred in farmers' production systems and the context they operate in."

52. E. F. Schumaker, *Small is Beautiful* (New York: Penguin Books, 1982).

53. Two important influences have been the work of Roland Bunch, former director of World Neighbors in Central America and the Latin American Consortium for Agroecology and Development (CLADES). See Roland Bunch, *Two Ears of Corn: A Guide to People-Centered Agricultural Improvement* (Oklahoma City: World Neighbors, 1982), and Miguel Altieri, *Agroecology: The Scientific Bias for Alternative Agriculture* (Boulder: Westview Press, 1987).

54. Emilia Velázquez, Luisa Paré, F. Ramírez, "Los retos en la sierra de Santa Marta, Veracruz," *La Jornada Ecológia*, November 11, 1993, p.6.

55. For agrarian wage-good strategies, see Albert O. Hirschman, ed., *Essays in Trespassing* (Cambridge: Cambridge University Press, 1981); Irma Adelman, "Beyond Export-led Growth," *World Development* 12(9), 1984; Irma Adelman and J. Edward Taylor, *Is Structural Adjustment with a Human Face Possible? The Case of Mexico* (University of California, Gianni Foundation of Agricultural Economics Working Paper no. 500, 1989); and David Barkin, *Distorted Development*.

56. So argue Daniel Goldrich and David Carruthers, "Sustainable Development in Mexico? The International Politics of Crisis or Opportunity," *Latin American Perspectives* 19(1), Winter 1992. See Robin Broad and John Cavanagh, "No More NICs," *Foreign Policy* 72, Fall 1988.

57. David Barkin and J. Edward Taylor, "Agriculture to the Rescue: A Solution to Binational Problems," in Daniel G. Aldrich and Lorenzo Meyer, eds., *Mexico and the United States: Neighbors in Crisis* (San Bernardino, CA: The Borgo Press, 1993). Irma Adelman and J.Edward Taylor, *Changing Comparative Advantage in Food and Agriculture: Lessons from Mexico*, Development Centre studies, OECD, Paris, 1990.

58. Bruce F. Johnston and William C. Clark, *Redesigning Rural Development: A Strategic Perspective* (Baltimore: Johns Hopkins University Press, 1982); Walden Bello and Stephanie Rosenfield, "Dragons in Distress: the Crisis of the NICs," *World Policy Journal* 7, Summer 1990.

59. David Barkin, "The End to Food Self-Sufficiency in Mexico," *Latin American Perspectives* 14, Summer 1987.

60. For a discussion of the limits of alternative agricultural practices within the current political and economic context, see Armando Bartra, "La sustentabilidad: Un concepto y su posible uso práctico," *Políticas hacia una agricultura campesina sustentable* (Mexico City: Red Interamericana Agriculturas y Democrácia, July 1993).

Conclusion

1. For a valuable overview of food security problems and a review of policy options, see Solon Barraclough, *An End to Hunger: Social Origins of Food Strategies* (London: Zed Books, 1991).

2. For an analysis of Pronasol see: Denise Dresser, Neopopulist Solutions to Neoliberal Problems: Mexico's National Solidarity Program (San Diego: Center for U.S.-Mexican Studies, 1991), and Julio Moguel, "El Programa Nacional de Solidaridad, ¿para quíen?" in *Los nuevos sujetos del desarrollo rural*, Cuadernos Desarrollo de Base, 2, 1991. Also see Wayne Cornelius, Ann Craig, and Jonathan Fox, *Transforming State-Society Relations: The National Solidarity Strategy* (San Diego: Center for U.S. Mexican Relations, 1994).

3. Chiapas was clearly an exception to this success story. Part of the problem was that the program was less successful in places where the local political elites managed to thwart efforts to integrate independent community organizations into the Pronasol network and to succeed in using the program in more traditional clientelist ways.

4. *Mexico: Nutrition Sector Memorandum* (World Bank, 1990).

5. Although the targeting of nutritional subsidies to the most needy is a good idea, in practice such programs still often failed to reach the poorest of the poor. Consequently, the elimination of generalized subsidies in favor of more targeted ones may actually have a regressive impact. Nora Lustig, "Economic Crisis, Adjustment, and Living Standards in Mexico: 1982-85," *World Development* 18(10), October 1990, 335.

6. Baraclough, *An End to Hunger*.

7. These include Kirsten Appendini, Gustavo Esteva, David Barkin, José Luis Calva, and Cynthia Hewitt de Alcántara.

8. For an insightful, balanced evaluation of Mexico's food security options see Ana de Ita, *Dilemas y opciones de la política agropecuaria actual* (Mexico City: CECCAM).

9. An early proponent of a peasant-based development strategy was Andrew Pearse. See Pearse, *Seeds of Plenty, Seeds of Want: Social and Economic Implications of the Green Revolution* (Oxford: Clarendon Press, 1980). Irma Adelman and J. Edward Taylor, *Changing Comparative Advantage in Food and Agriculture: Lessons from Mexico* (Paris: OECD Development Center Studies, 1990).

10. See discussion of the "war economy" approach to development in David Barkin, *Distorted Development* (Boulder, CO; Westview Press, 1990), Chapter 7.

11. David Barkin and J. Edward Taylor, "Agriculture to the Rescue: A Solution to Binational Problems," in Daniel G. Aldrich, Jr. and Lorenzo Meyer, eds., *Mexico and the United States: Neighbors in Crisis* (San Bernardino: The Borgo Press, 1993).

12. See UNORCA, *Una propuesta para el movimiento campesino* (Mexico City: Friedrich Ebert Stiftung, 1993).

13. See Raúl García-Barrios y Luis García-Barrios, "Subsistencia Maicera y Dependencia Monetaria en el Agro Semiproletarizado," in Hewitt de Alcántara, ed., *Reestructuración económica*, 229.

14. For a critical view of peasant-based strategies that do not take into account class stratification and the importance of establishing new forms of productive organizations see Henry Bernstein, "Taking the Part of the Peasants," in Henry Bernstein, Ben Crow, Maureen Mackintosh, and Charlotte Martin, eds., *The Food Question: Profits Versus People* (New York: Monthly Review, 1990).

15. Robert L. Paarlberg and Merilee S. Grindle, "Policy Reform and Reform Myopia," *Food Policy* 16(5), October 1991.

16. Alain de Janvry, Elisabeth Sadoulet, and Erik Thorbecke, "Introduction," *World Development* 21(4), 1993.

17. John. W. Mellor, "Agricultural Development: Opportunities for the 1990s," prepared for International Food Policy Research Institute, 10, June 1989.

Glossary of Terms and Names

agrarismo	Policies affecting land tenure
cacique	Local rural boss
campesinistas	Those committed to the promotion and protection of campesino interests and who believe in the endurance of the peasantry as a special social sector.
campo	Countryside
comunero	Member of an indigenous agrarian community
comunidad agraria	Indigenous agrarian community
concertación	Process of government consultation with different social sectors
descampesinistas	Those who believe that the peasantry is a state of disintegration and that campesinos are becoming primarily proletarians, not farmers.
comisaridos ejidal	Ejido directorate
ejidatario	Ejido member
ejido	Category of land tenure that grants use-rights to agrarian reform communities in which there are usually individual parcels and common lands.
haciendas	Large rural estates
hectare	2.47 acres
indigenismo	Philosophy and policies about indian people in Mexico
latifundio	Large rural estate characterized by extensive (nonintensive) ranching and farming

maíz	Corn or maize
mestizo	Mixed-blood
milpa	Traditional corn field, characterized by shifting production and diversified cultivation.
minifundio	Small parcel used for subsistence or infrasubsistence farming.
oficialista	Associated with government
Porfiriato	Regime of Porfirio Díaz (1876-1910)
prestanombre	loaned name
proletaristas	Same as descampesinistas
sexenio	Six-year term of office
ARIC	Rural Collective Interest Association
CEOIC	State Council of Indian and Campesino Organizations
COCEI	Coalition of Workers, Campesinos, and Students of the Isthmus
CIOAC	Indepependent Central of Farmworkers and Campesinos
CNC	National Campesino Federation
CNOC	National Network of Coffee Grower Organizations
CNPA	National Network of the Plan of Ayala
EZLN	Zapatatista National Liberation Army
GATT	General Agreement on Tariffs and Trade
INI	National Indigenous Institute
NAFTA	North American Free Trade Agreement
PAN	National Action Party
PRD	Democratic Revolutionary Party
PRI	Institutional Revolutionary Party
Procampo	Program of Direct Support Payments to the Countryside
Pronasol	National Solidarity Program
SAM	Mexican Food System
UE	Ejido Union
UNORCA	National Union of Autonomous Campesino Organizations

APPENDIX 1

U.S. Agribusiness in Mexico

U.S. Company
(Mexican affiliate, subsidiary,
or joint venture partner)

Products

American Cyanamid	Pesticides and agrochemicals
Anheuser Busch (Modelo)	Beer
Arbor Acres Farm	Breeder poultry
Asgrow Seed	Breeders, Seeds
Basic Vegetable Products (Vegetales de México)	Vegetables
BASF K&F	Flavoring extracts, chemicals
Borden	Milk processing, dairy foods, specialty foods, chemicals, plastics
Cadbury Beverages (Extractos y Derivados)	Soft drinks
Campbell Soup (Distribuidora Camilar, Sinalpasta)	Canned fruits, vegetables, preserves
Cargill	Food products, animal products
Chevron (Insecticidas Ortho)	Pesticides, agrochemicals
Claude Laval (Separados Lakos)	Farm machinery, equipment manufacturing
Coca-Cola (Femsa)	Flavoring extracts and syrups
ConAgra (Univasa)	Grains, foodstuffs, pork, poultry
Continental Grain	Grains, field beans
CPC International (Productos de Maiz)	Consumer food products, corn refining products

Deere and Co.	Farm machinery and equipment
DeKalb Plant Genetics	Hybrid corn, sorghum, sunflowers, soybeans
DeKalb-Pfizer Genetics (Semillas Hibridas)	Seeds
Dexter Midland	Sausages, prepared meat products
Fermenta ACS	Pesticides and agrochemicals
Harris Moran Seed	Farm supplies
H.J. Heinz (Holdinmex)	Food products
Hershey International (Nacional de Dulces)	Chocolate, food and confectionary products
International Multifoods (La Hacienda)	Prepared feeds, feed ingredients
Intl Flavors & Fragrances	Flavoring extracts and syrups
J.R. Nor/ton	Horticultural processing
Kellogg	Breakfast food products
Corona Cookies (Industrias de Cordoba)	Cookies and crackers
Lance	Consumer food products
McCormick & Co. (Herdez, Grupo Pesa)	Seasons, flavorings, specialty foods
Monsanto [Nutra Sweet]	Pesticides and agrochemicals, sweeteners
RJR Nabisco (Marcas Alimenticias)	Food products
Oscar Meyer (Sigma Alimentos)	Processed meats
Peavey/Conagra Trading	Flour, feeds, and seeds
Pepsico Foods (Sabritas, Gamesa, Geupec)	Beverages, food products, services
Pet, Inc. (Almacenes Refrigerantes)	Specialty foods
Petoseed	Seeds
Phillip Morris	Soft drinks, cigarettes, dairy products, canned fruits and vegetables, dehydrated fruits, vegetables, and soups

[Kraft Foods, General Foods, Birds Eye, Oscar Meyer]
(Cigarros La Tabacalera, Sigma Alimentos)

Pilgrim's Pride	Poultry hatcheries

Pillsbury Co. (Pacific Star)	Frozen fruit, juices and vegetables, frozen foods
Quaker Oats (Fábrica de Chocolates La Azteca)	Breakfast cereal, chocolate candy
Quality Baker of America Bread (Bimbo)	
Ralston Purina	Animal feed, cereals, food products
SAF Products (Safmex)	Food preparation
Sara Lee (Kir Alimentos, Grupo Bimbo-partnership)	Food products, processed meats, baked goods
Seagram (Grupo Gemex)	Beverages
Tate and Lyle	Sugar
Tootsie Roll	Candy and confectionary products
Tyson Foods (Trasgo Group)	Poultry
United Brands (Numar)	Palm oil, food products
Universal Flavors [Warner Jenkinson, Felton Chemical]	Flavoring extracts and syrups
Universal Foods	Food products
Warner Lambert (Chicle Adams)	Candy and other confectionary products

* Not included are the many food distributors and fastfood and restaurant chains that are moving into the Mexican market.

Sources: *Directory of American Firms Operating in Foreign Countries, 1991*; *Business Mexico*, Special Edition 92; *Companias americanas que operan en México, 1991* (American Chamber of Commerce in Mexico); "Las 500 empresas más importantes de México," *Expansión*, August 18, 1993; Business Latin America, October 11, 193; *Directory of Corporate Affiliations, 1994*.

Appendix 2: NAFTA's Trade Effects on Selected Ag Products

Product	Avg. value of exports, 1989-199 (millions of US$)	Pre-NAFTA Tariff	Tariff Phase-out Schedule	Other Pre-NAFTA Barrier	Initial Quote	Quota Phase-out Schedule	Long-term Impact of NAFTA
Major US Exports to Mexico							
Corn	$328	none	none	Import permit	2.5 million MT	15 years	Large
Sorghum	325	15%*	Immediate	none	none	none	Moderate
Soybeans	273	15%*	10 years	none	none	none	Moderate
Beef	113	0-25%	Immediate	none	none	none	Mixed
Sugar	82	107%**	15 years	none	none	none	Small
Poultry	66	none	none	Import permit	95 thousand MT	10 years	Small
Dry Beans	63	none	none	Import permit	50 thousand	15 years	Small
Pork	52	20%	10 years	none	To be determined	15 years	Moderate
Wheat	51	10%	10 years	Import permit	none	none	Small
Cotton	50	10%	5-10 years	none	none	none	Small
Major Mexican Exports to US							
Live Cattle	355	6.3%**	Immediate	Quota threat	none	none	Small
Tomatoes	355	6.3%*,**	Immediate	Mrktg. Order	337,800 MT*	10 years	Small
Orange Juice	161	19.5%**	15 years	none	40 M gallons	15 years	Moderate
Peppers	111	6.1%**	5-10 years	none	29,900 MT*	10 years	Small
Cucumbers	74	14.5%*,**	5-15 years	none	none	none	Moderate
Onions	72	14.5	5-15 years	none	none	none	Moderate
Frozen Broccoli and Cauliflower	65	17.5%*	10 years	none	none	none	Moderate
Cantaloupe	54	35%*	15 years	none	none	none	Large

* = seasonal   ** = 1991 average tarif   MT means metric ton, or 2,205 pounds

Sources: "North American Agriculture Fact Sheets: Commodities and Other Topics,: USDA, FAS, April 26, 1993; "Effectsw of the North American Free Trade Agreement on U.S. Agricultural Commodities," USDA, ERS March 1993.

SELECTED BIBLIOGRAPHY

Appendini, Kirsten. 1992. *De la milpa a los tortibonos: La restruc-turación de la política alimentaria en México*. Mexico City: El Colegio de México.

Autonomedia. *Zapatistas! Documents of the New Mexican Revolution*. Brooklyn: Autonomedia.

Barraclough, Solon. 1991. *An End to Hunger: Social Origins of Food Strategies*. London: Zed Books.

Barkin, David. 1990. *Distorted Development: Mexico in the World Economy*. Boulder: Westview Press.

Barkin, David, Rosemary L. Batt, and Billie R. DeWalt. 1990. *Food Crops vs. Feed Crops: The Global Substitution of Grains in Production*. Boulder: Lynne Reiner Publications.

Barry, Tom. ed. 1992. *Mexico: A Country Guide*. Albuquerque: Resource Center Press, 1992.

Barry, Tom, Harry Browne, and Beth Sims. 1994. *The Great Divide: The Challenge of U.S.-Mexico Relations for the 1990s*. New York: Grove/Atlantic Press.

Bartra, Armando. 1985. *Los herederos de Zapata*. Mexico City: ERA.

Benjamin, Thomas. 1989. *A Rich Land, A Poor People: Politics and Society in Modern Chiapas*. Albuquerque: University of New Mexico Press.

Calva, José Luis. 1991. *Probables efectos de un Tratado de Libre Comercio en el campo mexicano*. Mexico City: Fontamara.

___. 1993. *La disputa por la tierra*. Mexico City: Fontamara.

Collier, George. 1994. *Basta! Land and the Zapatista Rebellion in Chiapas*. Oakland: Food First.

DeWalt, Billie R. and Martha W. Rees. 1994. *The End of the Agrarian Reform in Mexico: Past Lessons, Future Prospects*. San Diego: Center for U.S.-Mexican Studies.

Esteva, Gustavo. 1983. *The Struggle for Rural Mexico*. South Hadley, MA: Bergin and Harvey.

Fox, Jonathan. 1993. *The Politics of Food in Mexico: State Power and Social Mobilization*. Ithaca: Cornell University Press.

Gates, Marilyn. 1993. *In Default: Peasants, the Debt Crisis, and the Agricultural Challenge*. Boulder: Westview Press.

Grindle, Merilee. 1986. *State and Countryside: Development Policy and Agrarian Politics in Latin America*. Baltimore: Johns Hopkins University Press.

Harvey, Neil. 1994. *Rebellion in Chiapas: Rural Reforms, Campesino Radicalism, and the Limits to Salinismo*. San Diego: Center for U.S.-Mexican Studies.

Hewitt de Alcántara, Cynthia. 1976. *Modernizing Mexican Agriculture*. Geneva: UNRISD.

___. 1984. *Anthropological Perspectives on Rural Mexico*. London: Routledge and Kegan Paul.

___. ed. 1994. *Economic Restructuring and Rural Subsistence in Mexico: Corn and the Crisis of the 1980s*. San Diego: Center for U.S.-Mexican Studies.

Katz, Friedrich, ed. 1988. *Riot, Rebellion, and Revolution: Rural Social Conflict in Mexico*. Princeton: Princeton University Press.

Moguel, Julio, Carlota Botey, Luis Hernández, eds. 1992. *Autonomía y nuevos sujetos en el desarrollo rural*. Mexico City: Siglo Veintiuno.

Redclift, Michael. 1987. *Sustainable Development: Exploring the Contraditions*. London: Methuen.

Rubio, Blanca. 1987. *Resistencia campesina y explotación rural en México*. Mexico City: ERA.

Sanderson, Steven. 1981. *Agrarian Populism and the Mexican State*. Berkeley: University of California Press, 1981.

___. 1986. *The Transformation of Mexican Agriculture: International Structure and the Politics of Rural Change*. Princeton: Princeton University Press.

Womack, John. 1969. *Zapata and the Mexican Revolution*. New York: Knopf.

Selected Journals

Cuadernos Agrarias (Mexico City)
El Cotidiano (Mexico City)
La Jornada del Campo (Mexico City)
Latin American Perspectives (Riverside, CA)
Ojarasca (Mexico City)

Sources for More Information

Center for U.S.-Mexican Studies
Ejido Reform Research Project
U.C.-San Diego 0510
La Jolla, CA 92093-0510
Fax: (619) 534-6447
Phone: (619) 534-4503
Email: dmyhre@ucsd.edu
Contact: David Myhre

Centro de Estudios para el Cambio en el Campo Mexicano (CECCAM)
Tabasco No. 262 Insurgente
Despacho 602
Colonia Roma
Mexico, DF 06700
Fax: (525) 514-0205
Phone: (525) 207-1072
Contact: Ana de Ita, Julio Moguel, Luis Hernández

Institute for Agriculture and Trade Policy (IATP)
1313 5th Street SE #303
Minneapolis, MN 55414-1546
Fax: (612) 379-5982
Phone: (612) 379-5980
Email: (EcoNet) iatp
Contact: Karen Lehman

Institute for Food and Development Policy (Food First)
   398 60th Street
   Oakland, CA 94618
   Fax: (510) 654-4551
   Phone: (510) 654-4400
   Email: foodfirst@igc.apc.org
   Contact: Peter Rosset

Interhemispheric Resource Center
   P.O. Box 4506
   Albuquerque, NM 87196
   Fax: (505) 246-1601
   Phone: (505) 842-8288
   Email: resourcectr@igc.apc.org
   Contact: Tom Barry

INDEX

A

Acculturation of indians, 174-75, 179-81

Agrarian bourgeoisie, interests of, 18

Agrarian communities, land-use planning by, 220

Agrarian policy, 11-12, 40

Agrarian reform, 2, 5, 226; amendment ending, 47; and Cárdenas, 21-23; control of campesino communities, 139; demands for, 17-20, 149, 165; foreign examples of, 226; lack of implementation, 4, 123; obstacle to development, 131

Agrarian reform law, revision of, 26, 36; under Salinas, 46, 68

Agrarian traditions and state involvement, 238

Agrarianism, 32-33, 36, 38, 232-33

Agrarismo, see Agrarianism

Agribusiness, 38-39, 42; and new migration patterns, 192

Agricultural Development Law of 1980, 42

Agricultural frontier, colonization of, 158, 160-62, 209, 216, 219

Agricultural sector, 31, 90, 118; dependence on foreign inputs, 90; environmental issues limited under NAFTA, 204; financing industrialization, 25; foreign control of, 68-69, 78; lack of infrastructure, 81; lack of research and development, 87-88; policy, 11-13, 149; subsidies, 46-47, 101; sustainability of, 97-98, 209; treatment under NAFTA, 66-67; US model of modernization, 28; and women, 186; US-Mexican trade, 67 (table), 71, 80-81

Agricultural workers and national GDP, 198

Agriculture and food consumption, 222

Agriculture in Chiapas, role of, 159-60

Agrochemical use, costs of, 214-16

Agroexport, 29-31, 58, 77; and basic grains, 246; under Cárdenas, 21-22; and development policy, 55; under Echevarría, 39; labor force, 83-84, 189-91, 195; *Porfiriato* and, 16-17; trade, 87, 263n.14; and water crisis, 212

Agroexport-domestic food production strategy, 226, 241-42

Agroindustry, 58, 60-62

Agroprocessing and transnational corporations, 31

H

I

R

S

Tercermundismo, 36
Thatcher, Margaret, and neoliberalism, 54
Tlatelolco massacre and legitimacy crisis, 141
Toxic chemicals, US-produced, 214-16, 284n.25
Trade deficit, agricultural, 88-89, 94, 103-4
Trade liberalization, 43, 66
Transnational capital evolving agro-food system, 58
Transnational corporations, 237, 260n.20, 22; agroexport benefits to, 58; and agroindustry, 62-64; and agroprocessing, 31; contract production, 77-79; and market integration, 53-55
Transportation and storage needs in food distribution, 115
Trilateral commission, NAFTA and, 204
Trimodal structure of agriculture, 27, 231

agricultural development projects, 226-27; during the Salinas administration, 164; as policy source, 149; and sustainable development 221;
UNPH (National Union of Fruit and Vegetable Producers), 78
Urban dwellers, 192, 281n.60
Urban poverty compared with rural, 147-48
Uruguay Round agreement and agricultural trade, 66
US agroindustry, 63-64, 67, 88-90, 266n.9
US debate on immigration, 193
US distribution network of Mexican investors 264n.20
US food aid to Mexico, 99
US investment in Mexican agriculture, 76-79
US-Mexico border environmental commission, 204
US-Mexico productivity comparisons (table), 73-74
US-Mexico environmental groups, cooperation between, 204-6
Usufruct rights, 23, 119

U

UAIMs (Agro-Industrial Units for Women) and ejidos, 280n.56
UGOCM, 273n.20, 274n.1
UN World Commission on Environment and Development, 200
Unemployment, 30, 39, 85, 244
UNORCA (National Union of Autonomous Campesino Organizations), 132-33, 142-45;

V

Valley of Apatzingán, melon market in, 86
Vásquez, Genaro and Guerrero Civic Association, 155
Villa, Francisco "Pancho," 2, 17-18

ABOUT THE
RESOURCE CENTER

The Interhemispheric Resource Center, founded in 1979, is a private, nonprofit institute located in Albuquerque, New Mexico. Tom Barry is a founder of the Resource Center, where he currently works as an analyst. The Resource Center produces books, policy reports, audiovisuals, and other educational materials about U.S. foreign policies, as well as sponsoring popular education projects. It publishes three periodicals: *Borderlines* (a monthly that covers U.S.-Mexico cross-border relations), *Resource Center Bulletin* (a quarterly that features the institution's latest research findings), and the *Democracy Backgrounder* (a bimonthly that covers democratization issues). Recent books published by and available through the Resource Center include: *The Challenge of Cross-Border Environmentalism: The U.S.-Mexico Case; Crossing the Line: Immigrants, Economic Integration, and Drug Enforcement on the U.S.-Mexico Border; For Richer, For Poorer: Shaping U.S.-Mexican Immigration;* and *Mexico: A Country Guide.*

For more information and a catalog of publications, please write:

The Interhemispheric Resource Center
Box 4506
Albuquerque, NM 87196
Fax: (505) 246-1601

ABOUT SOUTH END PRESS

South End Press is a non-profit, collectively run book publisher with over 180 titles in print. Since our founding in 1977, we have tried to meet the needs of readers who are exploring, or are already committed to, the politics of radical social change.

Our goal is to publish books that encourage critical thinking and constructive action on the key political, cultural, social, economic and ecological issues shaping life in the United States and in the world. In this way, we hope to give expression to a wide diversity of democratic social movements and to provide an alternative to the products of corporate publishing.

Through the Institute for Social and Cultural Change, South End Press works with other political media projects—*Z Magazine;* Speak Out!, a speakers bureau; and the Publishers Support Project—to expand access to information and critical analysis. If you would like a free catalog of South End Press books or information about our membership program, which offers two free books and a 40 percent discount on all titles, please write to us at: South End Press, 116 Saint Botolph Street, Boston, MA 02115.

Related Titles from South End Press

Roots of Rebellion: Land and Hunger in Central America
Tom Barry

Democracy in Mexico: Peasant Rebellion and Political Reform
Dan La Botz

Mask of Democracy: Labor Suppression in Mexico Today
Dan La Botz

Haiti: Dangerous Crossroads
NACLA